SKID DOGS

SKID DOGS

Emelia Symington-Fedy

Douglas & McIntyre

DOUGLAS AND MCINTYRE (2013) LTD.
P.O. Box 219, Madeira Park, BC, VON 2H0
www.douglas-mcintyre.com

EDITED by Caroline Skelton
COVER DESIGN by Naomi MacDougall
TEXT DESIGN by Libris Simas Ferraz / Onça Publishing
COVER PHOTO by Emelia Symington-Fedy
AUTHOR PHOTO by zev tiefenbach
PRINTED AND BOUND in Canada
PRINTED on 100% recycled paper

DOUGLAS AND MCINTYRE acknowledges the support of the Canada Council for the Arts, the Government of Canada, and the Province of British Columbia through the BC Arts Council.

LIBRARY AND ARCHIVES CANADA CATALOGUING IN PUBLICATION
Title: Skid dogs / Emelia Symington-Fedy.
Names: Symington-Fedy, Emelia, author.
Identifiers: Canadiana (print) 20230440673 | Canadiana (ebook) 20230440681 | ISBN 9781771623643 (softcover) | ISBN 9781771623650 (EPUB)
Classification: LCC PS8637.Y45 S55 2023 | DDC C813/.6–dc23

Dedicated to all the girls

"We were made to bleed, and scab and heal and bleed again, and turn every scar into a joke."

—ANI DIFRANCO ("Buildings and Bridges," 1991)

Skid Dogs is based on real events. To protect the identities of the people involved, names have been changed and personal characteristics altered. For creative purposes, timelines have been condensed, flipped and stretched and some characters are composites of many different people. The telling is mine. My friends and Taylor's family have given me their consent. I respect that our memories may differ. That said, though artistic licence was taken, and fictitious scenes built for dramatic purposes, this is my attempt at the truth.

I KNOW IT'S OUR SPOT when I get to it by the curve in the rails that used to hide us from view. The moon is three-quarters full and gives off good light. I crouch, searching the gravel. I'm looking for a memory. Lip chap. A single button. Something to tie me to this place. But it's been two decades and there's nothing left of us here – just ice crystals playing tricks on me.

The night has a bite; that just-before-winter feeling that makes my eyes water. I tuck my mom's coat – a thin red wool – underneath me and sit with my head on my knees, taking on the perspective of a train, the same view I had the first day I met my girls. Four of them, dressed in crop tops and high-waisted shorts, long tanned legs, lounging along the rails.

A few feet down the tracks my eye catches a glint of something on the ground. I turn on my phone's flashlight and get onto my hands and knees to look closer. Tucked into the gravel is a piece of glass, and as I shine my light across the area I find another worn shard. Then another piece reveals itself, half buried and roughed up. It couldn't be. Squatting, I turn the few dull pieces over in my palm. How is it possible after all this time? But why not? And like they've been waiting for permission, I'm penned in again. My eyes close. The air is cigarette smoke and Juicy Fruit as the girls crowd around me, a knee pressing into my thigh as an arm slumps over my shoulder. Faint at first but like a radio dial made clear when I tune in to the right frequency, a giggle pops up beside me and a raspy laugh drops from above. Rowdy. As hell. I open my eyes a slit so colours and textures can come into view and see the wheat-white curls of Aimes's new perm, Bugsy's bare brown shoulders, Cristal's crisp plaid button-up, and there's Max humming like she always does: with us, but also far away. Aimes's knees knock as she settles beside me, a stick of a thing compared to the cleavage pouring out of Max's tank top. None of us are allowed to wear makeup in public yet. Bugsy and I are the only ones to have bled so far. No one has kissed a boy, and all we want to do is be together. The others plunk in a row alongside Aimes and Cristal lights another smoke. Max pulls me toward her and I can smell her Herbal Essences shampoo as easily as I feel the cold on my cheeks. Bugsy flashes me her thin-lipped grin and another squeal pierces the air. I feel a bit hysterical inside, like how it used to be when we'd sit here for hours, talking shit, sucking on slushes and throwing stones.

Curling the glass in my hand I look up to the cold, wide sky. On my fourteenth birthday we drank a bottle of vodka here. After we'd finished it, I smashed the bottle across the rails, ricocheting glass. I shake my head, not wanting to think about that night. An old instinct, what we did back then too: we shook the pain off, by laughing, and smoking and making fun. Everyone knows, a girl has to be killed before she's taken seriously; anything less is just called growing up.

I look down the tracks and I'm alone again. The ghosts of my girls are gone, but in my palm there's proof. This was us. We were here. It happened.

Mom moved us into a real house during a heat wave. When everyone else was living at the river, drinking warm root beer and languishing in inner tubes, in the two hot months before high school started, she packed up our Hyundai Pony and drove us load by load from our trailer in the bush, along the river and out of Ashton Creek to Armstrong, a farming town we'd never seen before, an hour away. She was excited, sweat on her upper lip, long brown hair, thick as a rope, pulled into a low ponytail overtop a men's shirt covered in flecks of paint. She yakked at my little brother, Grum, through the rear-view mirror – words like "ravine," and "attic," and "rose arbour" – while I pressed my forehead against the passenger-side window, the VCR on my lap.

When we pulled up to a shaded house – squat but regal with gingerbread spindles decorating the front porch and fish-scale shingles falling off the dormers – it reminded me of one of the cover illustrations in the books I read: an image of a young girl in an apron running down the crumbling porch steps, about to get herself and her furry sidekick into all sorts of mischief. The house was cream-coloured, Victorian era, with scrolls of flaking paint rolling up the boards. The window trim and doors, painted a dark brown, were shedding too. Grum rode his BMX across the overgrown yard yelling "We're rich," while Mom began to tug at the vines of wisteria that had spread across this real-life doll's house. When they linked elbows and began discussing a spiffy new paint job as a way of properly introducing ourselves to our new town, I set out down the driveway to explore Armstrong by myself.

Down the hill, past the Armstrong cheese plant, I saw the tracks. They were raised up off the road, set high along a gravel embankment. From where I stood across the street I could only see flashes of metal through the brown grasses. The road continued its descent toward a few small buildings, which made me think that if I climbed up onto the tracks I'd be able to get a view of the whole town. I crossed the road and scrambled up the scree, grabbing choke grass for the final heft onto the rails. The tracks were shiny and dry, partially shaded by blackberry bushes, so the heat throbbed less. I peered across to where I'd just been, the cement cheese plant with four chimney stacks on its roof billowing out a thick tang, the park roped off by a rusty chain, and I realized that if I hadn't been able to see the full rails from the road, no one could see me up here. Cars drove by below and a few peals of hoarse end-of-summer laughter blasted from the chipped-up-looking outdoor pool beside the park, but with the scrub on one side of the rails and more dense brush on the other, I was hidden. The tracks smelled of oil. No, it was heavier than that. There was black grease on the ties, train juice of some sort. I looked toward the heat shimmering off the flat-roofed buildings in the distance and changed my mind. Instead of discovering our new town, I turned toward the protection of the trees.

Following the curve of the rails away from the park and the pool and the new town noises, I headed into a tunnel of maples, which brought immediate shade. The large spikes that attached the rails to the sleepers were almost hidden by the dandelions growing between the cracks, making them feel old and unused. I raised my arms toward the trees, stretching out my sore parts from the past two weeks of packing, scrubbing and dragging furniture. Picking up speed, I jumped from one tie to the next, counting the boards as I leapt.

Because my head was down, I heard the girls before I saw them. Faraway chatter and laughter that sounded like a fast-moving creek. My head jerked up and I counted quickly. Four girls, about half a block away. They hadn't noticed me so I jumped off the rails and scurried into a ditch of brambles and crouched low like I was taking a pee. I couldn't make out the details of their faces but the picture they made – of bodies lazing, bright colours, legs in shorts spread wide – was beautiful. These were languid creatures and their repose scared me. I scooted farther back into the bush, ready like a deer, alert and poised to bolt.

The two girls closest to me were sitting between the rails, across from each other, knees bent and heels dug into the gravel for traction. It looked like they were lobbing small stones at each other's faces. One of the girls had short blond hair and by the wisp of smoke rising behind her, I guessed she was holding a cigarette. Her competitor was clutching a small bouquet of yellow flowers. Yellow Flowers hit the smoking girl above her eye and brought her hand to her mouth in alarm. Smoker laughed, took a drag, and picked up a couple more rocks to restart the game. Another girl balanced along one rail, her back to me. The girl cackled every time she fell off, which was often, seemingly tickled by her own failure. From the platinum streaks in her hair I guessed she came from a we-have-a-boat kind of family. Reflexively, I tucked my own hair behind my ears; the Sun-In spray I'd tried a few weeks ago had left it a tell-all brassy orange.

My eyes held on the last of the gang and the tiniest, a girl perched straight-backed like a squirrel, immersed in her friends' antics, but not joining in. A frizzy blond, this girl's legs were so skinny that they were hard to differentiate from the poplar branches behind her. She sneezed messily and I jumped, falling out of my crouch. As I tripped into a pile of dead brush, a crack rang out and all four girls turned like a pack of dogs interrupted. The tiny one leapt to standing, wiping the snot onto her shorts, squinted into the brush and pointed at my hiding spot.

"Someone's there," she yelled. "We're being watched."

The girls bunched together in the middle of the tracks and scanned the woods. Tiny stomped her foot on the tie once, like she was trying to scare off a tomcat. Her kneecaps were wider than her thighs.

"It's a girl," she said, pointing to me. "She's hiding beside the birch."

I looked behind me, then remembered I was the one caught.

"Hey pervert," the tiny one yelled, "we can see you."

I stayed put behind the tree.

"How do you know it's a girl?" the smoker asked.

"Because she's right there," the tiny one said, pointing again.

I was still far enough away that if they started to chase, I'd be able to outrun them, but Tiny raised her arm again, this time in a come-here motion. She seemed friendly but it could have been a trick.

As I emerged from my hiding spot, the gang opened their circle to stand in a line across the rails. The girl with the yellow flowers tossed her long brown hair over one shoulder. The short-haired smoker ground her cigarette into the gravel. Platinum Blond stood in the centre of the tracks, her Chucks spread as wide as her grin and Tiny cocked her chin and placed a foot on the rail, claiming it. *This is the moment where everything changes*, I thought, taking another step forward. Thinking of myself as a character in a story relieved some of the pressure I often felt in real-time situations, so I willed myself to rise up and out of my body just enough to watch the girl who was me begin to move independently of myself. The girls were still a little ways off and I didn't know where to set my eyes so I kept them on the planks. I could pretend I was just wandering. Yes, that sounded right. *I'm the new girl meandering along railroad tracks, coming upon my first adventure.* That's a fine way to start a story.

"Walk faster ya donk," Tiny yelled.

They'd started to jostle and shove, anticipating my approach, but I kept my pace steady, settled by the heavy track scent.

When I reached their line, the girls surrounded me in a huddle.

"You're the new kid," Tiny said, not asking a question.

"Do you know what your homeroom is?" Platinum Blond said.

"There's only one homeroom for grade eights, 'tard," Tiny said.

"Kill me for living," said Platinum.

They laughed like small dogs.

"I'm Aimes," the tiny girl said, grinning a mouthful of metal at me. "This is Bugsy," and she pushed the tanned blond from the edge of the circle out front.

Bugsy's eye colour was the same as a cat's, with yellow bursts at the centre. The tan lines underneath her Esprit tank top confirmed my assumption that she was the kind of girl who spent her summers bouncing on an inner tube behind a speedboat as her dad steered one-handed, gripping a beer. Bugsy's fingernails were stubby though, as small as nails could get without being gone, the thin moon indents painted a bubblegum pink that tried to distract from the ragged skin. Before I could look away, she tucked her fingers into a quick fist.

"Burns in the wind," the short-haired smoker said to Yellow Flowers and motioned for a drag.

"That's Cristal," Aimes said, pointing to the smoker.

As I'd seen at a distance, Cristal's blond hair was almost a buzz cut. Her shoes were Crest white. Cristal nodded without smiling and reached for the smoke.

"And Max," Aimes said, indicating the girl holding the yellow flowers. "She's an opera singer."

"I'm not a friggin' opera singer," Max said, ignoring Cristal and taking a drag.

"Max knows the entire CD of *Les Misérables* by heart," Aimes said.

Max rolled her eyes. They were the lightest of blue, like a glacier, and her brown hair matched the glacial look, lying flat like a sheet down her back.

"I love *Les Mis*" was the first thing I heard myself say aloud. "I have the T-shirt."

This was a lie. Mom had taken me to the touring show of *Les Misérables* for my thirteenth birthday but I hadn't dared ask for a souvenir.

Max looked me up and down while shaking her hair out behind her. She seemed unimpressed, which attracted me. She took another long drag, skipping Cristal again.

"Pass the fag, fag," Cristal said.

Max took another puff.

These girls acted like how I imagined sisters would be.

"What's your name, new girl?" Aimes asked and stepped closer.

"Uh, Emmy," I said. "I moved into –"

"– the olden days house across from the elementary school," she interrupted, as the girls made clucks of agreement.

Cristal sat down again and pulled out a pack of Du Mauriers. She counted how many were left, nodded to herself, pulled out another cigarette and lit it. She'd quit trying to make Max share and she hadn't made a fuss about it, which made her seem the most laid-back of the group.

"You want a drag?" Cristal patted the rail beside her.

I didn't sit down. I'd never smoked before and had assumed I'd have time to practice in private before trying it out in front of high-stakes strangers. I passed the cigarette along, with the dexterity of someone holding a live caterpillar, to Aimes, who stood beside me.

"Don't worry," she said. "Cristal's the only real smoker. We just do it to be cool."

The girls nodded again as they shuffled closer, trying to get a look at all sides of me.

"We heard from Ollie that there was a name change on his mom's paper route last week," Aimes said. "We were hoping you'd be a girl."

Realizing that my moving here was town news buoyed me up.

"Who's Ollie?" I asked.

"He's our best guy friend," Bugsy said. "Ollie Solly and his older brothers run this town. They're in a gang called the Raiders, so watch out."

"Ollie's mom grows a garden for food," Cristal said, standing up.

"She does seven paper routes every morning before work," Bugsy cut in. "My mom says it's a monopoly but my dad says it's called industrious and what else can a single mother do?"

"We have a garden for food," Max said, flipping her hair again.

"You have a greenhouse for cherry tomatoes, Max," Cristal said. "And your parents don't have real jobs."

Max scowled. "Being a ceramist is a real job."

"My dad said it's not a real job unless you hate doing it," Cristal said.

"That's what my dad says too," said Bugsy.

"Sucks to be you," Max said, and tossed the yellow flowers into the bush. "Can't be a single mom. Can't grow vegetables. Did you finally get your rag, Cris?"

Cristal laughed. "I wish."

Max stepped off the rails to reach a fanny pack that was suspended from a low-hanging tree branch. There was a detachment in her decision to leave that made me want to follow her, but Cristal interrupted the thought.

"So, where'd you come from?" she asked, taking a drag.

This was the question I needed to answer carefully. We'd just moved from our trailer. Townies didn't understand the difference between living in a trailer in the bush and renting a pad in a trailer park. We'd owned our land, but they'd still assume I was trash.

"Um, I lived in a place my mom built, in the woods, by the Shuswap River," I said.

I wasn't lying. Mom had built three separate additions to the trailer in the decade we'd lived there. First was the screened-in porch she'd tacked on to the front — for our shoes and coats and sick chickens and bad dogs and the seedlings we were trying to grow. A year later, she'd built another addition to the back of the trailer so she could have her own bedroom. A few years after that, Mom paid a church friend's brother-in-law in cash to pour a basement for storage and canning. Eventually there was nowhere else left to build onto and our mothership with its two space stations had reached capacity.

"Your mom is a construction worker?" Aimes said, tucking the frizz behind her ears.

"No, she's a nurse," I said.

"So, your dad built the house?" Cristal said.

"My dad lives in Victoria," I said, letting the word *house* slip off my radar. "But it's cool because I get double the Christmas presents."

"No shit, that's a silver cloud," Bugsy said.

"My parents never got married, so technically I'm a bastard," I said, hoping to sound provocative. The girls giggled, so I kept going. "I mean, what kind of an awful baby do you have to be for your dad to leave when you're three months old?"

"The worst kind," Bugsy said.

"Yer funny," Aimes said and grabbed her backpack. "My parents are probably getting a divorce." She stuffed her Walkman away and started to trot down the tracks, her backpack bouncing off her butt as she tried to catch up to Max. "Welcome to Cheese Town," she yelled over her shoulder, "where everyone knows you better than you do."

"And you get all the free curds you want," Bugsy with the cat eyes said, pointing down the rails to the cheese factory. "Grab a handful from the bucket. They never run out."

"There's not much else here," Cristal said. "One traffic light and three churches." She put her smoke out on the ballast and carefully set the butt on the top of the rail before starting off behind the others.

Bugsy was the only one left, sucking up the last sips of slush from the corners of the cup. I looked to her for direction and her eyes narrowed.

"You ever kissed a boy?" Bugsy asked.

"No."

"Me either — I wish. You ever been drunk?"

"No."

"Same here. You ever eaten shit?"

My breath caught.

"Just kidding!" Bugsy snorted and slapped me on the back.

"Come on ya bastard," she said, raising her eyebrows then turning to run. "We've got a whole day to waste."

If a bird had been flying above us on that first blazing summer day we met, it would have seen one girl in the lead, about a block ahead of the others, another girl running to catch up and three trailing behind, moving away from the protection of the trees and heading toward flat, open land. The bird would have seen our bodies gathering together in different formations then spreading out again, sometimes on the rails, sometimes moving straight down the centre of the tracks, always commanding the entirety of the space and staying within yelling distance.

"First thing to know is, adults don't use the tracks," Aimes yelled.

"So, if you see one," Bugsy said, "it's a pervert or the high school counsellor."

"But why up here?" I asked, pointing to the sidewalk below.

"It's faster than taking the streets," Bugsy said.

"Slash through the bush, cut through a backyard, jump on the tracks and get where you're going, ya know?" Aimes yelled. "Gives us more time to donkey around."

As we got closer to the main street the gravel embankment that kept us above the town started to grade down. We were still elevated over the cars and the few people walking along the sidewalk, but the trees had thinned considerably, so we had to rely on large blooming bushes on either side of the embankment to travel undetected. Soon there were no hiding spots left and we cut directly through the centre of Armstrong on a swath of exposed rail, almost level with the stores and businesses coming into view. The girls pointed out the important landmarks as we passed them. Short Stop, where the slushes were bought, the post office, an old brick building that had an awning in the shape of a cowboy hat. Tuckers was the diner they went to for fries and gravy on Fridays after school. There was a 7-Eleven in the distance. On our right we passed a grain silo.

"Sometimes Max lets us listen to her sing in there," Aimes said.

"My voice sounds clearest at night," Max said.

There seemed to be one of everything in the small downtown core: one pizza place, one pharmacy attached to one Video Express, one grocery store, one gas station and one junk shop – all sharing the same country-and-western theme.

"If we'd taken the road, we'd still be back by the post office right now," Bugsy said.

"And we'd probably have run into some dink-donk like Eli or Tyson. Up here, there's not so much BS to deal with," Aimes said.

In what felt like only a few blocks, the buildings stopped. A small bottle depot was on our left and then — open field. The town noises got quieter and the birds went back to calling out to each other and we were alone again, travelling alongside marshland and willow trees. At what seemed to be a pre-agreed-upon location all four girls stopped and circled a few times, like dogs do before finding rest. One by one we sat down along the rails, now on the opposite side of town from where I'd met them less than an hour ago. I was pushed to the centre, my thigh pressing into Cristal's. She lit another smoke.

As if unable to be still for more than a second, Aimes jumped up as soon as Bugsy sat down. She stepped onto a rail and started to balance.

"If I fall, Chad Chud is going to French me," she said.

"Chad Chud is a chode," Bugsy said, focused on an ingrown hair on her knee.

The girls laughed in concert again. There was something about making these sharp, harsh sounds together that seemed to excite them further. It reminded me of a crow's warning cry. *Don't get too close or we'll split your eardrums with joy.* Watching Aimes balance, Club Monaco sweater tied around her waist, logo facing out, it hit me: an hour ago, not only did these girls not have names, but the tracks didn't exist — and now I was in the middle of it all. We'd had friends in Ashton Creek, but the feeling — one I could only identify now that it was gone — was of goodwill. Letting us share in their Sunday family dinners and butchering days was an act of kindness for us to be grateful for. With these girls, I wasn't "being included"; instead I felt "part of."

A bit lower in the sky now, the sun was softer, and the only sounds came from Max snapping twigs into small piles.

"What's yer thing?" Max asked, glancing up with those ice-blue eyes.

I wasn't sure what she meant. A thick dandelion was growing out of a crack between a tie and its ballast. *Common*, I thought, but then I felt bad. The plant didn't know it was a weed.

"I like to read," I said. "I read a lot of books."

"Not what do you like *to do*," Aimes said, sliding into the conversation. "Who are you going to *be*?" she asked. "For example, Bugsy is going to have twins and marry her high school sweetheart – "

Bugsy crossed her eyes like a nerd.

" – and I'm going to have *two* sets of twins, marry my high school sweetheart *and* become a teacher for kids with learning disabilities."

I smiled at Aimes, this frizzy-haired, chicken-legged girl.

"I'm moving out of Armstrong and never coming back," said Cristal, running her hand through her hair, making it spike.

"That's not *doing* something, that's *not* doing something," Max said as she placed the sticks on top of each other, making a log cabin.

"Well, *not doing Armstrong* is my goal," Cristal said.

"Max is going to be an opera singer," Aimes said. "Obviously."

"Holy crapola!" Max jumped up, ignoring Aimes. "I knew it!"

We all rubbernecked.

"I knew I knew you from somewhere."

"Where?" I asked, relieved for a distraction from the interrogation.

"You were the White Rabbit, in *Alice in Wonderland*."

She was right. I had been. Mom had driven me to rehearsals at the Ashton Creek community hall three times a week for months. Even the morning Lucky got hit by a logging truck – after she pried Grum off his body, dug a hole and buried the dog – she got me to dress rehearsal on time. We'd performed the show for five nights and each performance I got more laughs. But then Mom told us we were moving and I'd forgotten all about it.

"You were good," Max said. "She was real good."

"You're going to be an actress then," Bugsy said.

"Actor," Max said. "She's an act-*tor*. Don't be sexism."

I looked to Cristal, hoping her cigarette wasn't out yet. If I took a drag and started to cough, the focus would shift.

"You did the splits," Max said.

I nodded.

"It was like, weird to do the splits," Max said. "But she got a big laugh. Dad called it 'absurdist comedy,' which I don't get. But. You. Were. Hilarious."

I looked to my jelly shoes, covered in dust and grime, and when I lifted my head I caught the girls making an agreement.

Aimes sidled up to Bugsy, her movements suddenly sleek. She wrapped her fingers around Bugsy's neck and Bugsy leaned into Aimes's butterflied palms as she ground her feet into the gravel. Aimes looked at me and smiled, then she began to push hard and slow on Bugsy's windpipe. Max started to count and Cristal watched. I'd not seen anything like this happen before, but their comfort within the motions put me at ease. At the thirty-second mark Bugsy's eyes rolled back into her head and she crumpled sideways. She wasn't faking it because just before she went limp there was a flash of panic in her eyes. She dropped onto the gravel with no great drama and Aimes followed her body down, placing her head gently on the ground. It was elegant to watch, this losing of consciousness. We gathered above Bugsy, her eyes half-closed with a bit of the whites peeking out, and waited. There was a moan and a twitch at her lips. Her limbs shook and tensed and she laughed at how her body could move without her permission.

Rolling over, Bugsy crawled onto her hands and knees and we all clapped as she toddled a few steps down the rails, like a baby, enjoying her lack-of-oxygen high. After Bugsy could stand upright, Aimes turned to Max – who told me that she was so good at fainting, she usually preferred to choke herself out. Max leaned into Aimes and we watched the choreography unfold again to its climax: one long sigh of release. Her face had gone pale and her jaw slack. Did Aimes go too far? Did Bugsy count too long? I looked to Cristal and she brought my attention back to Max – eyes glassy – with us again. A stunning performance. I dropped to my knees, wanting to help her stand if I could.

It was Aimes's turn next. She was nervous, so Bugsy and Max had to pin her arms down across the tracks. Forcing her didn't seem as much fun. She dropped too quickly, which meant she probably faked it but it's hard to tell what a body does honestly once it's down. Before we could surround her, Aimes jumped to standing and took a bow. Cristal and I looked to each other again and she shook her head in a private no motion, meaning she wasn't going to partake, which meant I didn't have to either, so I clapped even harder for Aimes. From the looks collecting between the girls, whatever ritual they'd just completed, my response had satisfied them.

"It's strange," Aimes said, squeezing in to sit between Cristal and me with a new level of comfort. "There's only been four of us since kindergarten and now that you've shown up, all of a sudden we're five. That's a club. It's going to be a lot easier for us in high school now. Don't you think?"

"Yes," I said, "it's strange, and easier." I stood up, uncomfortable with being wanted as much as I had want. "I need a brain freeze," I said, motioning back toward town.

"Come on skanks," Aimes said with a laugh, "I got all the change from my mom's purse," and she started to run.

It was probably my imagination but as the girls turned, the space above our heads started to glisten, like soap in a bubble, but with more density to it. It was as if I could reach out and grab the shimmering air, pull it down to wrap it around us like a blanket or a shield. But I didn't, deciding there'd already been enough weirdness for one day.

"Wait," Max said. She was looking down on her tiny log house, not yet finished. "Let's wreck it before someone else does." She ground the tiny building into the gravel with her sneaker.

We ran after Aimes, our feet pounding the planks while our T-shirts flapped in the breeze made by our own motion. The shimmering wasn't spoken of and I don't know if anyone else noticed it, but I could still feel its canopy as we ran back along the rails toward town, not stopping, fuelled by some sort of chimerical new magic.

I NEED TO MAKE A PLAN. My hands are numb and my feet feel like stumps. I slide the collection of glass into my pocket, tuck my nose back into Mom's scratchy coat – saved from her nursing days in the Arctic – and stride back to where the tracks hit the road. I've driven back to Armstrong too quickly and without thinking. When Mom called three days ago to tell me that a local girl was murdered on the tracks and her killer was still on the loose, I almost didn't believe her. Late for a live interview about an upcoming play I was in, I'd biked downtown to the CBC Radio building. After I'd finished, I headed back through the newsroom – where I heard two reporters talking, their heads bent.

"Her name was Taylor."

"What was she doing on the railroad tracks at night?"

"And by herself, too?"

I wanted to smash their foreheads together and yell, *Of course she was on the tracks, you fuck rods, she was taking the short cut.*

These people didn't know my town – how kids used the tracks to get around. We'd all walked on them alone at night, scooting through the underbrush on our way to a party or a friend's house. Every girl who'd ever come out of Armstrong was probably thinking the same thing: *She could've been me.*

I passed the reporters silently, went through the metal detectors, rode home and called Mom back.

"I'll be there tomorrow," I said.

Then I called my only contact at CBC Radio and pitched her a documentary, something I'd only ever seen on TV. I didn't know Taylor, and I didn't want to be an ambulance chaser, but she was killed on the same ground that formed me. It was where we went to get away – from home, and boys, and ourselves. This was our territory. Where would all the Armstrong girls go now?

The producer agreed immediately, as Taylor's murder was national news. I grabbed my Zoom recorder, packed my bag and drove home. But the decision had been rash.

Armstrong is in chaos — with reporters fighting to get interviews outside Short Stop, where Taylor worked, and police barricading the two exits out of town. No one's on the tracks. The place where Taylor was found, a depression in the ditch beside the rails, is cordoned off by sagging police tape, the grasses flattened by muddy boots.

As I head back along Rosedale Avenue, the street lamps don't lessen the new unease—their fuzzy hue only draws attention to the fog rolling in. Nailz and Cutz Salon is shuttered, its neon Open sign off. Down the block the yellow-and-green-striped house where I used to take piano lessons is dark, the blinds drawn. Beside it, the old mansion with its six weeping willows is still for sale. Everywhere I look a memory flings itself at me, but I'm not comforted by the sameness. The old buildings and storefronts are in their right places, but all familiarity has left Armstrong.

I head down the driveway to Mom's new house, the place she moved into twelve years ago, and the disquiet remains. In the carport I unlock the door that's never been locked before and creep into her dark and soft-smelling home, hoping the creaks up the stairs don't wake her.

———————

In the early light, after a few hours of restless sleep in the spare room, I crack Mom's door, lean over the bed and kiss her papery cheek goodbye. It was a mistake to come back. I'm not about to start interviewing people less than a week after Taylor was brutally killed. It doesn't matter how nostalgic I feel about the tracks.

Mom's eyes open and she grabs my arm.

"I've gotta go, Mom," I whisper.

She moans and rolls over, her disappointment clear, but within seconds her breath deepens back into sleep. I let my old chihuahua, Midge, take a pee, stuff her in her carrier and peel out of the driveway.

Now she's curled on my lap, snuffling in her sleep, and I turn on the radio to keep myself awake. Newscasters are reporting the events that led up to Taylor's murder and their voices seem unable to hide the shock that something like this could happen in a town as small as Armstrong. The live updates repeat what I've already been told by Mom and her neighbours: Taylor was strangled, beaten and left for dead, three days ago, on Halloween night. Her boyfriend had invited her to a senior's grad party, but she wanted to go trick-or-treating instead. She'd dressed up as a zombie, phoned her best friend and they'd made plans to meet up on Pleasant Valley Road. But at some point Taylor got a phone call from another friend, who convinced her to turn around and go to the grad bash. Taylor climbed up the embankment, jumped on the tracks and headed to the party, walking along the wooded corridor that led out of town. There were houses on either side of her and from the beginning of the corridor she'd have been able see its end. It was there that she texted her boyfriend.

"I'm being creeped."

Cresting over the mountains, I'm heralded into East Vancouver by the hundreds of crows that travel west to east every day, returning from the ocean to the protection of trees. It's a large, moving murder that takes about ten minutes to pass through the sky and East Van residents claim the daily trip as a point of pride. I pull into my housing co-op and watch the final few stragglers finish their commute before I unlock my door, drop Midge onto the couch and call Mom. She picks up on the first ring and tells me in fast whispers that she hasn't left the house since I said goodbye that morning.

"Mom, the killer is long gone," I say.

"You don't know that," she hisses. "He could be my neighbour."

"I don't think Grum's old hockey coach is a murderer," I say. "He would've killed someone years ago."

"You have no idea what'll make a person snap."

The next morning, groggy and late for work, I pedal fast through the rain, butt raised off my seat, pumping hard, trying to dispel some of the squall I feel inside. When I arrive at rehearsal, my co-director slides her laptop across the table for me to read. The police have issued a request that everyone in Armstrong stay inside their homes with the doors locked after dusk as the killer might still be in town, hiding. All strangers should be reported to the tips line. Near the end of my workday, while I'm trying to block a scene with an actor, my old high school drama teacher calls: men over the age of sixteen who live within town limits are being told to report to the Armstrong RCMP for questioning. After I bike home, she calls back to tell me there's a lineup of boys and their dads curling around the perimeter of the small cop shop.

"The line just keeps growing," she says.

It's around 10 p.m. when Mom calls me, frantic. Someone is outside her house, or it's many people – she can't tell. They're flicking her porch light on and off and banging on each door of the house, side, front and back – all at the same time.

"It's just a bunch of asshole kids with nothing better to do than terrorize old people," I say.

"You're not here," she says. "You don't know what's going on. We're all terrified."

"Mom, if the killer is still hiding in Armstrong, he's not after senior citizens," I say, having no idea if this is true.

As we talk, Mom climbs her stepladder and drives two nails into the plaster above all the windows in the house. She tacks wool blankets over the sheer curtains and crawls into her bed with a broom.

"I'll just stay awake till morning," she says.

It's this image, of Mom alone in bed, clutching a broom as a weapon, that makes the decision for me. I call my co-director and tell her that I can't finish the play and she should take my fee. I set my alarm and take a sleeping pill. In what feels like a blink, the alarm sounds. I put Midge in her carrier and start the seven-hour drive back home—again.

1991

On the first day of grade eight, an hour before the bell, we met on the tracks to prepare. I wore a Bart Simpson T-shirt, Hammer pants and a red beanie cap with a working propeller. Bugsy was more subdued, sticking to a B.U.M. Equipment tank top, but I'd noticed a few risks taken in her accessorizing. Her streaked bangs were sprayed higher than I'd seen before and she smelled of a new scent: Body Shop Dewberry. She reapplied her iridescent lip gloss as she glanced down the tracks, the pearl colour reminding me of a seashell.

"I'm not going to be late on the first day," Cristal said, standing in the same combo of 501 button-fly jeans, plaid short-sleeved shirt and gleaming white sneakers that she wore every day.

"She'll be here," Max said, cuffing her jeans. "We're not leaving the chicklet behind."

While my friends looked tucked in and crisp waiting for Aimes to arrive, I hoped that my bright colours and spinning propeller would evoke an untouchable confidence on this first day of school.

"Yoodle, doodle, hoodle" came a high call from behind us, followed by a laugh. Turning around, we saw Aimes running full tilt our way. "Yoodle, doodle, hoodle," she sang out again, her thin legs galloping haphazardly and her high pony bouncing in time.

Aimes skidded up, out of breath, and started rummaging through a small purple purse that sat flat against her chest.

"You guys, you guys," she started. "I thought you might've left already. I was freaking out but I needed a slush so we stopped at the Sev and then I got nachos and Mom was like, 'No way is *that* going in the car' – because of last time – so I had to finish them at the cheese machine." She pulled out a pack of unopened Trident and passed it to Bugsy to hold. "I ate so fast that the cheese burned the roof of my mouth, but luckily I still had some slush left" – Aimes opened her mouth and tilted back to show us the red patch — "so I chugged it and now I'm fine." She went back to digging in her purse. "Found it!" Aimes raised a tube of grape-flavoured lip chap. "My lips are dry like cornflakes." She circled the tube around her lips six times fast. "We've got less than forty minutes before we have to grow up. You ready?"

Bugsy shoved three pieces of gum into her mouth. "On the tracks we'll still be us, right?"

"We can always be ourselves here, duh."

Aimes swung around to start the trek toward the high school and we followed, gravel crunching under our new shoes, an airplane emitting its faraway drone above our heads.

Since the girls had caught me spying on them at the beginning of summer, we'd gathered in the same spot almost every day, to walk and talk along the rails for miles. While the girls told me which kids to steer clear of and which parents to behave around, I'd stopped thinking about the few friends I'd left behind in Ashton Creek. The promise I'd made to write weekly letters to my next-door neighbour floated away, and the deer runs and evening river swims seemed to quietly withdraw. As my comfort in a new skin grew, I turned my back fully on the land Mom had worked so hard on to make our home. My lack of filter seemed novel to these girls, and my bossy tendencies helped us to make decisions faster. Also, they hadn't found out I'd grown up in a trailer and enough time had passed that I could bet there wouldn't be any more questions. And so, while nothing tangible happened on our long days of walking and talking together, for me, everything was happening.

Hidden from the road by a bend in the rails, the spot had been chosen for its privacy. But there were other things I'd noticed being up here. The trees dampened the town noise, making us feel farther away than we actually were. On hot days, the sunlight only ever dappled through the maples, which provided shade and a softer light, and after dusk, once the air had cooled down, the rails kept their warmth for us, so we were comfortable in tank tops well after dark. I'd never had a place before, and here it was, without effort, ours.

Bugsy stopped walking.

"Did you hear Ryan finger-banged Twyla with her tampon in?"

Max froze.

Bugsy enjoyed her shock, then continued. "They were making out. She didn't want him to know that she was on her rag."

We gathered around her. This was what horror films were made of.

"He got down her pants. She tried to pretend everything was normal. But because of the tampon, he couldn't get his finger very far up inside —"

Bugsy started walking again.

"I'm never getting finger-banged," I said, rushing to keep up.

"Me either," said Aimes, following behind while tightening the pony on top of her head.

"Then he felt it —" Bugsy said.

"No!" Cristal and I said at the same time, and stopped again.

We were still hidden by the last few trees. I noticed a thistle growing along the rails and I started scuffing at it with the toe of my shoe.

"He felt the string," Bugsy said. "He didn't know what it was. So" — Bugsy paused for effect — "he pulled the tampon out."

I turned from the weed and faced Bugsy.

"He pulled the tampon out of her body?"

"Yeah. He. Pulled. It. Out. Of. Her. Vagina."

Aimes crossed her arms and looked to Max, whose eyes had gone dull.

"Max, did you know about this?" Aimes asked, sliding her tongue over her braces.

"Yeah," Max said. "Ryan told me about it. He was really freaked out. He had a shower and everything."

Ryan was Max's older brother so this was a direct confirmation of truth. We stopped touching and swatting, as if this information needed to be assessed by professionals.

"So, he saw Twyla's actual bloody tampon?" I asked, returning to the task of destroying the thistle.

"He saw the entire thing." Max shrugged. "He said it looked like a dead mouse."

Bugsy stepped up onto the rails to balance. I started using my heel to dig into the roots, which worked better. I was embarrassed for Twyla but also angry. How dare she expose the rest of us like that? Now Ryan knew what a period looked like, and he'd tell his friends, so soon they'd all know.

"He said he was so grossed out that he threw it across the room and it hit the wall," Max said, staring through the centre of our circle.

"Did he call her a slut?" Cristal asked.

"Yeah, duh," Max said.

Finally, the stabbing motion of my foot had decimated the plant. Twyla was a slut now. She'd brought it on herself.

"She's a skank for doing it on her rag." Cristal shrugged and stepped onto the rails to join Bugsy in balance practice.

Max stepped up behind Cristal, balancing easily. They started to travel, one foot in front of the other, continuing in the direction of the high school.

"Ryan said that when the tampon hit the wall, the blood exploded like a bullet wound."

"Grody," Bugsy said.

"Grody to the max," Aimes said back.

Now that Cristal, Bugsy and Max had moved from our circle onto the rails, Aimes and I followed, finding our spot in the line, while considering the ramifications this act would have on us. Twyla was the first official slut of grade eight – before grade eight had even started. *What a shit-for-brains*, I thought, but tried to understand the situation from Twyla's point of view. She couldn't tell Ryan that she didn't want to be finger-banged. She *definitely* couldn't tell him she had her period. She'd put herself in a no-win situation by being alone with him in the first place.

I'd only met Twyla at the park a week previous. She wore cakey foundation and lined the rims of her eyes with black. I thought that maybe we shared the same *more is more* fashion aesthetic, but the eyeliner should've been a red flag. She'd have that word tied to her for the rest of her Armstrong life and that's a long time to be a slut for – all the dick licking and bikini-line waxing she'd have to do now. I wondered if she even knew she was a slut yet?

I jumped off the tracks and sped past the girls, trying to get the high-pitched sound of fear out of my ears. I needed to state my position publicly and so far, explicit truth had worked the best. I stopped at the intersection.

"Okay," I said. "Here's the plan."

The girls caught up, eager.

"When I want to have a baby in my early twenties – only then – I'll have sex with my husband."

"Me too," Aimes said and punched the air.

"I'm never giving anyone a blow job," I said.

"Me neither," Aimes agreed. "Blow jobs are for skanks."

"I bet you'll both give blow jobs one day," Bugsy said.

"No. I swear it," I said, placing a hand on my chest. "It's porno and I won't do it."

I wanted them to know they could count on me to not put them in danger. I wouldn't make a mistake. I couldn't afford to. The labels *trailer trash* and *slut* didn't go well together.

I looked to my friends, their eyes still jittering from the news, and I raised my other hand in oath.

"Here, on the tracks, we solemnly promise that we will never get fingerbanged on our periods," I said.

Each girl nodded as I made eye contact.

"We promise to tell each other everything if a boy phones us or asks us on a date."

"If I don't get asked on a date in grade eight, I'm going to hang myself," Aimes said.

"We'll stick together if we get invited to a party and we'll leave together too."

None of these promises were hard to make as we'd not been in any of these situations yet.

"But what if I want to have sex before I get married?" Bugsy said. Her bangs had already fallen and she was trying to hide the fried ends behind her ears. Aimes threw her a hair tie to use.

I thought for a moment.

"How about: *if* we have sex, it will be *with* boyfriends, *after* grade ten only."

"Easy," Bugsy said, slinging her arm over Aimes.

Max reached across the circle, grabbed my hand and squeezed it. "I promise," she said.

"I promise," Aimes and Bugsy said at the same time.

"This is stupid, but I promise," Cristal said and shook her head.

"I promise," I said, last.

Our eyes sparked as we looked around the circle — safe.

Pushing through the slate-blue double doors into the main foyer of Pleasant Valley Secondary School, condensation and Pine-Sol greeted us. Linking elbows to stay attached, we were jostled into the student centre and as we slid our way deeper into the din we grasped each other's waistbands and jackets to stay close. I noticed some *How dare she?* looks coming off the older girls lounging on the carpeted benches, their legs spread in acid-washed jeans. My fashion choices seemed to be working. These older girls thought their back-to-school plaid flannel would get them noticed – but my tourist souvenir was stealing the spotlight. I didn't mind their scowls as it meant they'd seen me.

We kept to the edges and made sure no one was more than reach-length away as we travelled down the main hallway to find our lockers – across from the girls' bathroom and, thank god, beside each other. Comparing schedules we hurried to and from our new classrooms with their odd-shaped desks and already-tired-looking teachers. After each bell we rejoined at the bank of lockers, relieved to have five minutes to wipe our armpits with the toilet paper we'd stuffed inside our bras. Finally, the midday bell rang and we slid down the front of our lockers for lunch. In my periphery, a girl with glasses that sat low on her cheeks was staring at us.

"Who's that?" I asked, nodding toward the girl.

"Don't make eye contact. It's Cheralise. She smells like goat," Bugsy said.

When I glanced up at the girl again, books tucked tightly to her chest, she caught my eye and smiled. I couldn't risk being kind today. One mistake could push us off the rung of the ladder we were trying to climb onto. Removing the propeller hat, I stuffed it into the back of my locker, concerned that it might be attracting weirdos, then I glanced back to see Cheralise shuffling down the hall, searching for another host body to attach herself to. I felt for her, rejected and scanning for safety. She could have been me at my old school, too earnest, no sense of nonchalance. But instead of this similarity softening me, it bolstered my decision. Second place is first loser. Buck the fuck up.

Across the hallway, I noticed a pack of senior guys. One had a thin moustache. Another wore Oakleys, and the last had gold chains hanging over his Raiders jersey. They were sneaking glances at us. I tried not to pay attention but the intensity of their eyes felt like scissor snips. I reached into my locker and put my beanie cap back on, hoping that the flamboyance would deter them from approaching. This hat was quickly becoming an asset – something to catch attention or repel it, depending on my need. I wanted to be seen, yes. This was why I'd dressed so cartoonishly on the first day of high school. I wouldn't mind if the entire school noticed the new girl and respected her wild-ass style. But this wasn't how the boys were looking at me. They reminded me of a cat stalking a bird.

A scuffle at the end of the hall broke my attention. A group of senior girls, spread out, were moving fast, shoulder-checking doors as they sliced down the hallway toward us. I counted six, dressed in tight black T-shirts, heavy, dark blue jeans and cowboy boots. As they passed by, I saw a patch on the arm of a varsity jacket that read Brew Crew. I'd never seen these girls before but I'd met ones just like them. Back at the trailer I'd known farm kids who walked wide-legged and talked like grown-ups. They got off on tying lit firecrackers onto barn cats' tails and shooting pellet guns at toads. Once they decided to mess with you they didn't let go, and I'd endured enough taunting, rotten lunches stuffed into my desk and being pinned up against bathroom stalls to know that I needed a new tactic this time.

I pulled Bugsy to standing and the others followed.

"What the hell is a Brew Crew?" I whispered loud enough so the older girls could hear.

The girl with the Brew Crew patch stopped, spun on her heels and stared at me. Her eyes were brown with pouchy bags underneath. She looked older than grade twelve, her curly hair slicked back wet. Her black T-shirt showed big breasts and an even bigger belly that hung over her cinched-up silver belt buckle. Her jeans were boot cut, not for style, but to ride horses and tromp through mud. In a single motion she stepped out of the line and pinned me against the lockers.

"Who the fuck are you?" she said.

The rest of the Brew Crew surrounded us and we became a circle within a circle.

"She's so sorry –" Aimes said.

"Yeah, she's new –" said Max.

The leader pushed up close and I smelled cinnamon gum. She had a few drops of sweat dripping down where sideburns would be. I knew my only chance of not getting beat up on the first day of grade eight was to let shit fly.

"So what, you're like, the 4-H Club?" I said.

The leader kicked the bottom of the locker. Again, my friends tried for my release.

"She's not from here –" Bugsy said.

"She's retarded –" Cristal said.

"I love the colour of your eyes," Aimes said.

"Seriously. Who. The Fuck. Are. You?" the meaty girl asked again.

She shook me so hard that my beanie fell to the floor. I could smell her gel, Dippity-Do. A crowd had gathered around us now, excited for the first fight of the year. One of the Brew Crew took a step forward and touched the leader's back.

"Hey, Tonya, we're late for practice," she said. "You don't get any more chances, remember?"

Tonya pressed her forehead onto mine. From this close up her eyes merged, so she looked like an angry, wet Cyclops. I tried to focus on her one large eye. She was trying to decide if I was nuts enough to push it any further and I logged her momentary pause. She didn't want to fight me – she just needed a satisfactory subterfuge to walk away.

"If I didn't have ringette right now," she said, "I'd fuck you up."

Tonya released me onto the freshly waxed floor. I watched the cowboy boots turn and start down the hall to join the rest of the Brew Crew. "Forget them," I heard her friend say as she steered Tonya away by her shoulders. "They're just a bunch of skiddies."

The Brew Crew spilled down the hallway and out the double doors into the sunlight while the girls helped me onto my feet and the crowd of onlookers dispersed.

"Shit balls," Max said.

"I think I pissed my pants," Aimes whispered.

As they grabbed at me, they began to laugh, trying to release some of the tension I'd created. As it grew, I tried to join in, forcing the sound out at first but soon I caught on. We looked at each other and the laughter got more crazed. Bugsy grabbed my beanie off the floor. Aimes wrapped her arm around my waist and Max and Cristal fanned out on either end as we followed the Brew Crew's route down the hall.

The rest of the first day flew by on the wings of adrenaline. Most of our classes after lunch were together and we circled up in the back, replaying the scene.

"When she had you against that locker, I thought you were going to pass out," Max said.

"Her elbow was right in your neck hole," Bugsy said.

"Trachea," Cristal said, "it's called a trachea."

"Whatever dingus."

"And in my darkest hour, you told Tonya that she had nice eyes," I said to Aimes. "Ya suck-hole."

"I know, I know," Aimes said. "But she does have the prettiest brown eyes when you're close up."

"What did her friend call us?" I asked.

"Skiddies," Bugsy said.

"What does it mean?" I asked.

"No idea," Aimes said. "But it can't be good."

The last bell of the day rang and we pushed through the double doors differently than we'd entered that morning – taller, with more space between us. We had nowhere to be until dinnertime.

"Do you think everyone already knows what happened?" I asked as we walked through the concourse.

"Probably," Bugsy said. "You just messed with the scariest girl in school."

"Tonya was in the same swimming lessons with Ryan when they were kids and she used to hold him between her knees underwater," Max said. "He's still scared of her."

We passed through the student parking lot.

"Keep a look out, Sym," Bugsy said. "She's gonna be on your ass now."

My stomach jackknifed, but the feeling wasn't unpleasant.

"You guys wanna come over to my place?" Aimes asked.

Aimes had not yet shown us her new house and we'd been waiting for the invite.

"Did your mom do a Costco run?" Bugsy asked.

"Yep."

"When's she coming home?"

"She has teeth cleanings till eight."

We followed Aimes across the parking lot to where the school grounds ended and crossed over a freshly rolled-out rectangle of grass that stopped at a gated building. I hadn't noticed the small complex this morning, with butter-yellow plastic siding and small bushes recently landscaped in.

"Here we are." Aimes pointed to a sign that read Golden Acres. "It's only temporary," she said. "The manager is letting us rent a suite even though we're not sixty-five and up."

I giggled, but Bugsy shot me a look.

"It's close to school," Aimes said.

"That's for goddamned sure," Max said.

Two weeks earlier, when her dad had left on a work trip for the weekend, Aimes's mom had moved herself and Aimes out of their rancher in the country and into town. I'd only been to Aimes's rancher once before. It was a long, single-level home surrounded by fields, with multiple skylights in the kitchen and a sunken living room. She had a large stable with a single horse in it. Downsizing from the country to an apartment wasn't ideal, but it was only for a month or so, Aimes had told us, until her mom and dad made up.

"But we have to hide," she said. "Kids aren't allowed in the building."

We ducked along the plastic siding, making sure to be lower than the windows, so that the old folks watching TV didn't see us sneaking by, and slid through an unlocked screen door into a small suite that still smelled of paint, with a gas fireplace in the living room and wall-to-wall cream carpeting.

We threw off our shoes and ran to the cupboards, pulling out Fruit Roll-Ups and saltines.

"Gawd, you gunts, get out of there," Aimes said, as Bugsy threw a bag of salt and vinegar chips across the counter to Max.

On the kitchen island was a twelve-pack of large, cakey blueberry muffins and I ripped into the plastic wrap.

"Don't be pig dogs," Aimes said. "My mom's trying to pay the bills now, you know!"

"So's my mom," I said, lifting out a muffin.

"Let's go to your house then," Aimes said, "and eat all your food."

"Why?" I asked. "We don't have a Costco membership."

"Even if you did, your mom wouldn't buy good treats," Bugsy said.

"Which is exactly why we're being pig dogs here," I said, my mouth crammed with muffin.

I sprawled out on the couch in their grandma-sized living room. Bugsy took the two-seater. Aimes perched on its shoulder and began trying to tease up Bugsy's fallen bangs. Max threw pillows from the couch onto the floor in front of the TV and Cristal perched straight-backed on the piano bench. In the months since I'd met her, Cristal had always kept her cool, not letting herself spaz out with the rest of us. And she listened more than she talked, so when something made her laugh we'd repeat the joke for days.

Cristal looked at her watch and jumped up. "Crap. I gotta go."

"Are you kidding me?" I sat up.

"I gotta be home by four or else I'm grounded again."

She put on her Keds, noticed a dirty spot on the toe, licked her thumb and rubbed at it. I ran over and grabbed her around the waist, hoping to take her serious face away. She lay her head on my shoulder and nuzzled into my neck before she dipped out the door. The girls yelled their goodbyes with mouths full of chips as I flopped back down on the couch to watch *Oprah*. Today, she was interviewing a woman whose stepfather had raped and beaten her when she was a teenager. He'd held her captive in a pit he'd filled with snakes for six months. Because of the snake pit, Oprah said, the woman was different now.

The woman spoke slowly as she clasped her knees. She explained to the audience that in order to survive, she'd split her mind into multiple personalities. Now she had over ninety distinct people living inside of her and they all remembered different parts of her past. She paused a lot during the interview to put her head in her hands.

"I don't know," she kept saying when Oprah asked her a question, "you'll have to ask one of the others."

I was fascinated. I closed my eyes to imagine being her, inside a hole, plywood slats above to keep me from escaping. When she said *a pit full of snakes* did that mean they came up to her chest in a knotted mass? Or was it more like a thin bottom layer that she could differentiate when one slid under her thigh or up her shirt? Could she sit down? If she did, how would she not sit on the snakes? How could she sleep with all that wriggling around? Also, where did she poop? I wasn't frightened by these potentialities but I needed to figure out how it worked logistically, living in a snake pit.

There was a knock on the sliding glass door and Aimes lifted the blinds to show the shapes of three boys through the slats. It was Tyson, Eli and Ollie – kids we knew from grade eight.

"Don't let them in," Bugsy whispered.

"Too late, eye contact," Aimes said. "How do these losers know I moved here?" She slid the door open a crack and the boys ducked inside.

The smell of Drakkar Noir filled the room.

"Where were you guys?" Ollie asked. "We waited for you."

Ollie was a ruddy-cheeked boy, and it looked like over the summer his baby fat had tried turning itself into muscle. He wore a gold cross in one ear and had big blond curls, short on top, long in the back, the same haircut as his four older brothers, who also shared his barrel chest and high-pitched laugh. Seeing him reminded me that he'd lent me his satin Seattle Seahawks bomber jacket a few weeks ago when it had been windy on the tracks and I'd forgotten to give it back. I'd liked sitting beside him that night. He laughed at my jokes. He'd put his arm around me because I was shivering. I'd liked that too – his arm – just for a minute. His eyes crinkled when he smiled at me now, making me warm again.

"You live here now, Aimes?" Tyson interrupted. "We saw you sneaking over after school."

"Not for long," Aimes said.

It looked like Tyson had grown extremely fast this summer and his mom hadn't bought him new jeans to catch up – but he was the kind of kid who didn't care if we saw his bare ankles. Close up, mounds of crusty scabs covered his face. He had zits growing on top of zits.

"So," Eli said, stepping forward. "You girls wanna go to a party with us this weekend?" He spat some brown gunk into a soup can he was holding.

"Eli, that shit stains," Aimes cried and ran for paper towels.

Eli was an asshole. He had a crew cut. Even now he pretended I wasn't there, which made me want to kick him in the shins, or flirt. These boys had grown up with the girls before I'd shown up. They'd gone from kindergarten to grade seven in the same class. They'd played baseball and hung out in barn lofts while their parents had bonfires. That summer, they'd hung out with us on the tracks sometimes, wrestling and throwing rocks. But without mentioning it, we'd cut ties with these boys abruptly. They looked, all of a sudden, very young.

Aimes pushed Eli against the sliding glass door, so she could shove paper towels under his feet before he spat into the can again.

"Whose party?" Max asked, turning off the TV.

Oprah had ended and I'd missed the final wrap-up about the snake pit lady. Now I'd never find out how she fell asleep.

"It's the first grad party of the year," Ollie said.

"That'll be invite-only for sure," Max said. She rolled back onto her belly, ignoring the boys.

My insides started to grind – a similar discomfort as when the senior boys were staring at us in the hallway.

"Where's the party?" I asked.

"It's at my house," Ollie said.

We'd heard about how wild the Solly parties got: kids hanging out of the moss-laden window frames as AC/DC blared inside. Over the summer, a couple of senior boys got into a fight and kicked a hole in the plaster in the living room, revealing insulation made of horsehair. Kids liked it at the Sollys' because no one could make that house worse than it already was.

Bugsy smoothed out her eyebrows. "Tyson, we'll need three two-litre bottles of Rockaberry coolers."

The boys started to shift.

"What's in it for me?" Tyson asked.

"A blowjob from my dog," Bugsy said.

Aimes opened the sliding glass door and pushed them through it. "Friday night. Seven p.m. Meet us on the tracks."

The boys left the same way they came in, ducking across the lawn till they got to the hedge, and disappeared. Aimes jumped to the end of the couch and started doing gawky box-like figure eights with her hips.

"Friday's the night," she sang, rotating messily above me – no tits, no ass, no rhythm. "Someone's gonna wanna do something to me!"

All Aimes had wanted all summer was to get her period and kiss a guy and neither had happened. At the Sollys' she'd be sure to find someone drunk enough to take interest.

"But, Friday night's my birthday," I said. "We're having a sleepover."

"Perfect," Aimes said. "An alibi!"

Right then, we heard footsteps and keys jangling outside the door. The four of us froze – then moved quickly. We each grabbed something – the tray of muffins, our shoes, the pillows and crackers and juice – and we ran for the bathroom. If Aimes's mom caught us here on the first day of school we wouldn't be invited back, and this place was too convenient to give up. It was our new clubhouse. We could come here and take shits at lunchtime.

We scrambled inside, arms full, and stepped into the bathtub. Max and I kneeled as Aimes and Bugsy crouched overtop us. Like she knew what would happen next, Aimes slowly pulled the shower curtain shut, her finger to her lips. The bathroom door opened. Kitty was on the other side of the curtain – the only thing separating us white magnolias printed on plastic.

Convenience wasn't the only reason for our panic: Kitty was kind to us. She blasted Phil Collins when we'd hung out at the ranch house. She put ice in our drinks. She let us try on her clothes – the navy-blue power dress with scalloped neckline that fit me perfectly. Unlike my mom, Kitty treated us like we had something in common – a female-ness that was to be enjoyed. But mostly, even though we hadn't heard directly about Kitty leaving her husband, it was exciting to see a woman willing to blow her life apart like this. She didn't need us jumping out of nowhere and scaring the shit out of her.

Kitty unzipped the back of her skirt and pulled her nylons down. She let out a strong stream of urine and at the tail end came a tiny fart. We held our breath and looked to our sock feet, unable to make eye contact for fear of explosion. Through the curtain we could smell the musky scent moms make. She flushed the toilet and washed her hands for a long time. Then the bathroom door opened and she left. Taking a collective shallow breath we waited, still. The front door opened and shut. She was gone. She'd come home on her break from scraping plaque out of people's mouths to pee in private.

Listening in on her, an intimacy she hadn't agreed to, and knowing how humiliated she'd be if she knew, sedated the mood.

Aimes pushed back the shower curtain and stepped onto the bath mat. We followed. Bugsy put the sheath of crackers back in its box and closed it properly. Max filled the half-finished two-litre of juice with water, so it looked unopened, and placed it back in the door of the fridge. I grabbed the pillows and arranged them on the couch. Aimes handed us our shoes a pair at a time as we stood at the door.

"See you at school tomorrow," Aimes said, no longer high on the prospect of being felt up by a drunk guy.

We nodded and tried to smile but she wouldn't make eye contact. Sneaking out through the sliding glass door we sped across the shared lawn, bent at the waist, until we hit the bushes, then we ran.

When we hit Pleasant Valley Road we swung a right to head to the Short Stop for a slush. Max had softball practice so she peeled off to the left.

"Bye, Max," I yelled as she walked toward the field.

Her dad was the coach and he expected her to be there early to help him set up. She didn't like softball but she disliked her father's anger more, so twice a week she put on her glove and ran bases to keep the peace. She raised her arm and gave us a thumbs up as she strode up the hill. Max was only twelve, a full year younger than the rest of us, but she was already smarter. Putting her Walkman on, she started to sing. She was teaching herself French and Italian and she used every extra minute she had to memorize the words to the songs phonetically, not caring who heard her.

Watching Max walk away, backlit by the sun, I noticed she had The Sway. Her heavy brown hair going one way while her butt went the other. *If Max is a bowl of freshly picked strawberries, I'm a banana split with salsa on top*, I thought, feeling both protective and jealous at the same time. There was a sense of foreboding. I wanted to tackle her. I wanted to lay my body on top of hers before anyone else saw what I just had.

At the Short Stop Bugsy passed me a slush. I sucked on it till I got a brain freeze and handed it back, then we power walked to the tracks, only two now, clambering up the embankment to our spot.

"Is Aimes mad at us?" I asked.

"Nah, I don't think so," Bugsy said.

"Why'd her parents split up?" I said.

"Not my business," Bugsy said.

This was something else I didn't get yet. We spent all our time together but didn't share much at all and I was learning that I wasn't supposed to ask. Maybe that was why we were able to be so close, because we left the raggedy bits at home.

"Her pee smelled funny," Bugsy said.

"That's what happens when you become a mom: you get fat and your pee smells like skunk," I said.

"Are you gonna have kids?" she asked.

"Oh totally," I said.

"Me too," Bugsy said.

"Babies are sooooo cute," I said.

"I just wanna pinch them," Bugsy said.

"Twist their little ears," I said.

"Exactly. Or a nice, strong flick," she said.

Only here a few moments and the tracks had worked their magic. We brushed off our bums and I looked toward home.

"This is gonna be the best birthday you've ever had," Bugsy said, jumping off the rails, "'cause it's with us." She darted onto the shortcut that would take her home. "LYLAS bitch!"

"See ya later, skater," I yelled back.

Watching her leave, I realized what we'd just set in motion and my stomach dropped like the first hit of turbulence on a plane.

Four hours into the drive back to Armstrong, I take an Ativan to smooth my nerves. I don't play music or listen to the radio, aware that this is the last bit of silence I'll get. Making good time through the mountains, I take the first exit off the highway into Armstrong just after dusk and pull up behind a rusted-out truck. Police cars are blocking the T-junction up ahead. I guess they're checking all cars going in and coming out of town. I light a smoke, the last one before I can sneak out later. The line creeps forward slowly and when the smoke is done, I throw it out the window. Almost thirty minutes later, at the front of the checkpoint, a cop stands in the middle of the road, his belt heavy with a baton and a Maglite. He puts up his hand as he strides over to the driver's side. I recognize him instantly. Constable Green, a tank, with his thick moustache and crinkly blue eyes.

"I'm here to take care of my mom, Judy, from Zion United," I say as he scans the back seat.

Constable Green's son was in my high school graduating class and we always saw the Green family at church on Christmas Eve, that one night a year everyone tries to get a little holy. I must have been in grade eleven or twelve the night the doorbell rang and Mom opened the back door to find Constable Green holding up my very drunk little brother by his scruff.

"Next time I'll put him in the drunk tank to scare the shit outta him," Constable Green had said conspiratorially. "But I thought you'd want to sort him out this time, Jude."

Mom had forced a smile and grabbed her swaying son.

"Boys will be boys," he'd said. "I know it's hard on your own." He'd smiled again and we all felt hopeful for a moment.

"Okay. Pass," Constable Green says, waving me ahead, no smile this time.

I put my foot on the gas. At the turnoff to Mom's house I wave at her neighbour but he doesn't wave back. I'm not surprised. They all seem suspicious of me, watching through the windows of their cookie-cutter new builds when I let Midge pee on their lawns. Mom's decision to sell our family home had been sudden. After over a decade of restoring the hundred-year-old beauty to her original glory, she'd put the house on the market as soon as both of us kids had graduated from high school.

"I don't want to be married to nails and wood," she'd said, "so I'll sell her in her best condition."

"What about enjoying her in her best condition?" I'd countered, but Mom was too practical for that, and she'd quickly sold for under the asking price.

Almost immediately she'd regretted it and the ache of losing our family home was so real for all three of us that no one drives down Pleasant Valley Road anymore. It's been over a decade since Mom moved to the nondescript bungalow at the top of Okanagan Hill by the golf course. It's not her style, with taupe walls and shitty linoleum, and every time I pull into the driveway I feel a throb in my chest.

Mom's perched on a stool in the carport, ready to help me carry my bags inside, her dumb dog Zippy bouncing around her ankles. Even though it's only been two days, her thinness catches me by surprise. The skin on her neck flags and her dye job has grown out, showing a halo of grey. Five-foot-one and a steady 120 pounds, Mom has always prided herself on being mistaken for looking a decade younger than she is, but as she scurries toward the car she looks closer to eighty than her sixty-five years, and frail – a word I've never used to describe her before. I don't know why I'm shocked to see her failing. It's been almost two years since her diagnosis. I suppose it's because she's had cancer before so I know she'll beat it again.

Setting Midge down to unzip her bag, I lean in and tap Mom lightly on the back with one hand, trying not to let her get too much of a grip on me. Her neck smells like flannelette and she's trembling.

Midge pops out of her carrier and squats to pee and we break apart, glad to have something to focus on. There's still no snow in Armstrong, only a dry, dusty cold, and the naked old lilac bushes that edge the house look like they're shivering in embarrassment.

Mom leads the way through the side door and I kick off my shoes on the landing and follow her up the few steps to the kitchen.

"I didn't sleep a wink," she says. "I'm depressed."

"That's why I'm here," I say, lugging my suitcase across the blah-coloured linoleum. "Have you had dinner?" This is something I can do.

"I need to get prepared," Mom says as she pushes a shoebox filled with prescription meds and supplements to the corner of the table. "My affairs in order, that kind of stuff."

Picking up three hot pink Post-it Notes, she sticks them to her palm and turns them to face me.

"Anything you want," she says and spreads her arms wide to suggest the entirety of the house. "Put your name on the note and stick it to the furniture." She stops to consider. "Now, if you and Grum want the same item, we'll have to discuss that," she says. "But for now, I just need to know what I can start throwing away."

I don't want to indulge the drama. My mother is birdlike but also formidable, and this idea of packing herself up before she dies reeks of attention-seeking. I'd like to tell her so, but a cork has lodged itself in my throat.

"This is morbid," I manage to say. "I'm not putting sticky notes on furniture to pre-claim my inheritance. You're not going to die."

I can tell she's already fatigued by the way she looks at me, eyes dull and set back, but it's best if we keep moving. Stillness means contemplation, which might lead to talking, which could end in honesty and that'll do no good for either of us.

"The average lung cancer lifespan is four years and I've already used two years up."

"Dr. Google isn't a medical authority," I say. "Just look at you. Such a strong little lady, still bopping around."

Mom sinks into a chair and sighs. I wish I could sit down beside her, lie my face in her lap. But someone has to stay upright.

"Lydia and Hilda have taken to the streets."

Lydia and Hilda are Mom's church pals. They both live alone too, but seem a lot more content with it than my mother.

"They've decided to break curfew," Mom continues. "A bunch of them gather in the fairgrounds at dusk and walk across town with brooms, rakes, shovels – whatever they can find. To prove they're not scared."

"But they're probably scared, right?"

"No one's going to attack a half-dozen senior citizens at 8 p.m.," she says.

"Wielding garden tools," I say. "Probably not."

"This isn't a time for jokes," Mom says. "We're in the middle of a very serious tragedy if you haven't noticed."

"Yes, I've noticed. The whole country has noticed. I'm here, aren't I?"

Beelining for the guest bedroom, I close the door. There are fresh sheets on the bed and the room smells of lemon Pledge. She's turned on the bedside lamp and my eyes can't help but droop as I pull the sheets back. I can hear her slipping off her shoes and replacing them with her well-worn slippers. She travels through the kitchen, opens the fridge then closes it. The radio turns on.

"Punky?" she calls, then the slippers scuffle over to my door and I hear a light knock.

"Come in," I answer, bringing my computer onto my lap.

She opens the door and leans against the doorframe as if the trek from kitchen to bedroom has taken everything out of her. She's got an apron on, the one with the green flowers on it.

"You're always on your computer," she says.

"I'm right here, Mom," I say, but my eyes don't leave the screen.

"I want a visit with you."

"I'm working," I say, and my throat constricts.

She sighs and pushes herself off the doorframe. A few minutes later I hear her shuffle down the hall to her bedroom. The squeak of the brass bed means she's climbed into its saggy middle for her early evening lie-down. The house is quiet except for the sound of shame that's begun to seep under the door of my room – a high, seething hiss. The noise covers the floor like a thin wave and slowly rises up the side of the bed. After fifteen minutes of my guts twisting, they rumble. We haven't eaten yet. She'll be hungry and the food will serve as an apology.

But when I open the door, the kitchen is dark, the only light a blinking red dot coming from the clock radio. I'm too late. She's already tacked the blankets to the windows for the night. She must have climbed the stepstool silently, to prove a point or not to bother me. Both options hurt. I swallow, put my boots on, clip Midge to her leash and head out into the cold.

A block away from the house, I light a smoke, turn right onto Okanagan Street and glance behind me. Nothing. My mind jumps back to Mom in bed, beside her pile of medical journals. My presence seems to only emphasize how alone she is. At least when she's by herself there's no one around to let her down.

The shrine is where Mom said it would be, at the intersection where the tracks meet the road. In front of the teddy bears and cards, cellophaned roses overflow onto the street. At the base of the telephone pole three candles flicker on a prom photo taken of Taylor four months before. She's wearing a bronze satin off-the-shoulder dress and a thin tiara, her brown hair slicked back like a princess. Beside the picture, handwritten letters have been tacked up, the words mostly illegible from last night's rain but I can make out a few phrases. "I'll never forget you," "LYLAS" and "I guess God needs another angel," penned in loopy teenage handwriting. Collages glued onto cardboard have been tacked to the pole and jut out onto the sidewalk, making the shrine impossible to sidestep: Taylor at a birthday party with a decorative bow stuck in her hair, Taylor on a bench, her palm out, feeding a pigeon, Taylor in front of a school bus, an instrument case in her hand, someone doing bunny ears behind her. I tighten and shiver and stomp my feet to get the blood back into my legs. Her graduation picture looks a lot like mine — taken fifteen years earlier — the plastic flowers and cardboard hat, in the same room, probably sitting on the same stool, both of us fake smiling into our futures.

I back away from the telephone pole and hunch against the cold. Taylor hadn't been raped. This was what everyone was talking about: she'd fought him off.

On my previous quick trip home, I was in Askew's for groceries and I recognized one of the cashiers from high school. While scanning the meal replacements I was buying for Mom, she told me she knew Taylor's mom, Marie. I wasn't surprised to hear it and I leaned forward.

A few days after Taylor's murder, the cashier said, a police officer pushed through the media circus outside Marie's home and knocked on the front door.

"She'd already told the police everything she knew," the cashier said as she bagged my groceries.

That Halloween night, when Taylor didn't respond to her text messages, Marie had gone looking for her. On the tracks she found Taylor's broken cell phone. Then, Taylor's friends joined Marie in the search. When Marie found Taylor unconscious in the ditch she'd crawled to her and curled herself around her daughter's still-breathing body. "Hold on, hon," I imagine she'd said. "Stay strong for me, Tae."

Then she'd screamed at the girls to call an ambulance.

"Marie had gone over the night again and again," the cashier continued as I paid, "but this time she had a question for them. She wanted to know what would've happened if Taylor hadn't put up such a fight. So, she asked the officer: 'If my daughter had let him rape her, would she still be alive?'"

I imagine Taylor's mom standing in the front hallway of her darkened house. The officer quiet, considering what he knew so far.

"Yes," he'd said. "If the man had got what he wanted, he wouldn't have beaten her so badly. She might have pulled through."

I step away from the shrine. A girl was murdered because she didn't allow it.

The sky is cloudless and when I inhale the cold burns my throat. A police car drives by. He flashes his lights but doesn't stop.

1991

IT WAS 6 P.M. AND EVERYONE HAD ARRIVED except for Cristal, who wasn't allowed out, even though it was my birthday. From the window of my attic bedroom we watched Max's dad careen into the driveway. She got out of the car, yelled something we didn't catch and slammed the door, the gravel crunching as the Volvo sped off. What was he mad at her for this time? The screen door opened and I heard an indistinct greeting from Mom and then footsteps running through the dining room and up the stairs. My bedroom door opened and Bugsy and Aimes pounced on Max—the bearer of all information, as she'd been the one who'd talked to Ollie last.

Max put her backpack on the floor in front of her, then she put her head in her hands.

"We're uninvited," she said.

We looked to each other.

"Who says?"

"The Brew Crew said if any skidlets show up they aren't coming," Max said. "Ollie says sorry and happy birthday, Em."

"Those bitches know that the seniors will give us the booze they want for themselves," Aimes said.

"Will they beat us up if we show?" I asked, desperate to not spend my birthday at home doing vo5 hot oil hair treatments.

"They might," Max said. "I'm not risking it." She crawled across the carpet on all fours and shut the door. "Don't worry, Em," she said. "We're still going to throw you a birthday party." Her jeans pulled at her belly, so she lay back and shimmied out of them. She crawled pantsless to her backpack and pulled out a large bottle of clear liquid. "I stole it from my parents' wine cellar. They won't miss one twenty-sixer."

Max passed the bottle around so we could each hold it. There was a goose flying across the label.

"Is that enough for us all to get drunk on?" I asked.

"I think so," Max said. "It's stronger than beer."

She'd saved us. We looked around the circle in relief. We could still get shit-tanked for the first time with or without those fuck nuts.

Standing up, Max held the bottle above her head and wiggled for us in her high-waisted underpants. "We'll show them!"

An hour later, after saying a quick goodbye to Mom and promising we'd be home by eleven, we stormed up the street, arms linked.

"We'll show them, we'll show them!" we chanted as we lunged onto the tracks.

We ran to our spot, kicking up stones and gravel. Max unzipped her bag and pulled out the vodka, cracked open the sealed cap and passed it across the circle to me. I had no idea what "drunk" would feel like, but I was with them so I knew it would be good.

I lifted the bottle to the air. "We'll show them!" I yelled again and brought it to my lips.

Tilting back, I drank three big gulps. My eyes watered fire. Leaning forward, hands on my knees, I dry-heaved but didn't puke. Steeling myself with their shouts and rough smacks to my back, I chugged more of the molten liquid, wiped my face and passed the bottle to an outstretched hand. Aimes took the bottle and put her tongue down the spout. She gagged and passed the bottle along to Bugsy, who took a sniff.

"There's no berry flavour," Bugsy said, and without tasting it handed it to Max, who took a neat sip and then squatted down and tilted her head back to swig like it was summertime in a Coke commercial. I looked at my girls, laughing and dressed so pretty on the eve before my birthday. It felt like a miracle. The sky was light blue, on its way to dusk, and the air smelled of the sticky buds that grew along the ditch. I reached for the bottle but the ground was uneven and I fell forward onto my hands and knees. I reached out again, but misjudged Max's pass by a long shot. We found this very funny and had to stop everything and die laughing. I plopped onto my butt and squinted, trying to see how much alcohol was left in the bottle, then looked back to the group. Aimes and Bugsy shook their heads. They weren't going to drink tonight. We were already getting unruly and someone needed to get us home.

This wasn't spoken, just passed in a glance as Bugsy ran her fingers through her hair and raised her eyebrows at Aimes.

I chugged till my stomach burned. Putting my face in my hands, the world started to spin and when I opened my eyes I couldn't see my friends anymore, only blurs. Reaching up, I found hands that pulled me to standing. It felt like we'd been relocated to a ball pit on a trampoline. Even with my feet planted wide, I wobbled as I tried to raise the empty bottle above my head, but where my arms had been, they weren't anymore. I could see the hazy shapes of the girls but nothing further. Everything outside our circle had been caught in the flash of a camera, too bright and impossibly white. I couldn't place where the new and strange sounds were coming from, loud yelps and tinny, faraway laughter.

"Watch this," I said, and brought the bottle down hard across the metal rails.

The glass shattered and ricocheted up at us. The girls screamed and I covered my face, more afraid of the noise than all the tiny shards of glass.

With Bugsy and Aimes in the lead, we scrambled back to Rosedale Avenue, laughing at our inability to place our feet without rolling an ankle. In the short time between sober and drunk, the rules of motion had changed and lifting up an arm or leg had entirely different consequences now. I wasn't in control and I couldn't pretend to be and this was such a great amount of fun.

The sidewalk disappeared and the houses melted into lumps. Sounds became untrustworthy, too close by or way far away. I turned around slowly, or thought I did, and found myself on the ground again. The shape of Max pointed at me and I looked down at the two bendy straws that used to be my legs, the colour red pouring out of them. Without the constraints of muscle and bone I'd become a moving liquid.

Max and Bugsy grabbed me by the armpits and dragged me over to a lawn.

"Oh shit, she ripped her jeans," I heard Bugsy yell.

I tried to open my eyes, searching for a familiar road sign that would tell me where we were, but I'd lost the ability to read. This made me laugh. *Who cares. Who cares.* Someone grabbed my hand and yanked me up again. Aimes and Bugsy flanked us while Max and I accordioned into each other and more red poured out of our elbows and knees, making us laugh harder. Why did nothing hurt? Finally, we crawled up each other to standing and charged down the centre of the street, heading directly toward oblivion.

Headlights. Glare. Boys' voices. A rusty tan pickup truck. *We're having fun. We showed them. We showed them. We sure did.* A large white house came into view across the street, its lit-up windows making the front facade look like a face. I had to get closer to the feeling inside that home. My feet slipped along the pavement like I was skating. I stepped onto the gravel drive and sidled along the side of the house toward a large window, which I crouched under. All I could make out was gauzy white, but once my eyes found focus I recognized the pattern as lace curtains and I was able to see deeper into the room itself. A large table. Seven high-backed chairs. Seven old women sitting in them. A pile of colourful squares poured off the table onto the women's laps. A quilting circle.

My forehead leaned against the cold pane. These women could've been sitting in this wallpapered room, in the exact same chairs, for the past million years. Mom was probably in her chair too, working with a needle as well, on a sock, or a small hole in my favourite shirt. Grum would be on the couch beside her and our old dog Fred resting at her feet, her sentinels. Spying through the lace into this room I started to make horrible sounds. My cheeks were wet. Something was coming out of my nose. A woman from the circle looked toward the window. She was the owner of the house. I knew by the way she stood. I dropped down under the sill to hide. I wanted to go home but I didn't know how to get there and Mom would be so angry at the state I was in. All of a sudden I wanted to die.

I sat down on the gravel and wiped at my eyes. An engine revved across the street. Laughter. I ran down the driveway toward the sounds of my friends.

Awoken by loud music, I could feel the vibrations underneath me. I didn't know what time it was. I was cold, lying on something metal and bumpy.

"She's puking, get her out of my truck," a voice yelled.

Someone's puking, they should get her out of their truck, I thought to myself.

There was a sharp yank. I was being dragged by the hair. The grooves along the bottom of the flatbed shoved sticks and nails under my shirt as I was pulled forward and then I was weightless.

I woke up. What time was it? It must be before eleven. I had to get home before Mom started to worry. My hair was wet against my neck. Finding my hands, I brought them to my chest and trailed my fingers down my naked belly. My shirt was gone. I tried to open my eyes but they were stuck shut. I could smell soil. My cheek felt deliciously cool. Putting my hands to my face, I pried my eyelids apart and let my eyes roll around for a bit until I saw a long, green stalk in my periphery. At the top of it, if I squinted, I could see a blast of colour. What was the name of this beauty? What were the names of all the beautiful things I didn't know about yet? I heard a scream of laughter in the distance. The girls were here. I let my eyes go heavy, then close. They'd remember me if I forgot to.

I woke up again. There were loud voices above me but I couldn't decipher the words. I had to figure out where I was before the voices noticed I was awake. Something smelled antiseptic, or was it disinfectant? What was the difference? There was a long moan. Behind me a new baby cried. I wiggled my toes. I clenched and unclenched my fists. I wasn't paralyzed. Nothing was broken. I fell back asleep.

I woke to the sound of metal rings being ripped across their tracks, then the *shush shush shush* of slippers nearby. The voices were back around me, low but harsh like they didn't care if they disturbed me. There was a flash of light that made me flinch and behind my eyes, red. Another flash, closer this time. I thought I heard my mother's voice. She was here. She'd stop the vicious light.

"Take more pictures of her," a male voice directed. "So she won't forget."

"It's embarrassing how she looks," my mother said.

The bright punches of light continued, so I tried to roll over. The movement turned my stomach into an ocean and I vomited on myself.

"How did it happen?" my mom asked.

"They drank too much," the irritated voice said. "She's lucky she isn't dead."

"Is she hurt?"

"Looks like some boys got at her."

I touched my stomach under the blankets. I was naked. My skin tacky. I could taste a burning high note in my nasal cavity, acid at the back of my throat. *Who got at me?* I wondered. *What did they get?*

"Does anyone know how many girls were involved?" asked the same male voice I couldn't place.

"There were four of them but she's the worst," my mom said.

"Have their parents brought them in yet? To get rape kits done?"

"I don't think so. She's the worst," Mom repeated. I could hear her trying to match his clinical tone. "I had to hold her head up by her hair to drive her here," Mom said. "I thought she'd choke on her own vomit. She just wouldn't stop puking. Heads are very heavy."

"Heaviest part of the body," he said. "We've pumped her stomach. Her esophagus will be bruised, so only liquids, but she probably won't be able to keep them down. Don't clean her sheets. Don't wash her hair. Let her steep in it."

A kindness snuck into the man's voice. "She's lucky she's got a nurse for a mom."

"Thank you, Doctor," Mom said, matching his cold tone perfectly now.

I fell back asleep.

I woke up walking this time. Someone was pulling me faster than I could keep up.

"I can't open my eyes," I said, reaching to find a wall.

She started wiping at my face with a rough piece of cloth.

"Your eyes are caked shut with your own puke," Mom said.

Using the wall to steady myself, I was able to pry my eyes open with my fingers again, wincing at the overhead lights. There was a small figure bent over in front of me. She had short hair and was wearing a hospital dressing gown and her sneakers were unlaced. I leaned in closer to get a better look.

"You're looking at yourself, Emmy," Mom said.

Stooping toward my reflection in the hospital sliding glass doors, I saw that my long hair was plastered to my head like damp clay.

Mom grabbed me by the forearm and pulled me close. She was pinching me on purpose.

"I work here," she seethed. "My colleagues saw me drag you in. Bugsy's mom helped pump your stomach. How does that reflect on me?"

She was so angry. I could feel it in her hands.

"Do you see what you've done to yourself?"

The light was still too bright for me to properly open my eyes, but I could tell we were standing in the vestibule between the emergency room and outside. I needed to lean on her but she wouldn't allow it. She pointed the camera at me again and I raised my hand up to shield myself – but the flash hit my eyes, another violent smack.

When I woke up again, I knew more time had passed. My head was under the kitchen sink and hot water poured over me. Mom was scrubbing my scalp. She had yellow dish gloves on. The water raced down my forehead into my mouth and I had to turn my face so as not to swallow the sour she was rinsing out of my hair. I started to cry, not because it hurt but because it felt like she wanted it to. *I'm not a bad person*, I said to myself.

"I'll need to do this at least three more times," she said, fingers trying to pull apart the matted chunks. She didn't bother brushing out the tangles at the ends. They were too far gone.

The phone rang and Mom left me bent over the sink. I shivered, waiting. When she came back she wrapped my still-soapy hair in a towel.

"It's your dad," she said. "He wants to talk to you."

By her tone I could tell they'd already spoken.

"I hear you got into some birthday trouble," Dad said as I leaned against the wall, phone to my ear.

"Ya," I said.

"Sounds like she's pretty mad at you," he said.

"Mm hmm," I said.

I wasn't sure if he was going to scream at me or take my side. Both his temper and his kindness always took me by surprise.

"Not a happy birthday, hey kiddo?"

"Nope."

"You just wanted to have a little fun and it got out of hand."

"Yep," I said.

He was being nice. I tried not to cry.

"You're just a teenager. It's not your fault. When I come for a visit we'll celebrate for real, okay?"

Mom grabbed the phone and hung up.

I don't remember getting up the stairs or falling back asleep, but upon waking I heard the voices of men. There were fathers in the house. I smelled clean cotton and the window had been cracked. I brought my legs up and curled into a ball, opening my eyes. I didn't know what day it was but I felt awake, energized even. Rolling out of bed, my skin stuck to itself – when I stood up, I peeled my arm off my torso.

In the bathroom, the mirror showed a large gash that started under my nose and travelled across my cheek. My face was yellow. The whites of my eyes were almost entirely red from burst blood vessels and my hair was still stiff so I wrapped it in a towel again, splashed water on my face and tied my bathrobe, preparing for visitors.

One hand on the banister for balance, I followed the voices down the attic steps. As I rounded into the living room they all looked up in unison like gophers caught mid-dig. It's who I thought it would be: the girls and their parents had come by to see if I was alright. I edged my way through the living room and sat on the ottoman, tucking my legs under me, but no one met my gaze. The carpet had been vacuumed and the blankets were folded nicely on the back of the chesterfield and the room smelled of Pledge. My stomach rumbled.

Bugsy and her parents had claimed the high backs that mom had carried in from the dining room and were as stiff as the chairs they sat in. Aimes was perched on a footstool and Kitty stood behind her, a hand on her daughter's shoulder. Max's family had the window seat, her father's legs spread, his face red like usual.

Cristal and her parents weren't there because she'd been in her basement the night we'd gone out. How many days had it been since then? None of the parents were bothering with small talk and it dawned on me that this was the first time they'd all officially met. Bugsy's mom worked with mine at the hospital, but we'd never all been in the same room together.

Mom entered balancing a tray of mismatched napkins and her good tea-cups, hostessing like she was throwing us a party. Offering milk and sugar around, the parents leaned forward to get their tea while Aimes stood to pass around a plate of Mom's burnt raisin cookies. The room wavered for a moment so I focused on the carpet. The girls stayed silent, their eyes on the floor too.

"What do you want to say to the rest of the parents?" Max's dad leaned forward, elbows on knees. The colour in his cheeks bloomed upward toward the top of his balding head.

Max sat up straighter on the cushions but kept her eyes on her hands.

"I'm sorry I stole the vodka," she said. "I didn't know this would happen."

After Max spoke, the room became animated.

"I don't know why you even called us here, Judy," Bugsy's mom said from the high back. "My girl is not in trouble." She patted Bugsy's hand. "My girl didn't drink anything. She. Ran. For. Help." She looked to Bugsy and smiled. "But if Bugsy *did* drink, it wouldn't be a twenty-sixer of straight vodka around boys she doesn't know —"

"Are you suggesting they asked for it, Barb?" Max's dad interrupted. A muscle in his neck twitched.

"Thirteen-year-olds too drunk to say no *is* asking for it, in *my* opinion," Bugsy's mom said.

This was when I realized no one was here to see if I was okay. They were here to find out who was to blame.

"I've got to go to the bathroom," Max said, sliding down from the window seat. She looked like you did after riding a horse all day, stiff and bow-legged. Watching her waddle through the French doors into the kitchen, I saw streamers tacked up to the walls and another realization hit — today was my fourteenth birthday.

Max's dad leaned back and folded his arms over his large belly. "We want the facts," he said, "from who remembers them."

Did the hospital happen only last night? Were what felt like days of puking only hours? I shook my head, confused by how time could twist that way. So sly.

Aimes lifted a hand as if she had the right answer. Kitty smiled down at her daughter. Her short, black bob was pinned back like she didn't have time to blow-dry it, but her blouse and jeans were ironed, making her look equestrian.

I leaned forward, ravenous to hear what happened, and I smiled, encouraging Aimes.

"Em and Max got drunk on the tracks." She looked to the parents. "We didn't know what would happen," she said. "They started running through the alleys and jumping fences."

An image flashed by me. Falling down. No pain. Knees wet with red. Trying to keep up with the fun.

"Bugsy and I couldn't keep track. They were banging on doors and throwing rocks at windows."

Aimes was still in her pajamas – matching tops and bottoms that had a print of about a hundred penguins wearing red nightcaps. Her hair was lank.

"The girls decided they wanted to crash the Sollys' grad party," Aimes continued. "So we headed over to Fletcher Avenue – "

She looked to me and raised her eyebrows but I shook my head. No recollection.

"When we were a block or two away from the party, some older guys pulled up in a truck, so we all jumped into the flatbed." Aimes paused here, deciding what to say next. "Then Em started puking so one of the guys shoved her out onto her head."

Another flash. Lying on my belly in the dirt. Laughter above me.

"Whose party was it that you wanted to attend?" Bugsy's mom asked, pressing her highlights behind her ears. Her shirt was tucked into her slacks like she was on her way to a golf tournament, but from the expression on her face, she fucking hated golf.

"You know the Solly brothers," Bugsy said, head still down. "You work with their mom."

"Oh yes, those boys run wild."

"Ollie helped us last night," Bugsy said, crossing her legs. She was wearing what seemed to be her little sister's jogging pants, too small and stretched thin.

"Well, I wouldn't want to be the mother of five sons," her mom said. "Bound to be troub – "

Max's dad interrupted again.

"Let me get this straight. Max and Emmy got shit-tanked drunk?"

Bugsy nodded.

"And you all got into the back of a stranger's truck?" He took a napkin to his forehead.

"We knew them," Bugsy said, speaking again. "We knew who the boys were."

Bugsy nodded for Aimes to continue.

"Em was puking pretty bad so we rolled her onto her tummy," Aimes said. "And when we turned around, Max was gone."

"Why was Emmy's shirt off?" my mom asked from the doorway.

Aimes shrugged. "I don't know." She was bouncing on the footstool, then stopped herself.

"Em wouldn't wake up," Bugsy said, looking at my mom. "Then Ollie ran by. His mom had just busted up the party and he saw Em in the flowerbed." Bugsy's mom patted her daughter's hand again. "Ollie told us to run to the store and call you, Judy," Bugsy said, pulling her hand away. "He put his sweater over Emmy so she wouldn't get cold."

Mom's voice broke in from the doorway. "I just don't know how you imagined this would turn out."

"What happened to my daughter? Where did you find her?" Max's dad interrupted again.

"When we came back with Judy about half an hour later, Max was sitting in the flowerbed beside Em. The boys were gone and the pickup truck too."

"Poor Ollie was so distraught," my mom said. "He'd never seen a girl look so unladylike before."

Max limped back into the room and squeezed between her mom and dad on the edge of the window seat. I'd always dreamed of having a bay window. Mom had found a shiny fabric for the drapes and made cushions to match our sponge-painted walls almost exactly.

Max's dad stood up. "You girls think you can waltz around town, drunk off your tits, and nothing bad will happen?"

"I thought so," Max said.

Bugsy's mom grabbed her purse. "You know what?" she said, rising. "This has nothing to do with us. Punish how you see fit. And you're welcome for pumping your stomach last night, Emmy. It was not fun." She strode out of the room and her husband, not having said a word, followed behind. Bugsy scowled and slunk out behind her parents. We heard the screen door slam and then their engine catch.

Mom looked at me from the doorway and pointed to my grade seven photo on the mantel. "They did whatever they wanted to you," she said. "I'll never be able to look at that girl again." In the picture I was wearing a forest-green turtleneck and a gold locket sat centred on my chest. My hair was long and blond. "She's gone now," Mom said, speaking to me as if we were the only ones in the room. "How am I supposed to live with that?"

Looking at the photo, I didn't understand. I was sick. My mother shouldn't be angry with me.

Kitty wiped at her eyes.

"The girls are tired," she whispered to no one.

"Maybe this will teach them not to be pigs around alcohol," Max's dad said.

Max turned. "We didn't know how much to drink, Dad."

"Well, I assumed you'd know not to drink so much that you wouldn't remember who took advantage of you," he yelled.

Max's mom grabbed her husband's knee. "Joe. No one has any idea —"

"We know our daughter is limping. We know that." He stood up. "Enough of this. You got what you asked for."

He stormed out of the room and Max and her mom followed quickly behind. Max touched my shoulder on her way past.

Aimes's mom turned now too.

"Thank you for dropping them off, Judy," she said, laying a jean jacket across Aimes's shoulders. "I'm happy to pay for any cleaning costs to your car."

Mom nodded.

"Let's chalk it up to a learning experience." Kitty smiled brightly. "Maybe it's for the best no one remembers, right girls?"

I nodded too.

"Let me help you tidy up," she said, moving to the coffee table.

"Thanks, but I'm fine, we're fine." Mom shrugged off the offer and started to clear the teacups.

Aimes hugged me tight and Kitty gave me a long squeeze too. "I'm sure glad you're okay, sweetheart," she said, and brought her hand to my chin.

I began to cry then, big, sloppy tears, relieved that someone saw I was there.

"See you at school on Monday?" Aimes said.

Aimes and Kitty slipped on their shoes and quietly left through the front porch door. Mom waited till the screen door slammed shut and she could hear their footsteps on the gravel walkway.

"Well, I'm not cancelling dinner," she said, heading toward the kitchen. "Get yourself cleaned up. You can't smell like that."

I didn't understand.

"It's your birthday. I've invited friends from church," she said. "We'll have to pretend you have the flu."

Exiting the living room, I saw that in addition to the streamers hung across the kitchen archway, balloons had been stuck to the walls of the dining room. Sinking down onto the piano bench, I dropped my head into my hands and breathed into my palms. I was fourteen years old. I couldn't remember what happened to any of us. I felt good.

We'd been wild and bad and wrong. We'd shown them.

Like every other weekday morning, Cristal sped up on her racing bike, smoked a quick dart in the breezeway, opened the back door and came through the glassed-in porch into the kitchen, ready to walk me to school.

"Hiya Jude," she greeted Mom.

"Hi hon," Mom said, and smiled, the first I'd seen since Friday.

"Whoa, Scarface," Cristal said, noticing the cut that ran from my nose to my ear.

I was impressed by it too. Mom told me that it wasn't deep enough to scar and the worst of it would be gone within the week, so I figured today would be its best presentation.

"I heard you guys from my window," she said as we headed to school. "With the party at the Sollys' and you guys screaming down the street, my parents grounded me on Saturday night too."

Which was why she hadn't been at my birthday dinner, a silent affair of knives scraping, throats clearing and eyes cast downward onto plates.

"Sorry I got you grounded," I said as we trudged up the hill.

"My parents grounded me for something I wasn't even there for. That's officially fucking nuts."

Once through the concourse, Cristal grabbed my elbow and led us through the slate-blue doors into the high school foyer. Like she knew it would happen, all eyes turned to me. Word had gotten out. I saw the girls already on the benches, waiting for us to join them, and when I sat down I placed myself facing outward, so passersby would notice the cut.

Heads dipped, we tried piecing the night together before the first bell rang, while eyes continued to track us. Aimes and Bugsy had been running between Max and me, so they'd both missed large chunks of time. We all remembered the flowerbed. Bugsy had tried her best to stop Max from ripping all the flowers out but she loved the dirt octopuses she made when she got the entire root system out in one go.

"Do you know who the boys were?" Max asked.

"It was Luke and Jesse," Aimes said.

"Jesse with the tan colour truck?" I asked.

"Yep," Aimes said.

Both boys were in grade eleven and older brothers of kids our age. We knew the truck Jesse drove because he was always tinkering under it in the parking lot.

"What time was that?" Cristal asked.

We looked to each other and shrugged.

"We were on our way to the Sollys' party," Aimes said.

"And you were on Fletcher Avenue, so it must have been Mrs. Plum's flowerbed you pulled up," Cristal said. "I can't believe I could hear you from all the way over there."

It was nice imagining that Cristal was with us in some form, listening from a few blocks away.

"Do you remember why your shirt was off?" Bugsy asked me.

"No," I said, sliding my finger along the ridge that ran across my face. It was bumpy and raised from crusted blood and I liked the sensation of not being able to feel my cheek under the gash, like part of my face wasn't attached to the rest of me anymore.

"Well, Luke could've done something to you, Em. He was still in the truck when Jesse went off with Max," Bugsy said. She was back to her bright self today, lashes framing her cat eyes, bangs waterfalling off her forehead.

"Something happened," Aimes said, turning to Max. We leaned closer so she could lower her voice. "When we came through the hedge, Jesse was messing with you."

"What time did you call my mom?" I asked Bugsy.

"I was home by midnight – so it must have been eleven," she said.

"It's so weird," I said. "That means I was only in the hospital for – " I counted on my fingers, "twelve hours. It felt like days."

"Did Jesse get down your pants?" Bugsy asked Max.

"No, I don't think so," Max said. "I guess if I'm pregnant we'll find out."

"You can't get pregnant if you don't have your period yet," Aimes said.

"Lucky me," Max said, and we laughed at that one.

The first bell rang and we rose in unison, feeling the eyes of the stragglers on us as we grabbed our backpacks and swung them over our shoulders. Starting down the hall, the crowds parted with whispers of "drunk" and "hospital" and "cops." We spread out – not touching, but leaving no room for anyone to break though. I imagined we looked like small queens, slowly charging down the main corridor, heads high and eyes forward.

We were different now. We had something of value. Is this what it meant to become a woman? Whatever it was, the beast inside my gut that never stopped begging for attention was sated. And instead of worrying about a night not remembered, I revelled in being fascinating enough to be talked about.

We strode forward unhurried, Max and I marked by scratches and bruises, the awareness just dawning that our pain had given us currency. In being hurt, we'd gotten harder, and by becoming hardened, we'd gained control. It felt good to get stronger. More options would be available to us now.

I turned to see the girls striding alongside me, chins out, heads cocked. Who knew a night so bad would bring such good fortune?

"Do you wanna try again next weekend?" I asked.

"Hell yeah," Max said.

"How do we get the booze this time?" Cristal asked.

"Any grade twelve who wants down our pants will buy it, duh," Bugsy said.

"It's not breaking the pact if we don't remember, right?" Aimes said.

"No," I said, confirming the new rule.

"If you see any of them, will you say anything?" Bugsy asked.

"Why bother. What can we get mad about?" Max said.

"You're limping?" Aimes said.

"Whatever. Ballet class hurts worse."

"They at least owe us a twenty-sixer," Bugsy said.

By the time we reached our lockers I'd made up my mind without needing to say it aloud. Only a month into grade eight and we'd found the key to our immunity. If we gave the boys what they wanted before it was demanded of us, we stayed safe. This insight – that I had inherent value to trade and pawn and make alliances with – felt like a very useful discovery. The next time the boys tried to get at us, we knew to expect something in return.

"You girls want some Fuzzy Peaches?" Max asked, handing out the soft candies one at a time as we headed into our first class. She stopped for a moment to put the sweet on her tongue. "Better than sex," she said.

"You wouldn't remember," Cristal said, and we died laughing.

Mom's already up, bustling around the kitchen. The room feels damp as I try to disentangle my legs from her old quilt so I can grab my phone. It's already ten thirty in the morning. Why do I revert to being thirteen years old every time I come home? I reach for an old housecoat – Christmas themed, red with tiny snowflakes on the collar – and like she's been waiting to hear me stir, Mom pops her head in, scoots across the room and pulls up the shade.

"Look!" she says. "It's snowing!"

The lawn is covered in a foot of snow and from the look of the sky it'll be two feet within the hour. Mom starts to track the fat clumps as they float down, and soon I too become mesmerized. Snow means the investigation will slow down for the winter. I'd read that the RCMP had passed the case to some big city detectives and everyone was hoping for a break before the weather turned. I wonder what Taylor's mom is thinking right now while she watches it dump down.

Mom's still in her dressing gown, too, light pink and stained at the cuffs, made of something flammable, in use since the trailer days. Cinching my housecoat, I rise and follow her into the kitchen. Her hair is pressed flat like a crop circle against the back of her head.

"How about the writing desk?" she says, returning to the dozen Post-it Notes on the kitchen table. "Grum doesn't appreciate it and it's our only real heirloom –"

I breeze past her and grab the stovetop espresso maker I've brought from Vancouver. If we're going to get into this conversation again, I need backup.

"You've just started a new trial chemo," I say. "This could be the drug that works." I pack the grinds. "You could live ten more years – easily."

In the month since Taylor was killed, Mom's lost almost twenty pounds. She hitches her pants up with a belt that she has to poke new holes in weekly and her bum is flat where an ample booty used to be. In the bathroom last night I'd noticed three or four wet towels stretched the length of the tub, and I assumed they were there for padding, to keep her bones from bruising against the hard surface while she bathed. Her oncologist told us that the recent shrinking and thinning is most likely due to this trial chemo she's on. The dark thumbprints under her eyes and the aching-all-over feeling probably have less to do with the lung cancer and more to do with the experimental medication. As soon as she finds the right cocktail, she'll gain her weight back and feel more like herself again.

The espresso erupts, gurgling hot life onto the stovetop and I pour a cup, adding some steamed almond milk.

"You're a coffee snob now?" she asks, over my shoulder.

"No, a friend finally taught me how to make a good one and now I'm hooked," I say, glad for the diversion.

"A girlfriend or a boyfriend?" she says.

Mom's never been subtle in her hope of me finding a mate, but neither have I. At thirty-four years old, I haven't had the best luck, partially because I'm an angry feminist with a requirement for high emotional intelligence, and also because I can be an empty bucket with a constantly dripping tap of needs. I find it hard to trust, which makes me ornery. And since my last birthday, we've both started to panic.

"I'm doing the best I can," I say.

"All I know," Mom says, returning to the kitchen table, "is that my last wish is to have grandchildren."

I back up against the sink. All tender feelings fly away.

"What do you want me to do, Mom? Rape a dude?"

"Don't be gross, Emmy. It's the only thing I've ever wanted and now there's an expiry date."

I feel the blood inside my veins poke to attention like a million tiny needles, pricking me from a place I cannot reach or calm. I want to slap her; wipe that smug look off her face. Rushing into the bathroom, coffee in hand, I lock the door, unzip my toiletries bag and tip an Ativan into my palm. I have to be careful. It's still early in the day and there are only twelve left for this trip — but this is an emergency and if I don't take one right now I might have to start punching myself in the head.

She's outside the bathroom door, deep into a one-sided conversation about alternative medicine, and as she says words like *qi gong* and *damp lungs*, fluid churns in my belly. I close my eyes and lean my head against the bathroom wall but the rushes of nausea continue to rise. I've felt this same sea sickness before, in the same town, with the same mom – the only difference is two decades. I want to unlock the bathroom door – I want to cross the divide – but I've never been able to. I don't know why. I slip the pill under my tongue and as it dissolves I repeat the phrase that's formed in my head: "My mom will live to know her grandchildren."

I do the math quickly. If four years is the average lifespan after a lung cancer diagnosis, taking into account all her alternative therapies and trial drugs, she'll easily double that. So, minus the two years she's already used up, Mom has six more years to live, which means I'll be forty when she dies. I could have a four-year-old by then. She'll watch her learn how to figure skate. That's not tragic. It's almost normal. I say the phrase out loud, my forehead pressed against the bathroom wall. "My mom will live to know her grandchildren," and the rhythm of the words helps stop me from flying through the ceiling.

". . . he's sensitive." I hear her through the door, speaking about Grum. "Not like you, Em."

Her voice is strong.

"If he's going to take time off and drive in this weather we have to spoil him a little."

I can keep her this way.

"Are you listening?" she raps on the bathroom door. "I'm going out for groceries."

Looking out the bathroom window, I return to tracking the flakes as they fall against the backdrop of white, which brings symmetry to my mind the same way the pills do.

"My mom will live to know her grandchildren," I say for the third time – making the spell bind – and a calmness descends, the perfect mixture of lorazepam and God.

The Subaru starts and I can hear her brushing snow off the windshield. Grum is travelling from Red Deer for a visit this weekend and she wants the fridge full of his favourite food. She'll be gone till midday. Errands take longer these days, with so much information trading to do. Armstrong isn't going to wait complacent for an entire season to find out if the killer is grocery shopping among us.

My cell rings. It's the producer from CBC calling to check in about how the documentary is going. Sticking a microphone in people's faces feels wrong, I tell her, so I haven't begun yet. I wish I could tell her the whole project is cancelled. But it's a job, one I should be proud of, and I need the money. The producer asks if I can at least make a start by collecting some ambient sounds. Alone for a few hours, I dress, grab my recorder, tuck Midge into the front of Mom's coat and start the trek across town to secret-smoke my face off and try to capture the sound of a train.

Past our old spot, down the untouched tracks, the sun breaks through. Armstrong is insulated and the air warms up fast. I consider dropping my coat but decide it's better to be wearing red so I'm not mistaken for a deer and shot by a hunter. I unclip Midge from her leash and let her plow through the drifts, her little black butt the only thing visible.

Midge barks and runs into the underbrush. She's either a good ratter or going blind and if I had any money I'd take her to the vet to find out which. For a four-pound chihuahua, she's brave as hell. The sun pauses behind a cloud and I sit to let her explore.

I can't stop thinking about Taylor's friends, and what happened that night after she didn't arrive at the party. Shivering fingers tapping their phone screens, they'd have gone to the tracks to start their search. They were relieved, I bet, to see Marie walking through the fog toward them. A mother was with them now. She'd bring the night back from eerie to practical. But after I don't know how long of calling out Taylor's name, she was found unconscious.

The girls would've had no idea what happened to their friend. Their best friend. What happened? What had happened to her?

Once the crowds of kids had swarmed the intersection, trying to glimpse down the rails at the medics and police and mess of bright lights, eventually, I don't know how, the girls would have managed to get themselves home. Locked the doors. Gone into their rooms. Needed hands and heavy blankets to weigh them down.

The cloud cover is gone and the sun bright. Closing my eyes, I tilt my chin to the warmth. The tracks were where we'd been happiest. Where we came to escape the boys' tedious picking over of our bodies: their fat tongues and pencil dicks, fast hands always trying to find something to pull on or flick. We'd meet here, my girls and I, to laugh it off, and in those moments the joy of being together far outweighed the pain of being practised on. A great dull flump of snow falls off a branch behind me and I wonder again, where will all the girls go now that the tracks are gone.

After lunch, Grum calls to cancel his visit. He does this sometimes, gets us excited and bails at the last minute, leaving me stuck being the asshole.

I pop another Ativan and head outside to call him in private.

"So, you're not coming?"

"Don't give me any shit," he says. "I got a work contract."

"Have you told the company that your mother has terminal cancer?" I say.

"You sound just like her. Guilt trips aren't good motivators, Em."

"I'm taking ten days off a month," I say.

"I'm the one paying for your gas," he says and hangs up.

The rage shutters in fast motion. He's left me on my own again, her perfect son.

Mom tilts her head out the sliding door.

"I'm going to start on dinner," she says.

Watching her turn away, I feel a spike of anger at her inability to walk upright. It's feeble, how she milks her illness for attention. These thoughts make me shrivel.

"My mother will live to know her grandchildren," I say again.

From now on all reactions must be swallowed. If I do the dishes and take her to church and listen to her worries and help her from her bath to bed; if I make sure she's sitting comfortably and eating high-carb snacks and has her hand cream nearby and gets some time every day in the sun; if I can take away her loneliness – I'll stall death, and she'll get her last wish. The prayer isn't just for her anymore. I've got to bury this fury. If she dies before I figure out how to, I won't be able to forgive myself.

Reaching into my pocket I let another Ativan fall out of its container into my hand. *They're helping me*, I think. *I can't quit now. This is when people use anxiety medication — during a crisis.* I put the pill under my tongue, needing my body to soften so bad. As it dissolves, I can feel it quietening me, which is the only reason I have the courage to tip the bottle and let all the little helpers drop out and disappear into the snow.

"It's a fair trade," I say aloud.

As I re-enter the house it feels like I'm walking toward a slow tidal wave, attempting, for the first time, self-sacrifice. I find her trying to defrost soup in the sink, chunking at it with a wooden spoon.

"I'll take it," I say.

She looks up at me.

"The writing desk," I say. "I'll claim it."

She smiles and pads across the kitchen to the Post-it Notes.

"Good girl," she says, and hands me a bright pink square.

IN THE KITCHEN FOR THEIR USUAL morning chat, Mom pressed Cristal for more information while I listened from the bathroom. Were the girls back at school? Was Max still hurt? Cristal told the truth but added no flourishes.

"After he pumped Em's stomach, I asked the doctor if we should get a rape kit done," Mom said, opening and closing cupboards, looking for something to stuff into my lunch. "He said there was no sign of penetration. Has she mentioned anything to you?"

"I think she was left alone because she was covered in puke," Cristal said. "It was Max who got taken to the bushes."

I felt a flutter of embarrassment for not being chosen.

"Did *her* parents get a rape kit done?" Mom asked.

"I don't think so," Cristal said. "She wasn't as sick as Em, so they let her sleep it off at home. But she's grounded."

I pulled my hair into two low pigtails and pushed my bangs off my face. The cut across my cheek looked worse than it had a few days ago, puffy with a light spray of blood at my temple that I'd chosen not to wash completely away.

I grabbed a granola bar from the breadbox and yelled goodbye to Mom without looking at her, a signal for Cristal to follow, and we left, the screen door banging behind us.

Walking through the high school foyer, my change in status was immediate. I'd been noticed the day before, but today's reactions made it official. It was as if through the alchemy of alcohol and turning fourteen, a red stone had started pulsing inside my crotch and was now transmitting a frequency. As Cristal and I beelined to the girls on the benches I saw that the same new charge was shared and our collective throb seemed to have a magnetizing effect, attracting the gaze of anyone who walked by. For the first time in my life, without the aid of exaggeration, I was seen.

The first bell rang and I stood up, curious to test my new power. We started down the hallway, not needing to be raucous because all eyes were already on us, and a great brick lifted off my chest and floated up through the high school ceiling. If all I had to do to feel this good was give them my body, the decision was easy.

In the week that followed, Bugsy and Aimes began sneaking makeup to school, applying it in the bathroom before class. They rimmed their top and bottom lash lines in black eyeliner and mascaraed their eyelashes into spider legs. Aimes carried Revlon's Toast of New York lipstick in her thin purple purse for touch-ups during the day, and, instead of toilet paper, she began stuffing her bra with her mom's nylons. The makeup and the fake boobs aged her at least a year and gave her the confidence to sit at the end of our line when we ate lunch at our lockers, making herself accessible to the older boys who smiled when they walked by. Bugsy got the idea out of *Seventeen* to buy her jeans two sizes too small, which meant she couldn't run up the bleachers anymore and she had to lie down on the bathroom floor to zip them up every time she peed, but she suddenly had a bum and a waist. Aimes and Bugsy began to prance past the machine shop during lunch, on the pretense that they wanted another iced tea from the vending machine, so the senior boys could stick their heads out of the shop doors and tell them about bush parties on the weekend. Soon invites started to roll in.

Between classes, hidden behind her locker door, Max would brush her hair sleek, and when she caught a boy staring, she dared herself to hold his gaze for three seconds before breaking it. This led to complications because making eye contact could be read as an invitation to approach and then we'd have to run down the hallway squealing like pigs. She didn't want to make out with a guy – none of us did. We just appreciated the recognition.

I tried to capitalize on the attention by increasing my vulgarity, adding words like *cunt* and *dick cheese* into my daily vocabulary, and I presented a gaudy confidence, wearing sequined blouses and puff-painted bell bottoms that I borrowed from the costume room at Asparagus Theatre.

It was Cristal who watched this all play out from a distance. She didn't seem to care about the motivation we'd found in the opinions of older boys. She didn't take personal pride in acquiring their attention, tallying up who might like us, who'd do us and who it would be best to align with so the creeps stayed away. So, as we turned toward the trial and error of exposure – planting ourselves in high traffic spots along the hallways – Cristal turned toward the camaraderie of girls' rugby, an outside sport, with only girls watching, that her parents didn't have to drive her to, or pay for, or watch her play.

On Friday, instead of circling up after school like we always did, with no real plans but to be together, we went our separate ways for the first time. Aimes walked home with Timmy, a cute grade ten guy, and Bugsy caught a ride with Timmy's best friend, Jimmy, a farm kid who drove a low-rider so who could blame her. Max waited by the smoke pit for Eli and the rest of the stoners, with the plan to head to Eli's rec room and listen to Nirvana. Cristal and I were left to walk home by ourselves. We didn't talk about this new fissure. It was only a small cut and it didn't run too deep.

We made a snack of crackers and cheese and she followed me around while I vacuumed and washed the floors, chores I did solely for the pride in seeing our one-hundred-year-old floorboards gleam. She helped me fold the laundry Mom had left piled on the wicker couch in the kitchen while we waited for *Oprah* to start and she smoked in the breezeway during the commercial breaks – making herself a quiet, easy companion. That night I had speech and drama lessons in the next town over and Mom was still at work. When Penny, the older girl who I carpooled with, honked, I ran out the side door, leaving Cristal to put the potatoes on to boil and set the table for dinner.

When I came home later that night I found Cristal and Mom sitting knee-to-knee in our screened-in front porch, spooning up the last bites of ice cream from shallow bowls, talking in hushed tones. I'd seen them together like this before, my mother nodding as Cristal spoke to her – about what? I was never told. But tonight, when I walked in on them like this, closer to each other than they were with me, I couldn't let it slide. Inside Mom's single-parent chutzpah hid a fragile bird and if I ever truly cranked the engine, I'd flatten her. I wanted to eat ice cream and get all soft-hearted, but I also wanted to punish her for not being able to withstand my big bulldozer self.

"I'm home," I said, interrupting their close-knit whispers.

"Hi Punky, come join us," Mom said.

"We're watching a movie. Let's go."

Cristal followed, not having much choice in the matter.

After *Ghost*, we spooned in our sleeping bags.

"Have you felt the crotch pulse yet?" I asked, turning to face her.

"I don't think so," she said.

"You could get a boyfriend if you wanted to."

"I don't want a boyfriend," she said.

"Me neither," I said. "Let's be gay together."

The sounds of the words made me laugh, nonsensical and a bit dangerous.

"That wouldn't make anything easier," Cristal said. "We'd get beaten up."

As my muscles twitched into rest, she whispered the phrase back to me. "Let's be gay together."

I smiled into my pillow and snuggled my butt into her tummy. Maybe her breathing changed. I couldn't tell. She hadn't moved a muscle, but her arms around me had become heavy and – vibratory. I giggled again, wanting her to know that I was fine, but unravelled myself from her legs to starfish on my tummy in the middle of the foam. I started breathing slow and deep, steady in rhythm, so she'd think I'd fallen asleep.

Just before noon the next day, we all gathered at Aimes's, slathered on our Hawaiian Tropic and raced for her mom's car. A late September heatwave was passing through Armstrong and we'd decided to go for one last swim while the weather held up. Aimes ran for shotgun but I hip-checked her and climbed into the front seat. Aimes sat on top of me and rolled the window down. It was hot as hell out and she was mad as fuck.

"What do you mean you did it without us?" Aimes said.

"It's no biggie," Max said, climbing into the back seat of the hatchback. "Take a pill."

"It *is* a biggie," Aimes said. She wasn't going to let this go.

Bugsy climbed over top of Max to sit beside Cristal, who was already hanging out the window, trying to get some air.

"But where did you smoke the pot?" Aimes asked.

"At Eli's house. We walked over there after school to jam."

We couldn't believe she'd broken the pact so soon into grade eight. We'd promised to go to parties together and watch out for each other. This was flagrant dissent.

"Why didn't you invite us?" Aimes asked. She'd started to pick at the broken-down seat cushion, pulling the stuffing out through the cracked vinyl.

"They didn't mention you."

There was a bead of sweat running down Max's neck. Aimes's thigh was stuck to mine. Cristal looked like she'd just run a race, her hairline wet. It was so goddamned hot in the car.

"What was it like?" Cristal asked.

"They put on *The Wall* and then Eli pulled out a joint from his guitar case and they started passing it around."

She was reliving something we weren't all reliving together – for the first time. She was about to tell a story we should have been adding our own details to – like how much earwax Chad had and how Eli lived in what looked like a rabbit warren and how we couldn't tell who but someone smelled sour like piss. I didn't like these dudes. They were snobs. They looked at me like I was either a piece of meat or a piece of shit. I wouldn't have wanted to try pot with them for the first time – but we should've been there.

Max found the tanning lotion she'd been searching for and started applying it.

"How did you feel after you smoked it?" Aimes asked.

"It was by far the best movie I've ever seen," Max said.

I crossed my arms and looked toward the house, praying for Kitty to come out. My back was stuck to the seat and I could feel sweat dripping into my ass crack. I still couldn't understand: how could anything be better without everyone there?

I reached behind me to Bugsy's feet and grabbed a bag of Cool Ranch Doritos.

"A moment on the lips, a lifetime on the hips," Bugsy sang.

On cue, Kitty appeared, trotting down the driveway with a large woven bag over her shoulder and sunglasses resting on her head. She jumped into the front seat.

"Ouchy! Those seatbelts are hot," she said, clicking herself in.

Kitty was a young mom. She and Aimes behaved more like sisters than mother and daughter. Kitty didn't give curfews. She bought razors for Aimes to shave her legs. She home-permed Aimes's hair.

"You girls ready to hit the lake?" Kitty said, starting the engine. "Joyride" blared on the radio.

Whenever Kitty drove us around, I grabbed shotgun so I could sneak a peek at her thighs while she drove. They were thinner than mine with tiny freckles on the tops and she wore shorts that barely covered her butt cheeks.

I started to cram chips into my mouth while hands reached forward from the back seat trying to grab the bag from me.

As we swerved down the gravel road that would take us to the lake, Max continued to explain loudly over the music that the previous night at Eli's had changed her. She'd seen a new dimension. She didn't think we were ready for it. I caught Kitty rolling her eyes.

"Those dudes are going to die in a drunk-driving accident, you know that right?" Bugsy said.

We bumped down the potholed beach road until the view opened up to Bugsy's old 1960s cabin, peeling orange paint, sitting squat on the lakefront. Before Kitty could turn the engine off, we ejected ourselves in a race to hit the lake. Sunlight clipped the surface as I ran in, the water swallowing my shins, thighs and tummy before I dove, arms in front of me, wrists thick with friendship bracelets and my fingers contained in many silver rings. I came up for air and heard Bugsy scream as Aimes jumped on her back. The water was just cool enough to take the car ride away.

Cristal and I swam fast into the dark part of the lake – where the lake-weed couldn't get our toes – and waited for the rest of them, our knees bonking as we treaded water. The sunlight only passed down a foot, revealing flashes of skin, but all light stopped before it reached our bellies. Arriving next, Aimes pushed her bangs back against her skull, making her look eleven years old. Bugsy was wearing her new swimsuit, a black one piece with a neon pink working zipper, which looked to me like a fluorescent dare.

"Synchronized swimming competition," Max said, rolling on her back to catch her breath.

"Watch me, watch me!" said Aimes.

"Let's do it together," Bugsy said, and slapped the surface.

"Point your toes."

"Now rotate, three times in a circle."

We shouted instructions at each other until Aimes yelled, "I've gotta shit!"

"Hold it," Max said.

"I can't," she said.

We all turned to look at Aimes. I could tell by her face she was sucking it in.

"Swim back," I said.

"I can't hold it in. The water —"

"She's shitting," Cristal said.

"She's shitting right now?" Bugsy asked.

"Look at her face."

"She just shat in the water," I said.

"She didn't."

"There it is, a log of shit," Max said.

The excrement was floating to the left of our circle. It was long and light brown and had tiny specks inside it that seemed to refract the light.

Aimes scooped her hand under the log and threw it at Bugsy.

"Get it away," Bugsy scream-laughed.

Bugsy shoved the water and the log bobbed toward Max.

"It's ginormous."

Cristal looked disgusted with how much fun we were having.

I smacked the surface of the water and this made me swallow some lake and choke, and I had to roll onto my back to get a breath. Ears under water, I could hear muffled laughter and more screams. I came back up. I didn't want to miss anything, not a moment. Too much fun.

Max swam toward the floating excrement. She cupped the log, lifted it out of the water and threw it toward me. As it released, the log broke into two and one piece dropped mid-air while the other sailed overhead. The girls screamed and swam away but there was movement on the newly floating log that caught my eye. It was a fly. It had landed perfectly and was eating its fill of the shit, which was, against all odds, still holding on.

"You've got some on your shoulder Max," Bugsy yelled. "It's on your suit top."

Someone coughed. Max hawked a loogie. I looked back to the floating poop and it had disintegrated, the fly gone.

Spitting water, we breaststroked to the floating dock and heaved ourselves up. We checked our backs and faces but there was nothing left: the water had washed all the shit away. We lay down on the hot wood, tummies down, faces in the centre, like the rays of a sun, and breathed heavily together. A laugh erupted, then a giggle and another hacking cough, then back to breathing. We wouldn't tell anyone about the shit fight. Too holy. We couldn't have it misunderstood.

"I think you got some poop on your lip," Cristal said.

"Nah, it's just lakeweed," Aimes said, and wiped it off.

"You got any more to push out?" Bugsy asked.

We giggled lazily, wet faces pressed against the backs of our hands as we rested on the floating dock and listened to the creaks and bangs underneath us.

"I'll go get some chips," Cristal said.

She rose and stepped to the edge of the dock, her simple black racing suit covering her neatly as she dove and was swallowed with hardly a splash – not graceful, but precise.

Emerging from the lake, she walked to the picnic table.

"Grab two," Bugsy yelled from the dock.

Cristal held up two bags of chips. Bugsy gave a thumbs up. The door to the orange cabin banged open and Bugsy's cousins tumbled out, older guys that were way too hot to deal with, so Cristal bolted across the sand, put the corners of the bags of chips between her teeth and dog-paddled, mouth closed, back to us. We laughed, but not too hard – we didn't want her to lose her freight.

Cristal pulled herself up onto the dock, ribs heaving, and threw us the chips. The girls busted them open on the hot planks.

"So, are you going to apologize or not?" Aimes said.

"I'm not sorry I smoked the pot," Max said. "But I am sorry I didn't invite you."

"That's all I wanted to hear," Aimes said.

"It was stressful without you guys there," Max said.

Aimes lay her head on Max's wet bum and Max pushed out a fart.

"I'm learning how to fart notes," she said. "My butthole is my new instrument."

Cristal laughed, a bell tuned to the sparkles on the water.

Max dove in now, back toward the beach. "Smokes," she yelled after she came up for air.

"We should get drunk without her," Bugsy said when she was out of earshot.

"Why?" I said. "She apologized."

Bugsy propped herself up on her elbows. "Come to my house tonight for a sleepover and we'll figure out how to get the booze. Don't tell her about it."

Cristal shrugged.

"Okay," I said, relieved to be included.

"She should know what it feels like to be left out."

The drive back from the lake was quiet. Kitty had to stop at Askew's so we rolled down the windows while we waited in the parking lot, trying to catch a breeze.

"Is that Ollie and his brother at the Sev?" Bugsy said.

We stared across the street.

"It's all of them," Max said, and slid down the back seat.

I recognized Jesse's truck — a tan colour — as the one I'd been yanked out of.

"I'm going to ask them to buy us booze," Bugsy said, stepping outside. "It's the least they can do."

"I'll come with you," I said.

We ran across the street before the rest of the girls could join us. The older boys were huddled around the truck, heads bent under the hood. I tapped Ollie on the back and he sucked in his tummy reflexively. We hadn't talked since the drunken night — about the state he found me in or how he'd helped me out.

"Hey Ollie," I said. "Can you ask Dameon if he'll bootleg for us?"

He frowned, not wanting to ask his older brother for a favour.

"Only if I can come with you," he said.

"We'll tell you where we end up," Bugsy lied.

Ollie nodded. I saw him steel himself as he entered the tightly packed group of large, hairy almost-men.

"What's in it for me?" Dameon asked, not looking up from under the hood. Aimes had said he'd been there that night too, but I didn't remember.

"We could buy you some beer," Bugsy said.

"Sweeten the deal," a voice next to him said.

I couldn't see his face but I recognized the voice. It was Jesse, the guy who had gone after Max.

Dameon turned around, trying to place us, and smiled, his nose wrinkling like his little brother's did. He was at least six feet tall and looked how I imagined Ollie would when he got older: mountainous and dense, a protector or a destroyer depending on whose side he was on.

"Seb, do you know these chicks?"

A boy rolled out from underneath the truck. His hair was long and black, held in a low ponytail. His eyes were a perfect green.

"Are you the little bitches we keep hearing about?" he asked.

Holy hell, he was handsome.

"I don't know," I said. "What are you hearing?"

"The Brew Crew told me about you. Tonya said I might like the hippie. Which one's the hippie?"

"She is," Bugsy said and elbowed me.

"You?" Seb laughed and rolled back under the car. "No thanks."

I kicked the tire he was closest to.

"We'll get you beer," Dameon said. "Gotta start somewhere right?"

He laughed again and I laughed with him. Bugsy and I looked back across the street. From our view, Kitty's car looked empty, but we knew the girls were crouched down, watching us.

"Give me some cash and I'll pop over to the beer store," Dameon said.

Bugsy whipped out a twenty before he finished his sentence.

Dameon gave us a salute and the boys hopped in Jesse's truck and gunned it out of the Sev's parking lot. They drove across the main drag and parked between Askew's and the beer and wine store. We ran back across the road and crawled into Kitty's car to update the girls.

Our eyes at dash level, we kept watch on the store's front door.

"Seb is a babe," I said. "I can't look at him he's so hot."

"If you like goths," Bugsy said. "Jesse didn't even remember us."

"Maybe he's embarrassed about what happened?" Aimes said.

"Are you kidding?" Bugsy said. "He just doesn't care."

Kitty was pushing her shopping cart toward the car. Now we had a timing issue.

"I heard you guys on the dock," Max said.

"Heard what?" Bugsy said.

"Voices travel on water dumdums," Max said. "You're gonna ditch me?"

We were quiet for a minute, caught.

Kitty opened the hatchback. If she was done unloading the groceries before they came out, we'd lose our chance.

"I won't break the pact again. I promise," Max said.

Kitty finished packing the hatchback and started the engine.

"Where to next, gals?" she said.

We looked to each other, then to the truck in the parking lot beside us. It was still empty.

Bugsy panicked. "The girls are staying at my house tonight, Kitty," she said. "We'll just walk home."

"It's a long way. I'm happy to dri —"

"Thanks Mom, we're good." Aimes jumped out of the car and the rest of us followed, grabbing our backpacks.

"Take some junk food for the road."

Kitty got out of the car and began slowly digging through grocery bags to find chips.

"No thanks Kitty," we rambled, corralling her back into the driver's seat.

"My house has lots of treats," Bugsy said.

We waved as she exited the parking lot, sun visor over her perplexed look, and when we turned around, wet bathing suits up our cracks, Jesse's truck was gone.

"What the hell? Where'd they go?" I said.

"Probably their plan all along," Cristal said.

"Well, that sucks a dead dog's dick," Bugsy said.

We followed Bugsy to the road, feeling the frustration of a good plan foiled, but there was something else that trailed behind us too. A desperation. An inky shame. We'd looked stupid for those boys in broad daylight. And they'd duped us again.

At the gas station that marked the edge of town, we linked arms and ran across the empty two-lane highway. Sliding down into a small ditch, we pushed through the brush and in front of us lay the tracks, silver and gleaming.

Max stepped onto the rails and turned around. "We still have this little guy though," she said, holding up a Ziploc bag.

"You brought a joint?" I said.

"To share with you," Max said.

There it was. The next adventure.

Cristal jumped onto the tracks and started to run. She raced ahead gazelle-like, clearing two sleepers at a time. She didn't want to be caught up to.

Aimes and Max leapt onto the rails to start balancing. We took the sport seriously. If you could balance along the rails without wobbling that proved you'd spent a lot of time here, which meant the tracks belonged to you. Max was by far the best — arms out in a T-shape, she could sometimes run along the rails. Cristal and I tied for second place. Aimes and Bugsy didn't even place they sucked so hard, but they were still better than any newcomers to the rails.

Darting between sun and shade, Bugsy's body was turning into a replica of her mother's, the same curves on a tight frame. She lived in Armstrong's only subdivision, with houses that had built-in vacuum cleaners and RVs out front with hydraulic pop-outs that reminded me of Grum's transformer toys. Going over there always made me stressed out and starry-eyed. Bugsy had it the best, with parents who never seemed to be home.

We trotted until we found Cristal resting under a large fir, her eyes clear, like she could be with us again.

"Took you losers long enough."

Once we were all sitting in a circle of flattened brush, Max opened the baggie, put the entire joint in her mouth and pulled it out slowly between pursed lips — a move I didn't know the purpose of but she was in charge now. The lighter flamed and she closed her eyes and inhaled. Max held her breath while she passed the joint to Bugsy, who held it like a cigarette and pretended to inhale, then passed the joint to Aimes who took a tiny puff and coughed madly. I was getting antsy, wanting my try.

"Burns in the wind," I said.

Aimes passed the joint to Cristal who inhaled like a pro and passed to me. I held the joint as I'd seen Max do and inhaled. A dry fire rushed down my throat. I took another drag and it burned just as bad, but this time I liked the feeling.

"Don't bogart the joint," Max said.

I had no idea what she meant but I passed it back to her and it went around the circle again.

"Do you feel anything yet?" Aimes asked.

"I don't know," Cristal said, glancing to Max for a clue.

"It's subtle, I guess," Max said.

I looked up at the trees for anything out of the ordinary.

"I don't think it worked," Cristal said. "I feel normal."

We passed the joint around another time and I took an extra drag, trying to make it work. Cristal sucked till it burned her fingertips and then she threw the small bit left into the bushes. The nerves had left and a distant calm had dropped in their place. The light had changed from bright to soft apricot. Bugsy stared down the rails as she chewed on her nail beds, stumpy little slivers. Her mom had tried wrapping her hands in gauze overnight and had even soaked her fingers in a foul-tasting oil to deter her — but the need was so great she'd always manage to find a torn cuticle or strip of skin to gnaw on. Time had passed but I had no idea how much.

Bugsy jumped up.

"It's almost dinner," she said. "I've got to feed my grandma."

She took off down the rails and we grabbed our bags and chased her, needing to stay close.

"Don't tell the grandma," we could hear her muttering to herself once we had caught up. "Don't tell the grandma."

What she didn't want to tell her grandma, we weren't sure, but we knew it was our task to support her. Our arms around each other's shoulders, ten feet stepping in time, we became a machine, solid as steel. Impenetrable. There were no thoughts, only a boundless supply of force as we moved as one body. "Don't. Tell. The. Grandma," we chanted, interlocked, pushing forward toward the hill that would take us to her house.

Reaching the road, Bugsy looked around wildly.

"What if she smells my breath?"

When we dropped our clasp, an agitation descended. Even the air felt nervous.

Aimes threw her bag onto the ground and began digging through it.

"We brought gum remember?" she said, handing Bugsy a piece of Excel. "Here, chew."

The return was too abrupt. I stepped off the tracks and the stop sign felt as if it was trying to control me. I threw a stone at it. I didn't want to press forward into this landscape, on a road with cars. I didn't want to enter a house that had walls. The low horn of a train sounded, coming from somewhere behind us and long ago. I looked to my girls, their faces grey, and I needed them to know I'd take care of them.

"We won't tell the grandma," I said, and placed my hand on Bugsy's chest. "You can trust us."

"I do," Bugsy said.

Max jumped on Cristal for a piggyback. The whistle sounded and now we could hear the train itself, barrelling along the rails we'd just been on. The intensity gave way to laughter and we started to run, excited for blankets and pillows and Bugsy's waterbed. Past the clipped lawns and bay windows, we made it into Bugsy's garage, threw off our shoes and tiptoed down the carpeted stairs. I flopped on the couch in the rec room and Cristal lay beside me. Her leg looked like a chicken thigh. I pointed but couldn't get the words out and she put her hands on my tummy and massaged me until I could breathe again. Bugsy went upstairs to feed her grandma the anticipated meal.

"I hope she's not telling the grandma," Max said sincerely and we lost our shit again.

Aimes crawled back up the stairs and ransacked the pantry: chips, a plastic container filled with sour keys, Pepsi, a flat of brownies. Max grabbed the bag of Fuzzy Peaches and set it between her legs. She stuck out her tongue and placed one on it to press against the roof of her mouth. As she sucked, her cheeks inverted from the sour.

"Like I said, better than sex."

"How do you know if Fuzzy Peaches are better than sex?" Cristal said.

"Because *nothing* could be better than this taste," Max said from behind closed eyes.

"I'll ask you again in a few years."

"I don't have to have sex to know Fuzzy Peaches are better," Max said.

Aimes crawled from the beanbag chair to the stack of VHS tapes along the wall. She held out *Pretty Woman*. We shook our heads no, as we'd already seen it. She pulled out *Misery*. Too scary. She found a new release called *Sleeping with the Enemy*.

"Ooh, a romance," she said, reading the back.

The girls dragged pillows closer to the TV and began to pile on top of each other. My eyelids were dry and my brain felt like it was in a cloud; not uncomfortable, just slower than normal. I floated into the bathroom to pee and caught myself in the mirror. My face was red. I thought of Mom. *Should I call to make sure she's okay? Not too lonely?* I pulled on an old nightie I found hanging on the back of the door. There was a clump of Bugsy's bathing suits hanging stiffly on top of each other. When we woke up tomorrow morning, we could have a hot tub and there'd be one for each of us. Another adventure.

In the spare room I pulled back the sheets and crawled into bed, my cheek divine against the cool pillow. Someone came through the door and crawled into bed next to me. I could smell the Fuzzy Peaches on her breath. We curled into each other like spoons.

"Pass me a pillow," Max said. "I need one between my legs."

I reached behind me and tossed one over.

She began to rock her hips back and forth, the pillow between her knees, and my arms around her waist.

"Donkey riding," I said.

Max giggled. "It calms me down."

I rocked with her for a while.

"Max?" I said.

"Hmm?"

"Have you ever smelled your vagina?"

"Yeah," she said.

"What's it smell like?"

"Cookies."

I could tell she was smiling.

"I think mine smells wrong," I said.

"I'll smell it for you tomorrow," she said.

"Thanks Max."

We lay together, falling deeper into the mattress. Max rocked a bit more and the motion made me tired. Soon, there was another weight on the bed, and then another. Cristal was crawling in beside us and behind her came Bugsy and Aimes. We could hear the movie on in the other room — but here was the perfect place to squish together, legs on top of thighs, arms across chests.

"It's too bad the pot didn't work," Bugsy said.

"I heard they were filling joints with oregano," Max said.

"Let's punch their dicks and steal their money," Aimes said, and we laughed, but this time no sound came out, our bodies jiggling silently together.

2011

CHRISTMAS IS QUIET IN ARMSTRONG this year. There are a few multicoloured lights strung up along the main street, and Short Stop's put up an inflatable snowman on its front stoop, but no one wants to make a spectacle. Mom watches the evening news at five every night but there's nothing new to report in Taylor's case. No suspects. No leads. The city detectives have given the case back to the local RCMP, who state in a public announcement that they plan to resume forest-gridding for clues after the snow melts. Taylor's face isn't on the front page of every newspaper anymore but her killer is still out there.

On December 21 Mom tugs the fake tree out of its broken-down box and we unbend its branches to hang the old family ornaments. We putter through the weekend, strolling to the mailboxes and back with Zip and Midge, and wandering the aisles of Askew's, looking for garlic bread and organic chicken. Grum travels down on Christmas Eve and drives us to the evening church service in his big truck. The cab is so high off the ground that Mom needs him to piggyback her from the truck to the sidewalk and this makes us laugh, her little fiddlehead of a body curled around Grum's back.

On Christmas Eve our small wooden church is filled with all the once-a-year folks and their extended families, so our usual pew is taken. While I find us a bench to squeeze into, Grum walks Mom to the front so she can join the choir. There's no place to stuff our coats so we keep them on, already hot before the service begins. Rita, the accompanist, bangs out a piano solo and Mags, the weaver, apologizes for forgetting her glasses as she stumbles over the scripture reading. The order of events is the same every year – from the minister's performative oration to the out-of-tune children who play "Away in a Manger" on their string instruments. I lean my head on Grum's shoulder and my eyes drift between the scarves and wool coats up to Mom. With this bit of distance, I'm surprised to see changes that I haven't noticed closer up. Her glasses are far too big for her face and the surgical tape she's wrapped around the bridge to keep them in place isn't working – every time she looks down at the sheet music she has to hold the frames to keep them from falling off her nose.

When it's time for the choir to sing, Ruth, the older woman beside her, gives Mom an arm. Once she's upright, Mom clutches the railing like she's on a boat. Her hair is completely grey now and looks like wire. But what's most surprising is a new come-and-go glaze in her eyes. She seems unsure of what she should do next. Like a child in their first performance, she's relying on her surroundings for clues. I can't hear if she's singing, but the song, "Silent Night," is one of her favourites, and even in her confusion, a smile appears. This is what breaks me. Grum puts his arm around my shoulder as I sob as quietly as I can into his armpit. My mother looks like she's dying.

After the service we head into the hall for tea. Grum and I stand on either side of Mom, letting her show us off to the old folks who remember us as kids, and when I see the glazed look return I take her arm and lead her down the steps toward the parking lot. Grum hoists her up into the truck and drives us home, Mom and I staring out of the tinted windows, her searching for the few strings of Christmas lights while I try to understand how my volatility with her is in direct opposition to what I get on my knees and beg for nightly.

Grum helps Mom out of his truck and they teeter into the house together. I smoke a joint then follow behind. When I enter the kitchen she's got CBC Radio on already and she's humming along as she carries a plate of the reheated jalapeno cheese puffs she's saved since Grum's last cancelled visit to the living room. He's stretched out on the couch and she balances the plate on his belly so that he can eat while he watches hockey.

———————

We don't leave the house on Christmas Day, except for a quick grocery trip, and it feels like we're back in the trailer again, just the three of us, hemmed in but happy about it.

Grum's taking a nap so I bring Mom a cup of tea and sit down next to her. Once I've settled into the pillows on the couch she clears her throat.

"Have you ever thought about teaching?" she asks, as if the thought just popped into her mind.

Reaching for my tea I can't help but roll my eyes. Mom has pitched this idea at least once a year for the last decade.

"All I mean is, have you considered getting your degree so that you have something to fall back on?"

"I don't think spending $60,000 on something I'd be bad at is a good fall-back plan," I say.

"What about starting a theatre school then?" she says.

"I have a theatre *company*, Mom," I say. "It's an internationally touring organization that's quite well respected, actually."

"I just don't want you to always be poor," she says.

"You were a full-time nurse for forty years and your pension barely covers the bills. How's that working out?"

She grunts.

"I can't do something that I don't like for the rest of my life."

"Well, I hope you like the taste of cat food when you're sixty-five," she says. "I'm offering to send you to teachers' college. You can teach during the day and make your plays on the weekends."

Her disregard of my work grinds me down. If she doesn't intend cruelty, is she dumb?

"How will you ever buy a house?" she asks.

"I won't," I say. "A teacher can't buy one either."

It dawns on me that, although imperfect, we are having a conversation. An honest yak. I'll take what I can get.

"You know what *my* teacher told me on the first day of theatre school?" I say.

"What?"

"The sure way to be a successful theatre artist is to be the last one standing. To wait it out until everyone else has quit." I draw my legs up. "So, that's my plan. Get famous when I'm fifty."

I pull a blanket over us. Some daughters have moms they want to spend time with — going on wine tours where they discuss intersectional feminism and get a bit flirty with the waiter. I've never felt jealous of them — more gobsmacked. I cannot remember having a single fascinating conversation with the woman who birthed me. Maybe right now? Maybe this is it.

"I do worry about money," I say. "I wonder how I'll ever afford a kid. But the trade-off is that I get to tell meaningful stories. For me, it's activism. My attempt at counter-hegemony."

"Don't try to sound smart." Mom pushes herself off the couch. She starts to pace.

"I know what you can do," she says. "When the Vancouver Folk Festival is on, you can dress up like a clown and seat people for a dollar!"

"Sorry," I say. "Are you telling me to busk for a living?"

"No," she says, getting more excited. "It's not that creative. Your job is to find people seats."

"So, you're suggesting that I be a freelance usher at an outdoor music festival?"

"Yes," she says. "Everyone needs help finding a place to sit down."

The suggestion is so absurd I laugh. But it guts me too – that she has no idea what I'm trying to make with my life.

———————

Grum leaves Armstrong on Boxing Day, earlier than he agreed to but with the impenetrable reasoning of "Gotta catch the window of good weather."

Mom's becoming tetchy too, wanting me to go back to Vancouver, though she'd never say it. Her routine has been disrupted by my three-week stay, with luggage left around the house and me and Grum bickering. She has to start seeing her Chinese medicine doctor daily if she wants her lungs to dry out, and she needs to practice qi gong in a quiet house. These are all things that give her life force, she says, and more life force buys her more time.

The phone rings during dinner and I notice it's a colleague so I head into the spare room to answer it.

"Emmy!" he yells. "Happy Hanukkah. I've got a job for you!"

I sit on the edge of the bed as I listen to my friend Itai pitch an idea for a theatre show.

"It's a solo performance about how I helped my mom die of lung cancer," he says. "I have video footage – of shaving her head and talking about her regrets – even of her death. It's provocative, considering all the right-to-die advocacy. I need a producer on board and a co-writer and you're perfect and we start next week."

"Itai, don't you remember that my mom has lung cancer right now?" I ask.

"Oh shit," he says. "Isn't this divinely timed?"

I look to the ceiling. This man can make death sound exciting. But the story is compelling and maybe it will help me pre-process my grief. I'm reminded of the radio documentary I haven't started yet. This will give me an excuse to keep it on the back burner. Also, it's a job.

"Yes," I say. "The company is on board. Send me the schedule and we'll start on a budget."

I come back to the kitchen feeling lighter.

"I just got offered a gig," I say.

"That's nice hon," Mom says. "Does it pay in money?"

Mostly, though, I need a break from this shit. I'm of no use to her angry. In a few weeks I'll return clear-headed. I have to pace myself if I'm going to keep up my end of the bargain with God, so the next morning, I take Grum's advice and drive back to Vancouver, "during a clear patch – before the next storm hits."

1991

LYING ON THE SCHOOL FIELD, knees bent, thighs bare to the fall sky, we were finding shapes in the cut-out clouds.

"We have to stop acting like spaz attacks," Bugsy said. "If we want real boyfriends, we've gotta simmer down."

After we'd amended the pact to allow for time alone with boys, Bugsy and Aimes had officially snagged the full attention of Timmy and Jimmy, the farm kids they'd been flirting with. They'd been to a few pit parties, drinking and kissing in the cabs of their trucks, and I was sure Jimmy had touched Bugsy's boobs but I knew Timmy hadn't been allowed near Aimes's, as she was embarrassed there was nothing for him to paw at yet. With them flirting in the parking lot most days and Max busy with singing lessons after school, Cristal and I were on our own more often. Not unpleasant, but we missed the constant noise.

"There they are." Bugsy pointed to the boys throwing a football back and forth. "Aimes, if I get drunk this weekend will you watch out for me?"

Aimes sat up to watch the clean-cut boys play.

"Sure. Just don't leave me alone again." She patted vanilla lip gloss onto her lips. "Let's go flirt."

The two girls jumped up and ran toward their targets.

"They're going on the offence," Cristal said, watching Aimes and Bugsy prance across the field.

"Whatchumean?" I asked, my mouth full of the poppy-seed muffin Aimes had left behind.

"Aimes was playing defensively but she's moved into offence — it's a tactical choice," Cristal said.

"Is it a smart play?" I said, wiping crumbs from my face.

"She might as well dog pile," Cristal said. "No one's passing her the ball."

Cristal was quiet for a moment as she stared up at the sky. "Coach says the safest way to get through a scrum is to run into the action, so technically they're doing what's necessary to win the game."

I rolled onto my belly. "Has Trent come around again, Max?"

Ever since my drunken birthday night the senior boys had been pecking at us. Like minnows biting the bubbles off our underwater legs, their attempts were ticklish and constant. Bugsy and Max got most of the attention. All they had to do was sit on the top edge of the carpeted benches in the student centre and a boy would sidle up to them, offering a ride to Short Stop or the Sev. Bugsy would dip her chin and glow. Max would get narrow-eyed, beads of moisture popping off her nose as she glared at one of us to save her, while Cristal and I sat with our arms crossed, scowling at the dude who'd just interrupted our conversation. Aimes sometimes nudged me, braces gleaming, a reminder to smile. Even though none of us wanted to make out with any of these hairy-chested burn-outs, having them in our pocket to buy smokes and coolers made our lives easier.

But since last week, the focus had ramped up. An older guy we'd not noticed previously had started to circle Max, smiling when he passed by her in the hall and ignoring her the next time. Once he sat beside her after school in the concourse, waiting to catch the same bus home. The final lap was when he showed up at our lockers during a spare.

"Just killing time," he'd said, leaning against Max's locker, staring her down.

Max looked drunk all of a sudden. Her eyes went glassy and she wobbled. I put my arm behind her as a brace in case she fell down. Two red spots flushed her cheeks, making her look kind of perfect and I realized *she likes the way he's looking at her*.

His name was Trent and he was hot, with long hair and light brown skin. The rest of us couldn't look at him without pushing each other into a locker, but that didn't matter because he never acknowledged our presence while he hovered over Max, saying shit we couldn't hear. Max was trying so hard to take the heat he threw but we knew she was dying inside because her nose was sweating, her telltale sign of panic. He pointed out that their eye colour was the same piercing blue.

"And I'm in grade twelve and you're twelve years old," he said – suggesting, I think, that they had things in common.

Later, he'd left a wilted cosmos at the bottom of her locker, stolen, we assumed, from a garden near school property. And today, he'd stuffed a black miniskirt into a plastic bag and hung it off her locker with a note that read, "This will look good on you."

"It says *will*," I said, stretching out the tight tube. "This *will* look good on you. Like he's assuming you'll want to wear it."

Max hummed softly to herself.

"I don't like it," I said, throwing the plastic bag back to her.

Max pinched the bag like it was a diaper and walked into the bathroom. We sat on the bank of sinks while she tried to pull the skirt on. She was having a hard time stretching it over her hips as the band of Lycra kept rolling up her thighs.

"When someone gives you a gift, is it rude not to wear it?" Max asked, hands on her tummy, looking panicked in the mirror.

"That's what my grandma says," Bugsy said. "You look hot!"

Now, lying in the field during lunch break, enjoying the last few weak rays of sunshine, arms splayed across each other, a shadow came over us. I put my hand up to shield my eyes. It was him. He looked down at us and smiled.

"What are you ladies up to – out here all by yourselves?"

"We're maxing and relaxing," I said, annoyed.

"I like what you're wearing, Maxine."

"Thanks," Max said.

It was a bold statement to use her real name. Even her parents called her Max.

"It makes your body look good, like I said it would," Trent drawled like a fucking country-western singer.

"Thanks," she said again.

"You wanna go for a stroll?"

We went quiet, waiting to hear what Max would say. We knew she didn't want to go but we also knew if she didn't want to be labelled a snob or a prude she didn't have much choice.

"Sure," she said. "Where d'you want to go?" Trying to sound nonchalant about what she might be agreeing to.

"Let's go hang out behind the hill for a bit," Trent said. "I wanna see you walk in that skirt."

She rose to meet him, one hand tugging on the skirt, the other brushing the grass off her knees.

"You should wear it every day," he said and swatted her bum.

This was the first time he'd ever touched her, but the casual smack told us that a girl's body was common to him. She hopped forward, grabbed her bum and pushed out a giggle.

Max walked with Trent, away from us, toward the dip in the field that would hide them from view. Cristal and I watched them get smaller as he led her into the high grasses. We saw him sit and reach up for her hand to pull her down.

Looking back to the sky, I felt butterflies for her. *What would he do and how would it feel?* Birds flew past. Crows, and a few seagulls too.

"Why do seagulls live so far from the sea?" Cristal asked, reading my mind.

The clouds moved and the sun got brighter so we didn't see Aimes and Bugsy until they'd dropped back down beside us.

"Where's Max?" asked Bugsy.

"She went into the grass with Trent," Cristal said.

"That's brave," Bugsy said.

"Or dumb," I said.

"She's gotta kiss somebody sometime," Aimes said.

"And at least remember it," said Cristal.

A plane flew by overhead.

Another half an hour went by before Max rose from the dip behind the field. Trent reached for her but she pointed toward us. He stood and wiped his hands on his jeans. She pulled her skirt down as they walked out of the grass, his arm thrown over her shoulder. She batted his hand away from her breast and fake laughed again. Before they reached us, he split off to the smoke pit.

With his back turned, Max hoofed it toward us as fast as she could. We all sat up to meet her. Her lips looked puffier than before. The chubby parts of her cheeks seemed irritated and her eyes were very wide, like she'd just dunked her face in ice water. When she sat down beside me, I thought she smelled a little different. Salty or something.

"What happened?" Bugsy asked, pulling her hair back into a stubby ponytail.

"He put his hands in my pants," Max said, placing a palm over her crotch.

"Gross," we said in unison.

She was fidgeting like she needed to pee.

"I think he got some grass up there."

"Did you kiss?" Aimes asked. She'd just gotten multicoloured elastics put on her braces, which made her mouth look like a party when she smiled.

"Yeah, he kissed me!" Max said, surprised she'd forgotten.

"Did he kiss you before or after he put his hands down your pants?" Bugsy asked.

"After," Max said.

"Did you like it?" Aimes asked.

"It felt like he was trying to gag me," Max said.

Aimes frowned. Cristal leaned back on her elbows.

"When you kiss, do you have to use your whole tongue?" Max asked.

"If you want to turn them on, you do," Bugsy said.

Aimes leaned through the circle to give Max a high-five. "Well, tick that off the list," she said. "Gawd, I can't wait to get finger-banging over with." She tucked her top lip under her top gum and flashed us a grin.

Cristal didn't say anything. On her back, arms behind her head, she kept staring at the sky.

We were proud that Max had her first kiss and relieved that some parts of the event were romantic. A gift given, long grasses, his arm draped. But when I looked at Max, sunshine streaming by the edges of her limbs, I felt afraid. She'd been picked. I'd have to catch up.

"Are you gonna do it with him now?" Bugsy asked.

"We can't do it till grade ten," Aimes said.

"You're going to do it," Bugsy teased.

"I'm not," Max said. "I won't ever." She crossed her legs at the ankles and scowled.

I looked to Bugsy, trying to discern if she felt the same way I did about Max, a confusing combination of resentment and relief, but the bell rang. Jumping up too fast, Aimes, Bugsy and Max got dizzy, making them zig-zag their way inside. Watching them leave I realized that now all three had moved into offensive positions. I was the only one left standing on the side-lines, beside Cristal.

"Later," I said, running after the girls.

"Wait for me," Cristal yelled, scrambling to pack up her lunch.

I kept running, pretending I didn't hear her call.

After school, we all grabbed our backpacks and ran for the double doors, heading down the hill to my house for the first time in months. We could hear Grum in the ravine with his friends, and Mom wouldn't be home from work till six, so we had the place to ourselves. I made a few boxes of KD while Max beelined to our apartment-sized piano.

"Did you know if you type star sixty-nine before you make a phone call it can't be traced?" she yelled, beginning the arpeggios to Pachelbel's *Canon*.

"Really?" I yelled back, straining the noodles and dumping them back into the pot.

"My brother does it all the time," Max yelled over the first chords. "He calls girls and whispers that he's in their house – then he hangs up. They never find out."

"We should prank Ms. Titteski," Bugsy said.

Ms. Titteski was a substitute teacher we'd begun working over last week. There was nothing wrong with her specifically, other than she had skittish eyes and nervous hands and that particular pairing made us bloodthirsty.

A stillness came over us, in acknowledgement of a good idea. The girls grabbed their bowls of KD and we plunked down around the kitchen table.

Aimes grabbed the phone book to look up Titteski. There was only one in the entire Okanagan Valley and after a few rock-paper-scissors blow-outs Cristal grabbed the phone, making the decision for us. She dialled star sixty-nine and then the phone number Aimes read aloud. Waiting, breath held around the receiver, after five rings an answering machine came on. Cristal waved us away so she could focus. We shuffled back, impressed with her taking charge. Lowering herself down onto the wicker couch, she cupped her hands around the receiver and started to breathe heavily. We heard the beep then she began growling into the phone. No words. Just grunts. Moving the receiver to the other ear, Cristal began to whisper, slow and raspy, about how she was going to kill Ms. Titteski's dog and fuck her grandma. She put the receiver to her mouth, exhaled like she was trying to fog a window and then she screamed, the craziest high-pitched sound that made us lose it.

"Cristal!"

Aimes tackled her while Max squealed, proud of Cristal for being so impulsive. After hanging up, she too blushed at her own nerve. The bowls of KD were left half eaten on the kitchen table as we ran upstairs to my room and blared *Blood Sugar Sex Magik*.

On Monday morning, right as we pushed through the double doors, Cristal was called into the office and suspended for a week. Max had gotten it backwards: star sixty-nine was the number you called if you *wanted to know who'd just called you*. Ms. Titteski had brought the tape machine to school to play for the administration, and even though she was sure we'd all been involved, only Cristal's name had been screamed into the recording so she took the fall. Cristal was asked to leave school immediately. Her face turned the colour of clay. She knew what was in store when she got home. I couldn't guess what her parents would say; I only knew she'd be sent straight downstairs, grounded, no phone calls, no TV, no communication with any of us, and I'd have to wait at least a full week to find out what happened. I imagined her standing at the top of the steep staircase, about to descend into a long and silent week.

I'd only been invited into her bedroom once. It was cement with a single bed tightly made in the corner, and a small dresser to store her jeans and plaid shirts. There weren't any posters on the walls or anything that hinted of personality, and the only natural light came from a high rectangular window the size of a box of Old Dutch chips. If you stood on her bed and looked out the window, all you could see was a truck tire in their driveway. Her parents didn't abuse her from what I could tell, but the starkness of her life had an aggression to it. It was like her only option at home was to be a pencil: straight and fitting into a tight little case.

On the first day of her suspension, I sat in our corner of the student centre and wrote a letter to send home with her older sister, Ford, who didn't talk much but I hoped would pass my message along.

The next day, Ford found me in the student centre with the girls and handed me a tightly folded piece of paper. Opening it, I had to squint to read the tiny handwriting. The letter started simple. She was okay. Bored. They didn't yell as much as she'd thought. More concerning was their lack of anger.

After the first page, Cristal seemed to get more comfortable and the letter stretched into prose. She wrote for pages. She said she'd never had a best friend before and hadn't known the hole was there until it had been filled. I'd never heard her speak so extravagantly about something, let alone me. I didn't show Cristal's letter to anyone. It was private, a sensation I hadn't felt with the rest of the girls yet. Sitting with Bugsy and Aimes, half-listening to them banter about Timmy and Jimmy and the best night to officially let them down their pants, I missed Cristal's constant presence. Max had been ambushed by Trent right out of French class. She'd turned to us as he tugged her away, her eyes puffy from not sleeping the night before, still trying to figure out how get out of these lunchtime dates. It was strange that Max had no problem yelling at her dad or singing loud in the grain silo, but with Trent she played meek. I suppose at this point she had no choice but to go – otherwise she'd be a cock tease.

When the final bell rang, I headed straight home to write Cristal back. It was surprising what came out when I hadn't planned what to say. I wrote about how I missed our sleepovers, not that I was gay, but "let's be gay together." Hahahahahahaha. I asked her, "How is it decided what becomes a memory?" I wrote until the side of my hand cramped, then I neatly folded the letter into a rectangle, put it in an envelope and kissed it, like in the movies.

The next day after the last bell I found Ford waiting for me by the front doors, jittery to get home before her 4 p.m. curfew, and I pressed the letter to her palm, squeezing her hand in thanks. At lunchtime the day after that, Ford found me at the lockers and handed off a crumpled ball of loose-leaf papers for me to unfold carefully and pore over as I slid down the lockers. After school, Mom was already home when I came crashing in through the side porch, writing the next letter to Cristal in my head.

"I miss my other girl," she said, peeling potatoes.

A current shot through my spine, but because I missed her too, I let the jolt slide.

Max called me that night. She told me that she wasn't coming to school for the rest of the week. Her new plan was to tell her parents she was sick with a migraine and hope that Trent would lose interest after a couple days' absence.

"If I'm not at school, there's a good chance he'll pick someone else," she said.

"I doubt it," I said. "He lasered in on you."

There was a pause like she was thinking.

"How do you pretend to like something you hate?" she asked.

I thought about flying alone to Victoria to visit my dad – an unaccompanied minor sign the size of a placemat around my neck – to meet his newest girlfriend in his even newer apartment, and the gnarling in my belly that happened for days before.

"You have to shut off your mind," I said. "Like how soldiers do."

I thought then about the gifts he'd send home with me on the plane. "It also helps if you know you'll get a treat out of it."

"Thanks, Sym," she said.

"I can scare him off for you," I said. "I could act crazy, like I just shit myself."

Max laughed. We both knew it had to be his choice. If she rejected him, he'd make her into a Tampon Twyla.

"I think I'll try becoming a snail," she said.

In my mind's eye I saw Max peering into the glass hutch that stored her collection of tinies. She had a tiny dog and tiny dishes and even a tiny spool of thread.

"I'll tuck up inside my shell so he can't pry me out."

I stayed up late that night making a collage that Cristal could put on her wall if she was allowed. I included a picture of the time my dad came for a visit and took us hiking and she almost got bit by the rattler. We looked glassy-eyed in the photo, high off adrenaline. In another picture, Cristal and I have our arms around each other's shoulders, cheeks pressed together. Mom had taken that one, on Cristal's fourteenth birthday at Pizza Hut in Vernon. Sliding the collage into a manila envelope along with another letter, I placed the package beside my bed, set my alarm and brushed my hair across the pillow, so it looked like a bird of paradise while I slept.

The next day at school, I found Max sitting by herself on the floor, wearing the skirt Trent had given her. I slid down the lockers and leaned my head on her shoulder.

"You came," I said.

"They wouldn't let me stay home," she said.

We sat together for a minute, hands clasped.

"Why aren't you hiding?" I said.

"Someone took a dump in the girls' bathroom so I'm just waiting for the stink to clear out."

A shadow came around the corner. I knew it was Trent before I looked up. He didn't acknowledge me as he extended his arm for Max to grab onto, which she did. My stomach felt like acid. I didn't want him coming around our lockers anymore. He scared me, in the way nothing was off limits to him, how he so easily looked at our boobs instead of our faces, which made the girls stay away and Max even more aloof, her only means of defence.

With Cristal gone and Max acting defeatist I'd had enough. There was no way some piece of shit was going to wreck my crew. I followed behind as they headed toward the hill behind the field, his arm draped over her shoulder.

"Trent," I yelled, "Max hates that skirt you gave her."

He didn't turn around.

"Hey Max," I yelled again. "You look like a slut."

She kept walking.

"Watch your pervert boyfriend," I yelled louder.

I hoped that she'd be so embarrassed she'd have to run back inside, or maybe he'd turn on her. But the heckling only seemed to strengthen their resolve and she slid her hand into his as they walked faster toward the dip in the field that hid them from view.

She came back to the lockers earlier than usual. She was alone, flushed cheeks like usual, but with pep in her voice.

"Help me," she said, handing me her coat.

I draped it around her while she rolled down the black skirt and shoved it into her locker, then she grabbed a pair of baggy cords and pulled them up quickly.

"Much better," she said.

I was waiting for her to get mad at me for calling her a slut. Instead, she smiled.

"I can't believe I didn't think of it before," she said into her locker. "I'll start taking the gifted courses my parents have been pushing." She grabbed her lunch. "I'll tell Trent that I hate them for it, but I have to spend every lunch hour in prep."

She stepped back and knocked the locker shut with her hip.

"It kills two birds with one stone," she said, turning to me. "My parents will lay off if I'm in the accelerated classes and Trent can't finger-bang me if I'm in the principal's office doing a practice test."

Max's eyes lit up. She'd figured it out.

"But I called you a slut."

"That's the least of my problems," she said.

———————

After the last class, I waited by the double doors for Cristal's sister to bring me her correspondence, but Ford never showed up. This meant that I'd have to go the entire weekend without hearing from her, which was too long. I headed down the hill with what felt like two large birds flapping inside my chest.

The Hyundai was in the driveway but Mom wasn't in the kitchen. Following the phone cord, I found it stretched under her bedroom door, which was closed. I knocked and opened the door, revealing Mom in bed, the phone cradled between her ear and shoulder, her brow furrowed. She waved me away. I retreated, then turned back to press my ear against the door. By her tone I could tell it was an old friend. She had done this every few months since I was little – locked herself away in the closet or pantry to get some privacy and talked for hours. Snippets of words floated through the heavy wood. "I miss ... " and " ... lucky" and "yes, the river." There was a long sigh. She was talking about the trailer. I turned the handle so the door would open a crack without her noticing and the conversation became clearer.

"Yes, yes, exactly," Mom responded to the voice on the other end of the line. "Good people." Another sigh, then her voice dipped, "tired" and "no time." Silence for a while. "Of course, I know." A chuckle erupted, as if the woman on the other end of the line just said something true.

"I don't know how someone who grew up in the bush could turn into such a snob." An intake of air. "Em, stop eavesdropping," she called out.

I opened the door. She looked pale. Why was she in bed on a workday?

"Em's home," Mom said. "I'll call you when I hear more."

Hanging up the phone, Mom stretched and yawned. The skin on her arms looked floppy, like she'd lost some weight.

"Hear more about what?" I asked.

"Why I'm so tired all the time," she said.

Mom patted the bed. Fred rose to the command and I helped him hop up, then followed.

"Why don't you ever want to go back to Ashton Creek to visit?" she asked.

I looked to the ceiling. Cobwebs covered in dust floated from the corners of the room.

"I'm embarrassed," I said, surprising myself.

"What could you be embarrassed about?" she said. "We excavated stumps to plant our own garden. We controlled a burn pile the size of a Ferris wheel."

"I think it's the opposite," I said, recognizing truth as I said it. "I'm embarrassed we left everyone behind."

There are only a few rules to living rurally – so quiet, they're easy to forget. The main one is that if someone thinks you need help, you get it. Which was why we were always included in our neighbours' family reunions and spring clean-up days. I'd thought we'd moved because we'd physically outgrown our hot metal box, already packed to bursting with dogs and chicks and a kitchen table that sat only three. But having to rely on our friends for holiday meals and babysitting had become a burden for Mom. It was too much work being so goddamned grateful all the time.

Now, lying in the same brass bed, but in a proper house, with a chandelier and crown mouldings, words I'd not known a year ago, the feeling was sorrow. We'd turned away from kindness and I hadn't looked back. *How dare I think I'm better than the bush?*

"So, the next time Cristal comes over, if I tell her you shared a bedroom with meat birds, you'll be okay with that?" Mom asked.

"With Cristal – I'm fine with anything," I said. "It's Bugsy I'd worry about."

"Speaking of being embarrassed," Mom said, rolling over. "Can you guys fix dinner tonight?"

"Sure."

"Is Cristal coming over – oh right, I forgot." She puffed up her pillow.

"I miss her," I said.

"You should visit her," Mom said, closing her eyes.

"I can't."

But as I said it, an idea came. I could go to her house after dinner and deliver my letter and the collage through her basement window. That was romantic as hell.

Past the cheese plant, I crossed the road and jumped onto the tracks, starting down the corridor of trees toward the shortcut that would take me to Cristal's house. It had been weeks since I'd been on the rails and most of the bushes had already dropped their green, only the large woody rosehips were still hanging on. As the sun turned an orangey pink, I sat down and tucked my mom's old wool coat under my butt. The weather was turning. Snow would come any day. I chucked stones for a bit, to make sure I didn't interrupt Cristal's dinnertime. Then I balanced along the rails, just to say that I had.

When the sun dipped behind the treeline, I crossed the tracks, jumped off the rails, ran down the shortcut and crawled through the brambles to Fletcher Avenue, where Cristal's small yellow house sat at the end of a cul-de-sac. The sheers were drawn but there was a light on in the living room. I snuck up the driveway with the manila envelope in hand, and when I was between their Ford truck – Cristal's sister's namesake – and the house, I got onto my hands and knees and peered into Cristal's bedroom window. There she was, sitting in the centre of her twin bed, staring at her dresser across the room.

I tapped on the glass and she looked up, shocked, then she grinned. She stood on her bed and with the glass between us, pressed her hand to mine. She tried to open the window a crack, but it was hard to do – the bottom runner of the frame was bumpy from old paint and window sealant. I didn't bother trying with the manila envelope, but I slid the letter through the small opening. The content had been written in a fevered passion, re-proclaiming my love and reminding her that we'd make it through anything together. We touched fingertips.

I sat back on my heels and maybe because I was so close to the siding, my movement made the motion sensor light come on. As if she'd been standing guard, Cristal's mom banged open the side door and saw me crouched by the truck tire. She let out a holler and I scrambled up, bolted down the driveway and hit the road. She ran after me, screaming sounds rather than words as she chased me down Fletcher Avenue, across the road and into the alley, and what scared me the most was that she didn't give a shit who saw her in her bathrobe and slippers, trying to run down a fourteen-year-old girl.

After I crossed back over the tracks I stopped running. My hands were clammy – I knew I'd just made Cristal's night a lot worse. Continuing back up the hill, under the rose arbour, alongside our newly painted house, I entered our glassed-in back porch, lit by the kitchen. Even though we'd moved in months ago, every time I entered I had the same thought: *So grand.* A few Wheat Thins left on a plate and the skin of tomato soup at the bottom of two bowls told me that Mom and Grum had finished an early supper. Wandering into the living room I found them cuddled together on the couch.

"Hi," Mom said, eyes on the TV. "Did you get to see her?"

I grunted, my mood gone sour. I didn't know why. She'd done nothing wrong but the feeling was *mad at her.*

"I left you some soup on the stove, hon," she said. "I'll reheat it," and she moved to get up.

"Don't bother," I said.

"Have a cuddle," Mom said, patting the couch beside her. "We're watching *Cheers.*"

I imagined climbing onto the couch and resting my head on her shoulder. She'd smell like the floral soap she kept in her underwear drawer.

"Come here, Punky," she said again.

I couldn't. I didn't know why.

I climbed the stairs and spread-eagled on my bed, hands on my chest, and started the nightly scan of my room, to calm my breathing down. The desk Mom had found and coated a glossy white was still off-gassing paint fumes and the carpet was damp from being steam-cleaned, giving the room an all-over dewy feel. In the bush, my bedroom had been multi-purpose, filled with winter boots and Mom's unfinished weaving and a heat lamp over the baby chicks that would soon be meat birds – the sawdust sweet from their urine and tiny poos. When we moved, Mom painted my new room a dusty rose. She'd sewn curtains and a bedskirt in matching white eyelet. I kept it clean, like in a magazine, and laying my eyes on all that beauty every night brought about a lovely sedation. I looked to my ceramic happy and sad drama masks – the centrepiece of the room – my vanity and mirror, and finished the scan where it began, on the white desk covered in photos of camping trips and birthday parties and the words *Dream*, *Passion* and *Obsession*, cut out of magazines and lacquered on with varnish.

Flipping the pillow to rest my face on the cool side, I closed my eyes.

"Em?" Mom knocked gently on the door. "Are you still up?"

The door opened and I felt Mom move toward the bed. It was early but I pretended sleep. She leaned over and kissed my forehead, a dry, nervous peck.

"I love you with my whole heart, Punky."

I stayed still. It felt wrong to want her attention – and get it. Too exposing. Better to practice indifference. Mom turned and headed across the hall to kiss Grum goodnight.

On my side, I squinted through the trio of windows, framed by the country kitchen ruffs, past the glare into the night. I'd had the same fantasy since I was a kid, and even though we'd moved I left my daydream in its old location. Letting my eyes go soft, I imagine a girl sitting on top of the propane tank behind the trailer. She's waving to get my attention. It's a warm night. My window is Kleenex-box sized, perfect for collecting dead stinkbugs and moths in its screen, and I crank it open and press my face against the mesh. The girl on the propane tank smiles, reassured that I've returned. I wave back and as she settles I stretch out on my tummy, crack my book and we both return to the stories we're reading about smart-alecky girls and the best friends they rely on. The fantasy makes me ache but it also softens my breath, to pretend she's out there and we're content reading together into the night. The imagery never goes further than that. It starts and ends with being waited for.

2012

IT'S LATE JANUARY, THE DARKEST TIME OF THE YEAR. From the floor of my co-op apartment in Vancouver I'm watching Midge try to chew through a bone. Out the window is grey. It's rained for twenty-eight days straight since Christmas, the longest I've gone without seeing Mom since her diagnosis.

The neighbours below me bang on the ceiling with a broomstick. They called again last night to tell me that the sound of Midge's constant bone-gnawing was terrorizing them. I reminded them that she's a four-pound chihuahua with no teeth and after I hung up I told them to go fuck themselves in the head.

Midge is my little saviour. Six years ago, she'd been found in a ditch beside a four-lane highway with two broken legs, milk leaking out of her nipples and no babies in sight. The minute I saw her on the dog rescue website I knew she was mine to save. I carried her against my chest in a Baby Björn while her bones healed. I fed her from my fingers. I pooped with her on my lap. She's graduated to travelling in her mesh carrier when she accompanies me to rehearsal halls, where she curls up in a shell shape under the table, or to the Children's Festival, while I pretend I can teach a hula-hooping workshop, and the myriad other wack-a-doodle side projects I piece together to pay rent. When asked, I tell people I take her with me because she's high needs, but I'm not so obliquely referring to myself. Midge soaks up my nervous energy. She shakes it through her own little body and whimpers it out of her system in small squeals.

It was Mom who'd convinced me to get a dog in the first place.

"You just need another heartbeat in the house," she'd said years ago, during the rainy season, when I'd called to tell her about another romantic tropical vacation that had turned into yet another heartbreak. Where is the partner I don't hate myself around? Who is the communicative, easygoing guy that likes my big feelings? I don't know because I'm not attracted to that kind of man. I like men who have no patience for me. The kind ones, I find repellant to be around.

"I'll be the woman who never finds anyone," I'd said to Mom. "I just have to figure out how to be okay with that."

"You don't need a boyfriend when you've got a dog," she'd said. "That's the secret to a happy life. What can a man give you that a dog can't?"

I took a breath.

"Don't be rude, Emmy."

Six years later, I don't know how I lived so long without Midge.

Even though it's acceptable to stay put this time of year, as travelling the Coquihalla in late January is hairy and my Jetta is a bag of shit, the real reason I've not seen Mom is that most days I just can't get up off the living room floor. It's quiet down here and the carpet is soft. I make myself snack plates of crackers and cheese and eat them lying face down, my mandibles grinding against the carpet. I walk Midge around the block three times a day and I crawl upstairs to pee. I've been dragging myself to work in the evenings, but listening to an actor tell the story of how he dropped everything and moved home to Israel to capture his mother on film in the last year of her life and then assist in her death is heart-wrenching timing. As he runs his lines on stage I sit in the back of the theatre, holding my computer in front of my face so I can weep unnoticed.

Should I move back to Armstrong? The argument quickly sprays in all directions. *If you lose your co-op, you'll never be able to afford the Vancouver rental market. You can hardly make it through the holidays together, imagine the hell of cohabitation? She birthed you — get your ass home.* This loop is made more complicated by me being my mother's daughter — my mother, a woman who scrubbed her own amniotic fluid off the kitchen floor after her water broke, fed the animals, finished weeding, then travelled across the Skeena River by cable car, before Dad drove her to the Terrace hospital to give birth. She taught me to place the to-do list above the to-feel list.

I manage to tip my cell off the coffee table and call an old friend. Her mother has recently died so she's got a head start in the field of grief. I hiccup into the phone, begging her to tell me *when will I know it's time?*

"You'll just know, Em," she says. "It'll be clear when it's time to move home, so that means it's not time yet." She added, "You fight with her a lot and that's not going to change. She's used to living alone. You've got years left on this journey, so my suggestion is to pace yourself. I promise, it'll be obvious when the moment has come."

I need this answer. I can feel my skull loosen its grip from being told what to do.

Splayed out in the middle of the living room floor, more of my tears seep into the carpet as Midge licks the end of my nose – my teeny-tiny-nose-licker with her stinky-little-nose-licking tongue – and I pray out loud, because I was told once that the clearer you are the easier your prayers will be heard.

"May I have no regrets," I say.

If the first prayer two months ago was for Mom to live long enough to know her unborn grandchildren, this appeal is only for me.

"When she dies, may I know I've done my best. May I have no regrets," I repeat.

I know what living without regret would mean, but in this moment, looking slant across my living room floor, I can't follow the terms: *Get home. Now. Nothing will matter as much as these moments with her – ever again. Stroke her arms and thank her for making you and dealing with your bullshit. Plant her garden. Finish the quilt that hurts her fingers. Rock her and coo like she's the baby – and definitely don't feel weird or resentful about it. This is the normal, terrible stage of life when your mother needs you. Go. There's no more time to discuss what you never got from her during childhood. That ship has burned. She's going to be dead for longer than you got to be her child and the only way you're going to survive the rest of your life without her is if you do a good job now. Smell her. Feed her. Listen to her mythology. Because soon, you'll have no access to your great-grandmother's maiden name or how to grow a proper-sized carrot. She's been trying to teach you this wisdom her entire life, by the way, and when she's gone it'll be all you want to know. Like the recipe for those jalapeno cheese puffs that Grum loves so much: it will be lost, and you'll spend every yuletide of your life trying to re-create it. Get a pen and piece of paper and write that recipe down right now you sad fuck.*

I focus instead on manageable logistics. I can up my visits to two times a month. I'll hire a cleaner. Call her at nine and noon as well as our regular 5 p.m. daily chat. When I do visit I'll attend meditation classes with her instead of waiting in the car. These are tangible goals to accomplish and I'm buoyed that I have some agency over my prayer.

Crawling across the room to the sliding door, I crack it open to the grey outside. *This is the first step*, I say to myself. *Now take the next.*

1991

O<small>N</small> <small>MONDAY MORNING</small> Cristal picked me up, free from her lockdown. We embraced in the kitchen but didn't speak of the chase as I assumed her mother's open wrath would've embarrassed her. She stayed silent as we headed up the hill to school, her eyes trained on the icy sidewalk in front of her. It might have been that she was trying to keep her face out of the cold, but maybe, after a week of isolation, it was also hard to let in all the noise and colours of kids streaking by. Just as we made it to the school's concourse a freezing wind hit us and we ran, heads bent, toward the school.

At lunchtime – after the girls dogpiled Cristal and Bugsy bought her a Pepsi and Aimes gave her three lucky punches to the arm and we crossed legs over thighs and lay back against the carpeted benches – we started to discuss the most burning issue: Trent's impatience. Aimes heard from Timmy that he'd called Max a cock tease. The title hadn't leaked out past the senior boys, but it meant he was getting frustrated.

"I'm safe today," Max said, looking above her to the skylight. "He won't want to go to the field in this weather."

My friends looked tired. Max raked her hands through her hair, like her scalp was on too tight. Aimes nodded and threw me a gummy worm. Bugsy lay on one of the benches, her legs curled in a fetal position. Cristal was beside me, rubbernecking, trying to catch up on last week's events.

"You can follow Bugsy and I to the machine shop after school if you want to hide out till your dad picks you up," Aimes offered.

Aimes understood Max's predicament. She and Bugsy also felt the responsibility of giving their attention when it was required. Their free time was no longer free either. They couldn't meet up on the tracks with no agenda on Saturday morning anymore, as this was prime attention-paying time, to be spent at the hockey arena or on the rugby field, cheering and pretending to care about the score. I understood their need, to feel the boys' eyes on them, prickly and hot, but I was also relieved that right now was just us. After a weekend apart, we were crazed to touch each other again, sniff the mango hand cream and stroke Bugsy's new velvet choker. Huddled on the bench seats, ignoring what was outside our circle, we gorged – replenishing like a cactus plumps after a drought.

"We're going to walk past the shop now," Bugsy said to me. "If Max won't, you should come."

This was where she and Aimes spent most of their lunch hours now, cackling outside the machine shop door. But in fairness, their commitment to securing their first picks had shown results. Jimmy and Timmy weren't their official boyfriends, but since they'd both let them get to second base confirmation was imminent. Jimmy and Timmy lived in a hybrid territory – a bit cowboy but mostly jock, the boys loved to dirt-bike in the back hills behind their subdivision. Next-door neighbours and childhood best friends, they both got low-rider trucks for their sixteenth birthdays and they drank Bud and Pil interchangeably. Most importantly, as much as Aimes and Bugsy didn't want to be called sluts, Jimmy and Timmy didn't want to date sluts, so for the time being French-kissing and dry humping was satisfactory for all parties involved.

"I don't want my first boyfriend to be a jock," I said.

"Don't be racist," Aimes said and took off down the hall.

Like Cristal, I thought having a boyfriend seemed stressful, all the leg shaving and vagina washing required. But unlike Cristal, I *did* want to be singled out, to be chosen, and that hadn't happened yet.

I followed Bugsy and Aimes out to the machine shop, our breath visible as we crossed the parking lot. From the doorway we watched skinny bums poke out of car hoods and wrenches clang onto the cement. The smell of gasoline made us a bit silly and we started pushing each other through the garage doors into the large room. Bugsy gave me a good shove and I landed on the floor, which made a smallish boy, the runt of the litter, look my way. I scuttled back to the girls but after a few more glances, his friends shrugged their approval and a deal was made. He wiped his hands on a rag as they pushed him toward me. I wanted to run. I wanted to point and say "Fuck you, you fucking ass cheese," but I didn't, because I was getting what I came for.

"Bo," they laughed. "Go get her, Bo."

Bo grabbed my arm and led me to the back of the school where kids usually play murderball, but no one was out today because of the cold. He pressed me against the cement wall and I could feel a hard nut in his pants as he grabbed my thigh and raised it to hip level. I smelled bananas on his breath, and then he kissed me. His lips were thin and as soon as they touched mine, his tongue jutted out. I opened wider to accommodate. He tried to tug my leg higher up the wall and I did my best to help him lift it. His tongue started to roll around my mouth like a sock in a dryer. I felt a sharp pain and tasted blood.

"Your face," he mumbled, and tried to step back.

"What?"

"Your face is caught on my braces."

He ripped himself off me, creating a waterway of blood that ran down my chin.

I pressed the space between my upper lip and nose. The skin was ragged.

"Do you have a tissue?" I asked.

My cold fingers felt good against the cut.

"No," he said, wiping his mouth. "Your face got caught on my braces," he said again, then he turned back toward the machine shop.

I brought my sweatshirt to my mouth to stop the flow of blood and strode to where Bugsy and Aimes were waiting for me in the concourse. By the time I reached them I'd started to shiver.

Bugsy put her arm around my shoulder and they walked me back to the student centre, where the rest of the girls were lounging.

"What happened to you?" Max asked, pointing to my rapidly swelling lip.

"Runt-o-the-litter happened," I said, showing her the cut. "His braces attacked me."

"Look at her face," Bugsy laughed. "Her first kiss is going to leave a scar."

"He kept trying to lift my leg," I said, curling up beside Cristal.

"Must be a porn thing," Aimes said.

"Listen, Em," Max said. "Sometimes we have to do gross things so worse things don't happen."

"Exqueeze me?"

"She's talking about how she gave Eli a hand job — so Trent would hear about it and back off for good," Cristal said.

"Ew. Eli the stoner?" I said.

"Our parents are friends. We went there for dinner. As soon as he got me alone he whipped out his dick," Max said.

"What'd it look like?" Bugsy said.

"I didn't see it," Max said. "He grabbed my hand and told me to cup it."

"How'd it feel?" Aimes said.

"Like I was holding a candy cane," Max said. "But before I could look down, he sprayed all over."

"Sprayed?"

"His semen. *Psssttt*. Like a Windex bottle."

"Windex," Bugsy said. "What a perv."

"I'm playing the long game," Max said. "I'll cup Windex's dick a hundred times to get Trent off my tail."

"Well, Bo is never allowed to kiss me again," I said.

I was surprised to hear myself say something so definitive about the first boy who'd ever shown me interest, but after saying it, I knew it was true. The issue now was that he'd assume he could get more – and that would be a pain in my ass. My eyes landed on Max, her chin lifted to the skylight, the winter sun breaking through. I'd have to start doing the opposite to her strategy. If she could rid herself of an older boy's focus by faking interest in a younger one, I'd have to get an older boy interested in me so runt-o-the-litter would know his place. It was a pre-emptive strike.

Bugsy and Aimes spread out across the benches while Cristal checked my lip to see if the bleeding had stopped. The lunchtime announcements came on and because we weren't listening, all our heads jerked when my name was called on the school PA system. "Emmy Symington please come to the office," the loudspeaker repeated. I liked hearing my name amplified but the immediate thought was *Grum is dead*, so I jogged in the direction of the voice.

Bugsy looked up from her ragged nails. "Tell the secretary I think her son is hot," she yelled after me.

I gave her a thumbs up and kept moving.

"Your mother is waiting for you in the parking lot," Jimmy's mom, the school secretary, said without looking up from the computer, so I couldn't pass along Bugsy's message. I pushed back through the slate-blue double doors and headed to where I knew Mom would be parked, while considering what could be wrong. If Grum wasn't dead, could Dad be? Her car was idling in the visitor's parking stall and through the back window I saw her hands gripping the steering wheel.

I slid into the passenger seat. She kept her hands on ten and two and lifted her gaze to the field in front of us. Her neck was long and the skin under her chin — taut. From the side, she looked creamy and regal and for some reason that made me feel proud of her.

"I have breast cancer," Mom said.

I folded my hands in my lap.

"I just got the news and I wanted you to know first."

My fingers wove together into a grip.

"It's spread to my lymph nodes," she said, eyes still on the empty field.

I searched for what she was seeing — stalks of dead corn, piles of newly frozen earth.

"What are lymph nodes?"

"They're in your neck and armpits and groin," she said. "Little sacs of white blood cells that protect your immune system. It means that the cancer is travelling."

Is this what a nurse sounded like? She'd never brought words like these home with her before. She moved one hand to her chest and drummed there lightly with her fingertips.

"I've been set up with an oncologist and the plan is to have surgery and then do radiation and hopefully no more than seven or eight rounds of chemo," she said, her focus still on the chunked-up field.

"Seven rounds? Is that a lot or a little?" I asked.

"It's a good kick at the can," she said. "But I'm going to need your help."

She reached across the car for my hand, but pretending I didn't see, I looked out the passenger side window. *Why would she drive here and tell me this shit, in the middle of my school day? Could it not wait till dinnertime?*

"Em, it's okay to be scared," she said, patting my knee. "I'm scared too."

"I'm not scared. You'll be fine," I said.

It felt like someone had just placed a sack of flour on my sternum.

"The doctor says it's the best kind of breast cancer a woman can get."

"Good news," I said.

"But we're going to have to move quickly," Mom said, returning to her nurse voice. "I'll have surgery as soon as they can fit me in. Then we'll start radiation. At some point I'll have to travel to Vancouver for the chemotherapy." She looked out the window. "Maybe your dad can drive up from Victoria and live in the house while I'm gone." She rested her forehead on the steering wheel. Her brain already in planning mode.

I shook my head and looked down to my lap again.

"How long will you be away?" I asked.

"Seven weeks."

Mom preferred to do everything on her own. She never used the ruse of poor-single-mom, even if a mortgage payment was late or she had to take a day off to stay home with a sick kid. One Christmas morning, we'd opened the trailer door to find a food hamper on the front step. She drove it back to the church, furious. "Give your damn cans to someone who needs them," she'd yelled out the car window. "We don't take charity."

"I'm going to need your help, Em," she said again.

"Yep," I said. How was it possible to feel so vacant inside, so flat about the whole thing? "Can I go back to class now?"

I made myself smile. My lip cracked and I tasted warm blood.

"What happened to your mouth?" she said, reaching for my chin.

"Murderball," I said.

I couldn't chance seeing where her eyes rested and if there were tears in them, or getting a glimpse of her cheeks – I'd be a goner. I kept my eyes at half-mast as I stepped out of the car and as soon as I stood up, I felt dizzy, like I was going to puke.

"You okay, Punky?" she asked, leaning across the passenger seat.

My eyes started to sting. *Please don't cry. Please don't crumble*, I thought, not sure who I was speaking to. Turning back around, I saw that her hands had returned to ten and two. Her chin lifted. Imagining my friends on the benches inside, their minds easy, I clocked that I didn't get that anymore. In only a few minutes I'd gone from chewing a soft piece of gum to trying to swallow a tightly packed ball of screws. I had to be careful now.

Shutting the passenger door, I bent down and waved, a stretched smile, and wiped the blood from my lip. Thin slivers shot down my throat, adding to the metal pieces that were collecting in my gullet. She smiled back, strained too. Once I got back to the girls everything would be fine.

Moving through the loud din of students at lunch, I rose above and in front of myself so I could watch how the girl who was me was about to behave. By the way she dug her fingernails into her palms I knew she was trying to keep her arms from flying off her body. *Poor child*, I thought. *She is so sweet, trying to hold on to the many little explosions happening all at the same time.*

"Where'd you go?" Bugsy asked. "Why'd you get called to the office?"

"My mom has cancer," I said, looking back to my lap. My hands were real. I could see them.

"Ooooo, shit," Bugsy said. "That's bad."

The rest of the girls had left, on their way to our next class, but Bugsy seemed in no hurry. Her eyes were soft and it was nice to have them on me. She kissed my forehead.

"You wanna skip and go to the tracks?"

"Naw," I said. "But when she goes to Vancouver for chemotherapy we can have a party at my house."

The final bell rang and the last of the kids jumped up, crinkled chip bags and crushed pop cans thrown at garbage bins.

"You coming, Sym?" Bugsy asked. "It's a science test."

She ran, her jean jacket tassels swishing behind her. On the school bulletin board there was a large year-long calendar. Today was December 12. Tomorrow would be the thirteenth, twelve plus thirteen equalled twenty-five. Two plus five makes seven. Seven is the number of weeks she's having chemo. That's a good sign. I was able to take a deeper breath. I closed my eyes.

That night after dinner, when Mom told him she had cancer, Grum cried fat tears that looked nice to feel. She rocked him as he sobbed until her hands on his back brought him to rest. She told him that everything would be okay. She was his mom and she wasn't going anywhere. She promised him with all her heart. I sat stiff. Grum cleared the dishes as she headed into the living room to watch *The Cosby Show*. I stared at the hutch across from me, a wooden cabinet with glass doors, the top piled with bills and unfinished to-do lists and old pieces of fabric she was saving for when she got around to mending.

When we got the call from Mom's oncologist the care plan came together quickly. Mom would have surgery within the week and she'd heal at home for six weeks. Next, she'd have radiation, along with more bed rest, and finally the cancer would be obliterated by chemotherapy.

"They're going to cut off my tit, burn me from the inside out and poison my blood," she said after she got off the call. "Then, I'll be good as new."

The day Mom had surgery they kept her at the hospital overnight. Grum and I came home right after school. We watched *Law & Order* and ate popcorn for dinner. When Grum went upstairs to brush his teeth I put the house to bed, as Mom called it, closing the blinds and turning off all the lights. Dad wasn't coming for another week as he was winter camping with his new girlfriend, so I locked the front and side and back doors, just to be safe, and Grum and I headed into our separate bedrooms, on opposite sides of the small attic. We didn't say goodnight but we both left our doors open so we could hear each other shift in the night.

We stayed home from school the next day, not sure when Mom would be back from the hospital. Grum watched TV and I read *Anne of the Island*, trying again to finish the third book in the series. I was almost done but something always seemed to interrupt me, like summer camp, or the move, or meeting the girls, so I'd put it down for months – maybe because I didn't want the story to end, I so related to Anne Shirley, that "red-headed snippet."

Lying in Mom's bed, I read with Fred at my feet – the only sound his collar jangling when he scratched – until I heard the screen door open and slam slut.

"Em?" Cristal's voice called out. "Are you guys home?"

"In here," I yelled, and climbed out of bed, not surprised she'd come by after school to check on us.

"There's a car in your driveway and I think Judy's in it," Cristal said as she entered Mom's room. We peeked through the blinds and saw Lydia, one of Mom's church friends, trying to help Mom out of the passenger side of the car, both tottering.

"Grum, MOM'S HOME!" I yelled and he jumped up from the couch and ran for the door.

I hightailed it upstairs, terrified to see her weak and bleary, and peeked out the window to watch Cristal and Grum get on either side of her and help her into the house. I listened as they hoisted Mom up and settled her in bed, where I heard her giggle, then moan. After about fifteen minutes of silence, I crept down the stairs and opened the door to Mom's darkened room. Cristal was perched on the bed, giving Mom a sip of water. She hadn't said anything to me yet – about Mom or the cancer – but here she was, and her familiar shape in our house gave me space to breathe.

Cristal still had a strict curfew of 4 p.m. sharp on school days and since she'd been suspended, she'd developed the habit of constantly checking her watch. She placed the glass down on the nightstand.

"Okay, Jude, sleep good tonight," she said, watching as Mom slowly leaned back against the wall of pillows they'd built for her.

Mom's good arm cradled her sore one. She nodded and smiled, her eyes still closed. Cristal checked her watch again.

"It's five minutes to four," she said as she turned to me, "I gotta go."

I walked her through the breezeway to her bike. "Missed you today, Sym," she said.

"Me too," I said.

She threw her leg over her ride. "See you tomorrow morning then," she said, pedalling down the slick driveway.

I ran after her as she raced across the street and through the elementary school playground. She looked back – her butt off the seat – laughing as I tried to catch up. Once she made it across the frozen field I stopped and held my hand high. I hoped she made it in time.

The NEXT MORNING, FEELING BETTER with a new plan in place, I call Mom and tell her I'll be there as soon as the Coquihalla Highway is safe to drive. Up the steps two at a time, I decide that while I'm waiting for good weather, it'll be best to sweat out some of the terror energy, so I look online and find a yoga studio that offers two back-to-back power classes a day. If I can devote three hours a day for the next few weeks, yoga might be just the thing to wring me out.

That afternoon I cab downtown and follow the scent of lavender and sweat up the steps into the studio. This is a hot yoga power class, nothing like the more traditional systems I've practiced and trained in before. I open the studio door but no light or draft greets me. The room is windowless and crowded, the air still damp from the class before, and I find the controlled environment with no music or talking allowed perfect. I grab the last spot, shoved up against the wall, close my eyes and listen to the teacher's instructions. Her voice is kind but controlled. I hold the poses longer than she counts for and when she sets us up to do an inversion, I come down almost a minute after everyone else. I keep my eyes steady on the mat and my mind on her demands. I enjoy the sharp pain between my shoulder blades. It means things inside are changing. I backbend until I think my coccyx might split and while I move I pray for my mom. *This sweat is for her life. Every drop is to heal her lungs. The pain I feel is so that she suffers less.*

It's so much easier to drive myself to the ground physically than be present with my mom emotionally that I commit to the three-hour practice daily and in only a few weeks, I notice strength I've never had before. Within a month, my body is tighter and faster. I stop waiting for the torrential rain to stop and I start biking to evening rehearsals. I don't cry in the back of the theatre anymore as the actor speaks about his dying mother. The exhaustion keeps me sane.

In Vancouver fashion, crocuses peek out from the ground too soon to feel natural. The rains have ended, which means the mountain pass is clear. After not seeing Mom for over two months, I bring my yoga mat and spend hours trying to pin a handstand in the living room while she naps. When my arms are too shaky to hold my body up any longer, I collapse and crawl over to the couch to wake her. We take a short walk to the mailbox at the end of the cul-de-sac with Midge and Zip, which is just enough exercise to tire Mom out before lunch.

A cycle begins. I drive back to Vancouver on Tuesday and work for two weeks on the upcoming play, drive the seven hours to Armstrong for a long weekend, then drive back to Vancouver for another two weeks of rehearsals. In Armstrong I focus solely on completing the tasks I've laid out for myself: make food, drive Mom to her appointments and try not to be a snippy bitch. In Vancouver, I ask my co-op for a six-month rent reduction and they agree, so now I don't have to ask my brother for gas money. On the next visit, Grum meets me in Armstrong and takes Mom for a long drive while I make dinners to freeze. The flowers in Mom's garden start to bloom and I call Ollie Solly, who still lives in the old Fletcher Avenue house, to come over and do some yard work. And the cycle repeats.

On one of these afternoons, I set Mom up at the kitchen table near the stove so she can watch me make grilled cheese sandwiches. She looks the same since my last visit — wiry hair, sunken cheeks, belt holding up baggy jeans — but she seems a lot more with it, more here.

"It seems like this trial chemo is working," I say.

"I think so too," she says. "My hair won't fall out from this kind of chemo either."

"You look good," I say, digging through the fridge for butter.

"It's my Chinese medicine doctor," she says. "Whenever Nell gets a cancellation, she fits me in, so I've been going almost every day."

"That's great, Mama."

"You can tell?" she asks. "I look better?"

"You seem to have more energy," I say.

"It's called *qi*," she says. "Nell says every time I go to an appointment, I earn a day."

I put the sandwich in the frying pan and wait for the bottom to brown.

"You're doing it wrong," Mom says, from over my shoulder.

I flip the sandwich.

"I know how to make a grilled cheese sandwich," I say. "You taught me."

"Well, you've forgotten," she says, and pushes me out of the way.

As well as having more energy, she's becoming more forthright, and it's a pain in my ass. She grabs the buttered bread and cheese out of the frying pan with her bare hands, shoves it into the toaster and pushes the button down.

"You're going to start a fire," I say.

"And you're going to shut your trap," she says, watching the coils heat up.

The cheese begins to melt into a mass at the bottom of the toaster.

"Mom, this is crazy," I say. "It's not how you make grilled cheese."

"You haven't seen crazy yet," she says, waiting for the toast to pop.

I head back to Vancouver early the next morning. It's best to take her in chunks to mitigate the damage. I kiss her cheek while she pretends to be fine, then drive the seven hours to the coast with Midge nestled in my lap, licking her little paws. But I can't shake the grilled cheese scene from the day before.

"My mom will live to know her grandchildren," I say, eyes on the highway, still covered in gravel and salt. "I'll live without regret," I add, passing over a canyon of frozen trees, tall and still. "My mom will live to know her grandchildren and I'll live without regret," I say over and over again until my breathing regulates. Try. Fail. Feel like shit. Try again. I'm both grateful to be leaving her cloying touch and ashamed of the thought I've just had: *If the cancer doesn't kill her, I might have to.*

1992

THE MORNING AFTER WINTER HOLIDAYS ENDED – with Cristal digging through our kitchen cabinets for food and Grum putting out Mom's pills as she was still too doped up to remember them – we finally got out of the house on time. The world outside was quiet. The city grader passed by, piling more snow onto the sidewalk. Cristal and I made it to the locker room in the gym just as the bell rang and I was relieved to have the day away from Mom's needs.

The girls were already getting changed for PE. I hadn't seen any of them yet as I'd spent the holidays with Dad. Mom sick or not, it was his year for Christmas.

"You kissed Seb?" Bugsy said, pulling on her gym strip.

"What?" I said. "Who told you I kissed Seb?"

Seb was the hot guy in grade eleven whose tire I'd kicked in the Sev parking lot. He had thin black hair and liked a band called Skinny Puppy. I was more partial to Neil Young, but after runt-o-the-litter ripped my lip behind the school, Seb had asked Max for my name on their bus ride home. Even after the two-week break, this rumour that we'd kissed meant he'd been fishing for intel.

"Jimmy heard about it at rugby," Bugsy said.

"Not possible," I said. "I just got back from Victoria."

The trip had consisted of back-to-back visits with Dad's new friends, listening to them talk for hours, over tea, about their feelings, while I fiddled with their seashell and driftwood collections. He'd just started his master's degree in therapy and I'd noticed a sudden interest in discussing his childhood trauma, maybe to alleviate the guilt he felt for leaving us. This observation wasn't precociousness on my part, just what I picked up from being steeped in hours of adult navel-gazing. I was glad to be home.

"That's weird then," Bugsy said.

"Seb could be my first real kiss though," I said.

After gym class, Seb found me in the concourse as if he'd just heard the rumour too.

"Hey," he said, tucking a black strand behind his ear.

"Hey," I said, my voice lower than normal.

"You hacky sack?"

He dropped the sack onto the edge of his black Vans and flicked it into the air.

"Sure," I said, lifting a knee to catch it and missing.

"You wanna come to a movie with me tonight?" he asked, saving the sack before he flipped it to his other foot.

First contact. I'd been picked. My stomach dropped into my ass. Glancing behind, I hoped to see one of the girls emerging from the gym so she could testify to the moment, but we were alone, Seb bouncing the greasy looking sack between his knees, my butt cheeks clenched so I didn't shart. He liked me. He wouldn't have asked me out if he didn't. So why did I want to steeplechase over the benches and bolt for the field?

"What movie?" I said.

"No idea," he said, eyes still on the limp little ball. "I'll pick you up at six."

"Sure," I said, sphincter tight like a sea anemone.

He peeled into my driveway at six thirty and after giving Mom a quick squeeze goodbye on her good side I ran out the door. The hatchback opened from the inside and Seb leaned forward so I could squeeze into the back seat beside two large boys I recognized but hadn't met. I willed myself to act like Max, distant and serene. Seb didn't talk to me on the drive to the next town over; the music was too loud, a screaming kind of death chant. When we piled out at the theatre, he walked ahead with his friends through the slush while I searched the back seat for my wallet. I was relieved to see he'd saved me a seat beside him in the already darkened theatre after I'd bought myself a ticket.

Snuggling in, I tilted my chin up so my neck would look longer and placed my palm face up on my lap so it was easy to reach. The movie was about a guy who was trying to kill a woman. They were on a boat. The guy had been her husband once, but now he wanted her dead. I wished Cristal were there so I could bury my head in her shoulder for the scary parts, but Seb surprised me by bringing my hand over to his lap. I smiled in the darkness and slowly leaned into him. *Imagine if we became boyfriend and girlfriend? He has a car — that would make life easier. How long should I wait before I introduce him to Mom?* Two weeks sounded ballpark. My hand still lay open in his lap while my synapses superhighwayed new connections, building our world together, pond skates and dinners out with his parents — but then a movement interrupted me. The first thought was: he has a hamster in his pocket. The second: it's a penis.

I'd felt three penises before, one in the pool when I was eleven and an older kid pushed himself into me underwater, one on the grade seven field trip when a boy and I had been dared to full-body hug and, most recently, Bo's little nut. They'd felt similar, like ballpoint pens, but this one had reached out, like a goddamned pet. Which led me to my third thought: Seb must not know. All energy focused on relaxing my hand, I stared at the screen. Now, there were men swimming under the boat. One of them had a knife. It was very hard to focus on the plot when this rodent trapped inside his pants kept mawing for me. How could he not feel it?

After the movie Seb's friends decided to try and score some beer and go to the park, so Seb and I drove around the back of the theatre and parked behind a dumpster. I wished the girls were here to see it happen: my first real kiss. I'd call them as soon as I got home. Seb pulled me past the e-brake and I lifted my face to his. He was pale, with red bumps along his jawline and neck. He unbuckled his seat belt and tilted the chair into a recline while I kept my chest pressed against his, hoping I looked like a fawn, or a dove. He brought a fingertip to my chin while I heard his other hand unzip his pants. I smiled, wanting to telegraph that I was enjoying myself. He moved his hand from my chin to the top of my head. His eyes were kind. He gently pressed down on my crown. I don't know how, but I knew what he wanted me to do next. I didn't want to do it. It was our first date. But I'd already agreed by being here.

I started to kiss his neck, dodging the crusty bits. I pecked his heart, overtop the black shirt embroidered with flames. Like I'd seen in the movies, I kissed his chest and down the buttons, pretending to be in the moment, until his hand returned to my head, signalling me to pick up the pace. I kissed down his tummy until my face met his beltline. He lifted his butt off the seat and scootched out of his jeans so they sat stretched around his white thighs.

Closing my eyes, I hovered, awaiting instruction. My mouth curled involuntarily. I really didn't like this. Gently still, he pressed my head down farther. The cotton fabric of his underpants smelled a little of urine. I wished he'd kissed me before this part. What if my face smelled like piss now? I glanced up and caught him looking down at me. My breath caught, mortified that I'd made eye contact in such an unglamorous position.

"Lick it," he said.

His underpants were tighty-whities but blue — and the elastic was frayed at the top like my dad's old underwear. I licked the cotton and the hamster rose. I licked again and I could see the little guy poking through the fabric and the movement reminded me of — what was the movie called? All those cylindrical monsters burrowing tunnels underground until they broke through the surface and killed everyone?

Seb pulled his penis out of his underpants and flopped it onto his belly, knocking me in the nose. A penis. This was a penis? It was purple. It looked plastic. His hips tilted forward and I stuck out my tongue, to taste-test. The tip was warmer than I expected and there was a bit of wetness on the top, like he'd just peed. I turned away, letting the penis slap back onto his lap. I hoped not to get more pee smell in my mouth in case he kissed me later so I pressed my cheek against the length of it instead. *Tremors!* That's what the movie was called. He seemed to like my cheek pressing against the shaft of his penis, so I steamrolled my face back-and-forth over it a few times, holding my breath, but this too was proving hard to do, because the penis was acting like one of those inflatable punching bags — always popping right back up.

"Put your mouth over it," he said.

The smell got worse, like horse in the back of my throat.

I got onto my knees in the passenger seat, which made it a lot easier to put his penis in my mouth. He rose to meet me and for a minute I felt like a cobra on a nature show, unlocking my jaw, trying to swallow a live mouse whole. It took a lot of coordination to move my mouth up and down to the same rhythm of his hand tube but he was really enjoying himself now, shoving his penis farther down my throat than I had space to hold. I gagged. He let me up and I took a sip of air and then he pushed my head back down again. His eyes were closed and his head lolled to the side. There was a frown on his lips. I couldn't tell if it was pleasure or annoyance.

I just wanted it done and I had the gist now, so pushing his hands away I propped myself up with my elbows, made my hand into a tube and crammed his penis down my throat. He made a cry that was exactly like a newborn calf I'd heard last summer. I started to gag myself faster. The tip of his penis hitting my tonsils seemed to be the ticket, so I tightened my grip and jammed it toward the back of my throat again and again until my eyes watered and my hand tube cramped. He pushed my nose into his belly button and held my head still while he bucked. The action reminded me of what Aimes said farmers do to ducks to make pâté: they force-feed them. I counted to eleven. A hot liquid shot out of his penis down the back of my throat. His whole body shook and then he tucked his penis back into his underwear with an exhale. I wiped my mouth. It felt puffy like I'd just eaten a bag of ketchup chips.

"You swallow?" he said, stroking my bangs away from my forehead.

"Yeah," I said, no idea what he meant.

"That's cool," he said resting his hand on my back.

"I know," I said.

He lifted his butt off the seat to pull his pants up. I felt a hair far in the back in my throat and I wanted to hack it out but that would have ruined the moment so I swallowed and swallowed until it was gone. He unrolled the window and lit a smoke.

"Can I have one?" I asked.

My jaw hurt. My chin felt like road rash.

"I've only got two left," he said, "but you can have a drag."

We were facing a Dumpster and the smell of rancid oil came through the open window.

"I'm headed to Dameon's place now. I can drop you off," he said and grabbed my hand.

It was this gesture that made it all worth it. *He thinks I did a good job. I went further than most girls would have. This puts me in the lead.*

"Yeah sure, drop me off," I said.

"Watch the teeth next time," he said, putting the key in the ignition.

I unrolled my window to give myself something to do. When I turned back, Seb leaned across the seats and kissed me. His lips were dry and scaled. His tongue darted in and out like a baby snake. He held his mouth to mine and made a smacking sound, then he pulled away.

"Gross," he said. "You've still got cum in your mouth."

"Oops," I said, and rolled my eyes, like I was the dumbest one around.

I didn't feel the need to entertain him on the drive home. I watched the lights glaze past in the window, my mind quiet as I sat in the front seat, his friends all squished together in the back. Jumping out of the car I waved through the window and he grabbed my hand again and kissed it before he burned out of the driveway. *He likes me. He'll want more.* I felt like a jellyfish, electric and boneless at the same time. I ran through the breezeway, threw my shoes across the dark kitchen, stretched the phone cord into the pantry and dialled Bugsy's number.

"Have you given oral yet?" I asked.

This was the first time we'd had a chance to talk since gym class and it was her, not Cristal, I wanted to give my update to.

"I don't kiss and tell," she said.

Which meant she had.

"It hurt the back of my throat," I said, sliding down the pantry wall.

I didn't bother pulling on the light. The dark was nice.

"I think your throat toughens up after a while," she said.

"Do you swallow?" I asked, trying to figure out what he'd meant.

"My old babysitter says you only swallow if you really like the guy," she said. "Semen's got more calories than a bacon double cheeseburger."

"Oh shit, gross."

"I know, so gross. But if you catch it in the far back of your throat, you'll miss it hitting all the taste buds on your tongue," she said. "That's what I do when I eat cottage cheese."

"Great tip," I said. "Thanks."

It was nice to talk with someone who had some experience with what a boyfriend might expect.

"He said to 'watch the teeth next time,'" I said. "Like there'll be a next time – so that's cool."

I stretched my legs out underneath the shelves of canned peaches and stewing tomatoes. From where I sat, I could see layers of wallpaper peeling off the back wall of the pantry. These were the only walls in the house Mom hadn't sanded, painted or smashed down, and seeing the brittle prints of birds, velvet yellow flowers and geometric shapes, I knew why. The layers revealed a hundred years of women's design choices. She was keeping record of all the other proud women before her.

"Congrats on sucking a dick," Bugsy said, yawning into the phone.

"Thanks," I said. "He kissed me too," I added, just remembering.

"Kissing's nice," she said with a sigh.

This was the first time we'd ever talked, just the two of us alone, and it didn't feel uncomfortable or weird at all.

"I think I'll have a bath."

"See you on Monday then," she said. "LYLAS."

"LYLAS bitch. Forever."

On Saturday morning, bold rays of light streamed through my windows, waking me up in a squint. I'd been kissed. I ran downstairs to find Mom and Grum snuggling on the couch watching cartoons. They were happy so I let them be. Hoping to meet up on the tracks later for an impromptu hangout I called Cristal but she didn't pick up. I tried Bugsy then remembered she'd left early this morning to visit her aunt at what we now called Shit Lake for the weekend. Aimes's phone line was busy. I called Max and she picked up on the first ring.

"Please stop calling me," she whispered.

"What?" I paused. "It's me, Emmy."

"Oh, shit, I thought you were Trent again," she said, her voice returning to regular volume. "He's been calling. I don't know how to get rid of him."

"Don't pick up," I said.

"I tried that last night but he just biked over here instead."

"He biked to your house? What happened?" I asked.

"Ryan let him inside," she said. Max sounded like she was trying to catch her breath or keep up with it. "He came into my room and I rolled over and moaned like I was sick so he wouldn't try and kiss me."

"Were you in bed?" I asked.

"Yeah, I was lying in bed. I dry-heaved to make it believable."

I almost told her that I'd dry-heaved yesterday too, but I caught myself, not sure how she'd respond.

"Doesn't this guy take a hint?" I asked, returning to Trent.

"He got mad at me," Max said. "He said, 'I biked all the way over here and now you're sick?' He tried to crawl into bed with me so I pretended to puke again. Then he got even madder and was like, 'What, I'm supposed to bike all the way home now?' So I asked Ryan to drive him home in Dad's car. Now his bike is here. My parents are on their way home from an art opening. He's been calling non-stop."

Max started crying, loud and panicked.

"Okay," I said, straightening up. "First thing, before they notice, tell your parents it's my bike. I rode over last night and we watched *La Bamba* again." I paused, for inspiration. "I got my mom to pick me up because it was too slushy to bike home."

"But your mom just had surgery. She can't drive."

"That was three weeks ago. She's got one good arm," I said. "I'll tell them the same story if they call me."

"How do I get him to stop calling?"

I looked to the ceiling. "If your parents find out he's been calling, then they'll know you've been hanging out with him."

"Dad will freak on my ass."

Max's dad had an angry streak. Mine did too. I understood the consequences.

"They won't know, Max. I promise. It's my bike, okay?"

"But it's a boy's bike," she said.

"Tell them I got my bike stolen when I went to camp last summer so I ride my brother's bike now."

"You're quick at making up lies."

"I have a strong imagination."

"Okay. Thanks Sym." Max's voice sounded calmer now.

"Now go have a shower."

"He didn't touch me."

"Just to wash the feelings off."

———————

On Monday after school, we found Max sitting on the benches out front. Seb was standing in line for the bus. I'd been waiting to share the good news and I quickly pointed him out to the girls.

"My first real kiss," I said, again leaving out the other part of the night.

They pulled me down, hungry for details. Aimes took the barrettes out of my hair and ran her fingers through it so she could start a French braid.

"Do you like him?" Max asked.

I stared at his back, bony ass invisible inside his jeans, a bag across his thin shoulders. "No," I said, "his tongue was too skinny. I don't think I like kissing."

"You like kissing," Aimes said, hands on my crown, separating my hair into sections, "Or, you *will* like kissing."

"Well, not tongue kissing," I said. "I'm not doing it again."

It was strange — with the girls I had opinions. I could disagree and gain their respect. I never considered not speaking my mind and they valued the audacity. It was only the boys I dulled myself down for, deferring to their needs. When the girls weren't nearby I seemed to lose my compass and float away.

"How are you going to get out of kissing him again?" Max asked, rolling onto her tummy. "Or worse?"

Bugsy and I caught eyes. She wouldn't give me up.

"Well, if he whips out his dick, I'll bite it off," I said. "Just the tip, like a hot dog."

Cristal and Max threw back their heads laughing.

"You are one sick fuck," Aimes said, putting an elastic on the finished braid.

I felt full up again.

Cristal and Bugsy and Aimes walked me home through the crusty snow. Bugsy and Aimes left shortly after for slushes and I watched Cristal smoke until she had to bust it back before curfew.

When I came inside, Mom was calling out for Grum and me, so we crawled up onto her bed. The room smelled medicinal, and also of farts. Crumpled napkins filled with yellow fluid were scattered on her lap and the bedside table. There were no groceries in the house. Grum hadn't changed his clothes in days. She'd considered calling Dad to ask him to arrive earlier and help out but then she decided it would be easier if he just didn't come at all. He'd get too overwhelmed. The chaos was easier to manage on her own. The incision was healing well but she still needed a lot of pain meds, which made her cranky and dumb at the same time. And she was already being bombarded by visitors.

"There are too many well-meaning people in this town," Mom said. "I don't want them to think I live in my nightie."

"But you have cancer, Mama," Grum said. "You're sick."

Her eyes turned from drowsy to pin pricks as she started to fidget with the raised bumps on her quilt, her knuckles bigger than I remembered.

"I'm not sick," she said. "They cut it out and I'm recovering. The radiation is only precautionary." Then, "Honestly kidlets, sitting still all day is harder than getting your boob cut off."

Grum's eyes widened but the announcement made me smile. I'd never seen the woman sleep in. She was up and gone to work before Grum and I had risen, two bowls of congealed cereal on the table and two tomato and mayo sandwiches, uncut, wrapped in wax paper beside the front door.

"I've got people coming by at all hours to drop off prayer shawls and casseroles. I'm not saying I'm not appreciative," she said, reading my mind, "but I don't like handouts, and I can't keep track of all the Tupperware I'll have to return."

"It's okay, Mama," Grum said and slipped off her bed. "Come outside, to the front porch."

He helped her hobble out and sat her down in the big velour chair, then wrapped her in a quilt. This was Mom's favourite room in the house. Screened in, it wasn't quite outside but breezy, not yet inside but cozy. She'd tried to build a porch onto the trailer, as the aluminum door opened directly into our living quarters, making for mud under the kitchen table and blasts of snow and ice. But the makeshift room quickly filled with pets and storage. "Humans need a space between inside and out. A middle-place," she complained. "It's what separates us from animals."

So, when she found a house that had both a glassed-in back porch and a screened-in front porch, that's what decided this was the home for us. After an afternoon of gardening I'd find her out here having a quick doze — feet on a stool, strong tea on the side table, sun hat thrown onto the floorboards — and

I'd think *this is what satisfied looks like.* Before she'd been diagnosed, Mom used the front porch daily, like how most people smoke cigarettes: a few drags between jobs.

"You're safe," Grum said and pointed through the screen. "No one can see you out here."

Mom peeked over the ledge, trying to get a view of the road, but she couldn't see much past the snow-topped bushes.

"Well, just in case, get the drill. We're screwing the screen door shut till summer."

She lay back in her chair, her privacy intact. "I never wanted children until I had them," she said, and fell asleep.

After a week stationed at the smoke pit during lunch then near the concourse after school, on Friday morning I woke up with my stomach in knots. Grum brought Mom breakfast in bed. Lightly burnt toast with chunks of cold butter ground into it and some orange juice from a can. I felt no similar impulse to help. Any softness I had toward Mom had been driven out by the more pressing concern of why Seb hadn't acknowledged me since our date eight days previous. If he didn't look at me today that meant he was purposefully ignoring me. I picked out a corduroy skirt and a yellow turtleneck to wear under my nicest patchwork vest. I didn't have time to peek in on Mom and as soon as I heard Cristal bang through the side door I ran for my boots.

We walked up the hill to school in silence, entered through the big double doors and saw the rest of the girls stretched out in the corner of the student centre. Our spot now. No one else sat here, even when it was empty. I grabbed Cristal's arm and strode toward them, needing my mind busied.

An hour later, in social studies class, Mom popped into my head again. Was she sleeping? Did Grum leave apple slices she could reach if she got hungry? Placing my forehead onto the cool of the desk I started counting. *I'm fourteen. Mom is fifty. That's a thirty-six-year difference. So that means in thirty-six days she will be fine.* It wasn't working today.

After school, Max and I headed outside. She was waiting for her bus and I wanted to give Seb one last opportunity to talk to me. We'd been on a date.

He'd kissed me. I assumed he'd want to at least try for third base again. Max pointed him out in his hacky-sack circle and I gave her hand a squeeze and started toward him, but as I approached he turned away. He'd seen me alright. I knew because his friend with the undercut had looked over and laughed.

I retreated back to the benches.

"He's telling everyone that you sucked his dick on the first date," Max said. "That's why he hasn't talked to you."

"Who told you that?" I asked.

"My brother heard about it in rugby."

"I didn't," I said. "He's lying."

"I know you didn't," Max said. "Who would suck a dick on the first date?"

"Not me."

"Seb's a skid," she said.

Max's bus pulled up.

"Max, wait," I said. "Can you ask him to stop talking about me?"

She smiled but I couldn't tell if it was for me or at me.

"It's the worst when people think things about you that aren't true," she said, and grabbed her bag.

"Do I call him?" I asked.

"Not unless you want to suck his dick again," she said, and ran for her bus.

I looked down at my boots and frowned. They were ankle high and had hundreds of tiny little holes punched out of the leather. Dad had given them to me for Christmas. No one else in school had a pair.

Cristal pushed through the double doors and came over to sit down.

"Hey ho." She leaned into me.

"Don't," I said, scooting down the bench.

If Max knew I'd done it, who else knew? The winter sun was beating down but a wind whipped through the concourse, like the weather was trying to fuck with me too.

"Wanna go home and catch *Roseanne*?" Cristal asked and kicked a pine cone.

I tucked my hair behind my ears, wishing I could plug them. Her voice grated. She had no idea what was going on. How lucky must that be?

"I told your mom I'd stop by for a quick visit."

"Not today," I said standing up. "She wants her privacy."

"Not privacy from me?" Cristal said.

"She doesn't want anyone coming over," I said, eyes on the cement.

"Okay," Cristal said. "I'll just walk you home then?" She elbowed me softly, trying to get a smile.

I needed to feel worse than I was already feeling. I had to dig a hole deep enough to crawl inside and curl up in.

"Just take a hint," I said. "Leave her alone."

I grabbed my backpack. I didn't look back. I didn't need to. I'd done the damage intended and it did feel better.

When I got home, Mom was sitting at the kitchen table, surrounded by loose-leaf paper, a calendar and highlighters.

"Where's my other girl?" she said, looking up from the stack.

I frowned. She looked better today. Her eyes were less clouded and she'd been able to have a shower since the home-care nurse had taken out her stitches the night before.

Before I could think up a lie about Cristal, Mom continued. "Good news," she said, circling a day on the calendar. "There was a cancellation. Radiation starts in a month. I just got the call."

She was chipper and she'd somehow gotten from bed to kitchen by herself, but I was shocked to hear she'd be starting radiation so soon after surgery. But what did I know? Cancer was a fast-moving train.

After dinner she let us stay up late with her again, watching TV, because she said the house felt too big with just her awake in it. This was what she used to do when I was a baby too, after Dad left. She'd light the wood stove and rock me into the night, for company. But tonight, I couldn't sit still. I climbed the stairs to my room and starfished in the middle of the bed.

In the darkest part of the night, I awoke to a sound. It was that point of sleep where you're down so deep that if woken, you aren't sure where you are. I sat up. There was a sound downstairs. I couldn't decipher it. The sound was quiet.

I waited for a minute, frozen, and the sound became clear.

"Please, Em, can you help?"

She was crying. Her arm was probably stiff from the incision healing and she needed help changing positions. Her voice got more desperate.

"Em, I need you."

I lay there. I couldn't get up.

"Em – hon – please?"

My body felt like it was made of a bag of dirt. It couldn't move but I also didn't want it to. So, like a ghost, I rose off the bed and floated up through the roof until I could look down between the open rafters at our home, a girl above her dollhouse. Mom was in her bed downstairs, calling out for me, but still. I was curled up on the floor above her, not moving either. I watched us from above like this, little dolls lying down, waiting for someone to animate our needs. Mom tried to roll over. I shook my legs out and tightened back into a ball. Mom pulled the blankets up with her good arm. I dug myself deeper into the sheets. She stared at the ceiling. I kept my eyes shut. She looked distressed but it didn't seem to be about the surgery, it was worse than that. And this made me even more rigid.

As the watcher I felt no need to comfort either of us. Our pain was different but both made sense. Eventually Mom stopped whimpering. Her body softened under the blankets and her breath deepened. I floated down into my own bed. My eyelids were sore from all the salt leaching through. Our big house was quiet again and I felt a breeze come through the window onto my cheek. Rolling over, I splayed onto my stomach and fell back into sleep.

One month later, on the first day of Mom's radiation treatment, Cristal and I got home from school and tiptoed into her room. She was out cold, snoring heavily through her throat. By the looks of things, it had wasted her. I stood at her window. Spring was trying to arrive early, the first shoots of daffodils poking up through the snow. Grum was in the ravine with the neighbour kid and he'd be out there till dark, and Cristal didn't have to rush home for her 4 p.m. curfew anymore. We'd never talked about why it had ended – possibly, I thought, because her parents would just rather not have her around so much.

The phone rang and I ran, hoping to grab it before it woke Mom up. Cristal went out to the breezeway and lit a smoke. Aimes was on the other end of the line and I brought the phone outside on its extension cord so that Cristal could join in our chat. Aimes and Bugsy were hanging out with Jimmy and Timmy later tonight. The boys had bought something they called panty remover, and Aimes was trying to figure out what kind of alcohol it was so they didn't look stupid.

"Is it like nail polish remover?"

"Tell her that as soon as she takes a sip her panties fall off," Cristal said.

"Geez Louise, I'll pack another pair in my purse, just to be safe," Aimes said. "I hate all the preparation that goes into a Wednesday night."

Cristal and I laughed, happy to have no plans. I hung up the phone and started coiling the cord back into the house when I heard Mom call out.

"You girls wanna know what radiation feels like?" she said.

"Mom, you're not supposed to be up."

"It feels like a fire hose," she said. "Not one that's used to put out fires, but an actual hose in my body, full of fire. Cristal, where's my magic bag?"

Mom had started to augment her doctor's orders with more natural healing modalities. A woman down the street suggested she try using tuning forks to de-stagnate her blood and the top rack of our fridge was devoted to mushroom supplements and fractionated oils. Cristal and Grum took pride in being able to remember which bottles were to be taken before or after meals, on a full or empty stomach, but I was more focused on trying to memorize my lines for the upcoming O-Zone Drama Festival, mouthing the monologues silently between bites of dinner, before my ride, Penny, honked to take me to my weekly speech and drama class.

"Maybe we should just switch homes," I joked after I returned and found Cristal eating popcorn on the couch with Mom and Grum.

Cristal looked confused. She didn't have to keep her distance, like I did, to protect Mom as much as myself.

"Join us, Punky," Mom said and patted the couch.

"I've got homework to do," I said, and I headed upstairs, leaving Cristal to let herself out.

The next morning, we sat in the student centre, waiting for Aimes and Bugsy to join us, but they didn't spill through the double doors like usual.

"Where the hell are they?" I said.

Cristal shrugged. She'd been at my house till nine the night before so her guess was as good as mine. We headed to our lockers and I gave her butt a little kick to let her know we were okay and she turned and curled her top lip to let me know the same.

Aimes showed up in English class fifteen minutes late and tucked in beside me. She smelled of toothpaste and peach, almost too fresh.

"Panty remover works," she whispered.

So far, Aimes had been the most prudish of all of us. She wouldn't let Timmy down her pants, and even though she'd attended every party this entire school year she hadn't officially gotten drunk yet, only got her buzz on. On weekends she'd been charged with keeping watch over Bugsy, sitting in the flatbed of Timmy's pickup as she watched her best friend dance by the fire, later making sure she put on her PJs and peed before she stumbled to bed. The theory we'd come up with was that because Aimes didn't have her period, her red stone hadn't started pulsing yet. This was why she felt no interest in going further than letting Timmy do figure eights with his tongue in her mouth.

Aimes giggled into her hand.

"It's not called 'panty remover' on the bottle. It's called lemon gin and it tastes like pop," she said.

"What happened?" I asked, cocking my head so it looked like I was paying attention to Mr. Wyatt.

"Jimmy and Timmy snuck it over to Bugsy's and we drank it in the hot tub," she giggled.

"What'd you do?"

"Honestly, I don't remember much." Aimes squeezed her legs together. "It was like, I just didn't care anymore. Like, all the stress of should I? or shouldn't I? was gone. So, I crawled –"

Aimes stopped mid-sentence as Mr. Wyatt turned away from the blackboard to catch our eye, then returned to scratching in chalk.

"– I crawled onto Timmy's lap," Aimes said.

"Where were Bugsy and Jimmy?"

"They were in the hot tub too, but then Jimmy was like, 'It's go-time bud,' and he hauled Bugsy out, who was totally loosey-goosey too, and then I grinded on Timmy and it was So. Much. Fun."

Aimes looked radiant. Or like she had a fever.

"Bugsy and I woke up in bed this morning with our panties off – which is funny, right?"

"Did you guys have sex?" I asked. "No," Aimes said, "definitely not. It was just cool not to care anymore, you know? Like, whatever he did to me was fine."

Aimes knees were knocking together under the desk.

"I just cannot tell you what a relief it is to get that over with. I'm drinking panty remover for the rest of my life," she said. "It's my signature drink."

I turned back to the blackboard. It did sound like a relief to not have to care anymore. To be able to give someone exactly what they wanted, and then feel free.

ON THE COAST, SPRING IS IN FULL FORCE thanks to the moisture from the old-growth and ocean. It's the opening night party for the Dying Mom show and even though I've managed to slink away from most of my responsibilities to the production, I decide it's best for optics to attend the celebration on the beach. I tie a kerchief around my neck and do my hair in two low braids. Fashion has always moved too quickly for me so my go-to look is small-town hick, which I suppose I am. With Midge in a bag across my chest I speed across town on my bike.

A beach fire is roaring and I make the rounds, mustering a jubilant "Happy opening." It feels good to be in a celebratory environment even if I have to push it. Tucking Midge up to a pile of coats, I find a patch of sand and place my head on my sweater and roll up to a headstand. A pair of legs wearing yellow pants blocks my view of the ocean and a man bends to my level. I know him but not well. He's my best friend's old high school friend. He moved to town a few years ago but we've never properly met.

"Christie," he says, "remember me?"

"Christie is a girl's name," I say before I can stop myself.

He throws his towel down beside me. "It's also Irish."

Christie is not my type. He's excessively attractive, with a chiselled jaw and eyebrows that arch perfectly over terribly blue eyes. He looks like a Banana Republic model, an obvious kind of hot I'm not comfortable with. Men like him are soft on themselves, which makes them boring. They coast through life on their good looks and supportive parents, and for the same reason I chose Midge I prefer the second-hand, broke-down cases. But we practice headstands during the cutting of the opening night cake and we keep at it when the dancing starts, and even when the cops interrupt the party, I try to teach him some simple acrobatics and he's a good sport about it. Eventually, the star of the show, Itai, saunters over to comment on our clique behaviour and we laugh and go right back upside down. With only a few stragglers left around a pit of embers, I introduce him to Midge, who he holds easily while we climb up a small hill to smoke some grass and watch the sun set. When we return to the party, everyone's gone and the fire is out and Christie asks if he can bike me home.

The next morning, he meets me at my power yoga class and keeps up. I buy him a coconut water from the 7-Eleven across the street.

"Did you know in the Vietnam War, coconut water was used as an alternative for blood transfusions?" I say. "It's the closest thing there is to plasma."

The next day I invite him to my apartment for lunch and Christie arrives with unwashed hair and stained sweatpants. He kicks off his shoes in the doorway and it's the easygoing-ness that makes my stomach jackknife. We haven't touched. As far as I can tell he's a friendly guy who wants to make a contact in the theatre industry. His relationship with the prettiest, most mysterious girl in the world has just ended and he must still love her because tomorrow he's helping her move out. I've got to drive back to Armstrong this weekend as Mom has already called with a list of spring cleanup jobs. But after he fixes my wobbly kitchen table leg, he offers to re-pot the plant I've had since I was nineteen and I can't stop myself.

"What are you doing this weekend?"

"Something with you," he says.

"Do you wanna meet my dying mother?"

"Sure," he says, matching my flip with tenderness. "I'd love to meet the woman who made you."

We drive his yellow Volvo through the mountains with the windows down and Neil Young blaring a tinny "Harvest Moon." It feels like we're old family friends after a long time apart and I talk so fast my jaw aches. He's wickedly funny and shares a similar upbringing, growing up in a smallish town with little money. At a rest stop I buy him a large magnetic sticker of two mallard ducks and thwack it onto the back of his Volvo.

"Ducks mate for life," I say.

As he drives, I keep side-eyeing his hot-as-fuck face, thinking *not my style*. Mostly, though, the road trip is fun, something I haven't had in a while.

Mom's waiting in the carport, ready to flag us into the driveway. I've brought men home before and she's gracious, but I'm wary as to how she'll behave, especially since the grilled cheese incident. Christie steps out of the car and she stands, arms open for a hug.

"Thanks for bringing Punky home safe."

"Thanks for having me for the weekend, Ms. Symington," Christie says.

"Call me Judy."

As they chat, I haul a duffel bag and suitcase inside. Through the screen I watch her cluck away while she shows off her flowerbeds. He makes us spaghetti and meatballs for dinner and Mom is relieved to hear I'm eating meat again.

"I just don't know how she got enough protein when she was a vegetarian. It was always such a worry."

"Well, Judy, I'm sure you already know this but legumes *are* higher in protein than most meat products," Christie says. "And cheap."

She dips her head at his frugality, and I think I see my mother blush for the first time.

That night, we watch *This Hour Has 22 Minutes*. It's her favourite show and I'm squished between them on the couch, popcorn on my lap. Mom and Christie and I laugh at the skit about the "GD clicker box," and something inside me corrects. My mind scans for a time I've felt this *me* around a man. It's always been an effort — an attempt to present a version of myself that's palatable. For him to see me in my natural state and be tickled by it makes me want to laugh louder and eat more.

We sleep in the spare room. We could've put a mattress on the floor but we pretend there's no choice but to spoon. I snuggle my bum into his crotch and he squeezes me around my waist but makes no other move. I wonder if he might be gay. The bum wiggle is universal in meaning. He shifts his body away from me.

At breakfast, I watch my mother revel in having a man around who enjoys being useful. It's as if her entire life of homesteading drops away and suddenly she can't open a canning jar. She's lived a life of militant self-sufficiency and as I watch her pour syrup onto the pancakes I realize that although it came naturally, her competence hasn't been a choice. It's pure pleasure to see such a capable person sink into reliance on another. Christie notices that when she leans forward to read, her glasses fall off her face and the tape around the bridge isn't helping, so he walks Midge to the pharmacy and returns with an optician's kit to tighten the frames, along with a handsome beaded chain, as he's also picked up on her routine of pacing the house, "trying to find my goddamned specs."

Christie's happy to putter alongside Mom in the afternoon, hearing the histories of each plant in her garden. She points to the blue and purple ground cover she originally planted the morning after I was born.

"When Emmy and I left the North, she was only a few months old, and about 250 miles out of town I slammed on the brakes. I'd forgotten the deadnettle. So we drove all the way back, crossed the cable car, dug some roots up, and I've brought it with me to every place we've lived since." She strokes the early leaves. "Plants are like family," she says. "You don't leave them behind."

Everything about Christie being in the house feels dizzyingly good; like we've found a maypole that works dual-action as a grounding rod. But I worry that I've misread him. This guy's got style. He hangs around with contemporary dancers. He's not made a move on me all weekend. I may have been relegated to "scrappy pal."

On our last night, I lie in the single bed and watch dusk arrive while Christie helps Mom prune the front hedge. The chatting is back and forth and I remember what she said to me the day my brother was born.

"You and I are good friends, Em, but with Grum, we've become a family."

I'd been hurt. I'd wished that I were enough to be a family on my own. But now, thirty years later, I understand what she'd been trying to say: a third person takes stress off a duo, like how a triangle is stronger than two straight lines. With Christie here, my body is quiet. I don't want to reach for my computer. And for Mom, too, it's easier for her to imagine her job coming closer to completion with him around.

We pack the car after breakfast and Mom hugs Christie and whispers something in his ear. He nods his head. They've made an agreement. She waves us off from the carport and I cry, worried about leaving her again, as he starts to drive us back to the city.

We pull up to my co-op building, carry my bags up the two flights of stairs and drop them in the front hall. I turn to hug him goodbye and I lay my head against his chest. I can feel his heart beating. He pulls me in tight. Squeezes me. Solid.

"Can I kiss you now?" he says.

I frown. Is this a mind game? I've spent the entire drive trying to be okay with the fact that the funniest, hottest, kindest man I've ever met finds me unfuckable.

"Why didn't you kiss me two days ago?"

"Because on the ride there, you said you didn't want to rush things," he says.

"*Some* things. Not *everything*."

"I thought it was romantic."

Never. Never in my life has a man heard a boundary and not tried to supplant it. While I'd pawed at him incessantly, talking into the night, he'd still not overridden the request. Even after I forgot I'd asked him, he held us to the deal. This patience with my body makes me so horny.

The kiss is awkward, the only thing to remind me it's our first one. There are no clothes being ripped off, tripping into the other room, horn-dog couch grinding. Our lips stay pressed together for a long time and we sway back and forth. He rubs my back and I can't not smile, making our teeth bonk, so nervous that he's here.

1992

On the final day of grade eight our English class turned into a feeding frenzy. Max had just presented a literary essay about a mouse who lived inside her vagina. The mouse had a very long tail, which she felt squiggling around inside of her and one day, when the sensation was simply too much to bear, she pulled the mouse out of her vaginal canal and threw it against the wall – in an act of bodily autonomy. I giggled and looked at Mr. Wyatt who, legs up on his desk, was smiling too. Mr. Wyatt didn't bullshit us with words like *responsibility* and *respect*. He seemed to know that this class was useless to us now and would also be meaningless in our futures, so he punched in like we all did, valuing our sass as a potentially stronger life skill than How To Write An Essay.

The final sentence she read was: "And then the blood from the mouse's exploded body dripped down the wall, along with my innocence." She'd obviously been inspired by Twyla the Slut and the end of *her* own childhood. We thought it was quite a layered piece of writing and Mr. Wyatt must have agreed because he took out his marking pencil and scrawled a large A+ over her cover page. This was what had turned the class wild, his absolute okayness with her smartassed-ness.

When the bell finally rang we high-fived him and ran to the lockers. The girls were hanging out and I couldn't contain myself. I'd been desperately trying to learn how to be better contained, but containment wasn't my natural state. So to have a few hours together before we left on our separate summer adventures – with the plural goals of getting and keeping boyfriends – was glorious.

We linked arms like we used to and charged down the hill, ignoring Dameon and Ollie Solly and their buds calling out to us in the parking lot. We'd worked hard enough gaining their favour to deserve a day off. Besides, the summer would be filled with bush parties and drunken lake swims, so tonight was ours.

I opened the back door of the house and we ran through the glassed-in porch, kicked off our shoes and headed for the living room. No matter how many weekends we'd spent apart, no matter what cracks had developed and sealed over, when we came back together, the same thing happened. As soon as the back door slammed shut and the kitchen curtains were drawn, we unzipped the bullshit we'd stuffed ourselves into, shook out our hair, undid our button-fly jeans and spread the fuck out. We seemed to need each other to become ourselves again. After we disrobed, we entered buck-wild territory: Max trying to lick a forehead, Aimes on the back of the couch cawing like a crow. Bugsy pretending the remote control was her dick.

"Mom's moving us again," Aimes said.

"Where to?" I asked.

"A basement suite on Okanagan Street," Aimes said. "The new place has air conditioning."

Cristal had gotten her first summer job picking strawberries. She had to get up at five every morning and ride her bike for an hour to get to the farm on time but the harder she picked, the more money she made.

"I'll have $3,000 saved in three years to buy a motorbike, and that includes money for smokes and beer," she said, patting her belly.

"I'm at Shit Lake all summer," Bugsy said. "If anyone wants to join. You remember where our cabin is? The third turn. Past the sign that says free tires."

We nodded, knowing no one would stop by. Her older boy cousins had grown even hotter over the year and there was no way we could act normal around them.

"How long's opera camp?" Aimes asked Max.

"All summer. Eight weeks," she said. "I'm sleeping in a college dorm with a roommate."

She didn't explain any further, like it was too smart of a place for us to understand.

I cooked up a few packages of Lipton Noodles & Sauce for us to eat and Max went upstairs to try and take the shit she'd been holding in for a week. Cristal turned on the TV and half-watched *Oprah*.

"When are you going to camp, Sym?" Aimes asked.

"In a week. I'm an LIT this year," I said, taking a mouthful of sour cream and chive noodles.

"Camp sounds gay," said Cristal, sinking deeper into the couch.

"Camp is fucking rad," I said, sitting up. "The Symingtons are a camping family."

This was the phrase Mom always used. Her dad, my grandpa, had worked for the YMCA in Ontario and had led summer camps her entire childhood. Now she used her summer holidays to volunteer as a camp nurse so Grum and I could go for free, which we'd done every summer since I could remember.

"We met you on the tracks last summer when you'd just come back from camp, remember?" Bugsy said.

"That wasn't last summer," I said.

"Yeah it was, dingleberry," Bugsy said. She grabbed Cristal's bowl and started shoving noodles into her mouth before Cristal noticed. She was wearing a silver bracelet Jimmy had bought her after she'd let him jerk off in her butt crack. She'd been clanking it around all week, demanding we comment on how pretty it was.

"You were trying to spy on us," she said.

"I wasn't spying," I said. "I was curious."

Was it only last summer? We'd just moved in. I felt like a very different girl now, or, more specifically, not like a girl at all.

"Oh shit, you were so funny," Aimes said. "You had this way too big T-shirt on and mom shorts."

"And your hair was in two low braids –" Bugsy said.

Aimes interrupted: "You looked like Anne of Green Gables."

That never-ending book. I'd been about to find out if Gilbert was going to die. But after Mom got back from surgery, I hadn't picked it up again.

"Does Gilbert Blythe die in *Anne of the Island*?" I asked.

"I can't remember," Aimes said. "I only watched the movie."

"He dies," Cristal said.

"He doesn't. He dies?"

"I'm kidding, Sym, I don't even know who you're talking about," Cristal said.

"Gilbert Blythe, Anne's beau! Her one and only true love. Gil proposes but Anne rejects him," I said, trying to recall the order of events.

"I can't believe you know all this," Bugsy said.

"It's Anne of fucking Green Gables, Bugsy, how do you *not* know?"

Aimes headed upstairs to check on Max's constipation progress and I stood up, preparing to re-enact the climax scene I'd rewound so many times on our VHS at the trailer that I knew both characters' lines by heart.

Aimes ran back down the stairs with three rolls of toilet paper in her arms, stolen out of the bathroom.

"Now she really can't take a shit," she said.

We all chuckled. Ganging up on Max always left us feeling impressed with ourselves because she played along so well.

"Is she mad?" Cristal asked.

"I don't think she noticed, her eyes were closed and she was humming and rocking."

"That's how she gets the poop out," I said. "Can we get back to the show?"

I readied myself in the centre of the carpet and imagined my feet were roots firmly planted, as my speech and drama teacher had taught me.

"When I stand here – I'm Anne." I pointed to the carpet. "And when I stand here – I'm Gil." I stepped onto the hardwood. "Ready?"

The girls nodded, happy to be entertained.

"The scene starts with Anne, all alone, in the mist, when Gil finds her on the bridge."

I closed my eyes, took a belly breath and began.

"I don't want any of it to change, Gil," I said, opening my eyes to the scene. "I just wish I could hold on to these days forever, but I have a feeling things will never be the same again, will they Gil?"

I turned around to become Gil, looking at the Anne I'd just been.

"Well, I'm not going to change, Anne," I said, lowering my voice. "I can promise you that. I know you don't think I'm good enough for you now, but I will be."

I traded spots again, getting into the familiar scene.

"No, Gil, that's not it," I cried. "You are a great deal *too good* for me. You want someone who will adore you, someone –"

A noise interrupted us from upstairs.

"Em, where's the toilet paper?" Max yelled.

We exchanged glances.

"Em, can you bring me some shit tickets?" she yelled again. "I'm done."

"Yep, I'll be right up," I yelled and returned to acting. The scene was bubbling inside me now. "This is where Anne turns her gaze to the water," I said. "She's wearing a high-necked lace blouse and a pin. The black and white one from the olden days, with a face in it? Her hair is pinned loosely on the top of her head."

Reaching across the bridge for Gil's hand, I pleaded with him. "We'd end up like two old crows fighting."

I stopped to look out over the creek and felt the tears rise, aware that I was feeling *and* performing at the same time.

"That's it?" Bugsy said.

"She denies him her love?" Aimes said.

"Cold-hearted snake," Cristal said.

"I don't know why she says no," I said, returning to my seat. "He's such a good man. In the book I'm reading now, we find out that she *does* love him, but it's too late because he's going to die. I can't believe I haven't finished it."

We heard Max yelling from upstairs again. "I know you're down there!" A pause. "I've got a shitty ass!" In the silence we could hear her figuring it out. "You bitches stole it!" she screamed.

I lay down on the couch. She'd be fine. Max was used to our tricks. She played into them, acting more upset than necessary to get us all riled up.

"That was good," Cristal said.

"Yeah, Sym, you're a good actor," Aimes said, nodding.

"Where's camp?" Bugsy asked, scooping the last spoonful of Cristal's noodles.

"Across the Shuswap River, at the mouth of Mabel Lake," I said.

"What's an LIT anyway?" Cristal asked, unimpressed that I was leaving her alone for the summer.

"Leader in Training," I said. "Next year I'll get to be a real camp counsellor."

"Next year?" Cristal whined. "You go to camp every summer?"

Aimes and Bugsy snuck to the bottom of the stairs to listen in on Max's progress, then flew back into the living room, Max chasing them.

"Aimes, you're a psycho hose beast," she said, lunging for the toilet paper. She turned to me. "I wiped my bum on your hand towel, by the way."

This was the problem. Even in her anger, Max delighted us.

But the teasing left a residue that made me want to leave Armstrong for the summer even more. I needed a pressure drop. Mom only had one more radiation treatment before she'd travel to Vancouver for almost two months of chemotherapy. At camp I'd think about her less, too busy with the pleasure that came every summer, being in total immersion. The schedule was predictable and so were my duties, and within the week I'd not know or care what day it was, or how Mom was feeling, I'd be so rapt with camp friends.

Every year, Grum and I hauled our sleeping bags up the hill to my favourite moment, when the faded buildings came into view. Eight cabins, an arts and crafts hut, a dining hall and the nurse's cabin – unfinished, its joists and insulation still showing, encircled by a wide-open field. I always prayed for cabin number three: one of the newly built ones. It didn't have electricity or a toilet but it wouldn't have mice or be overrun with red ants.

The LITs arrived the night before the campers, to meet the camp counsellors, and I was pleasantly surprised to find myself teamed up with the girl who'd been my counsellor last summer too, Michelle, a seventeen-year-old who was pretty like a porcelain doll, shiny and rosy-cheeked with natural ringlets. That night, we lit candles and walked down a path through the trees to the chapel, a small clearing with a circle of half-cut logs to sit on. When everyone had gathered she drifted to the front of the open-air sanctuary and sang "The Rose" like an angel.

As we walked back in silence toward our cabin Michelle put her arm through mine and whispered how she and her boyfriend, Doug, were still together from last summer – which was beyond romantic to me. Later that night, as we snuggled into our sleeping bags on our respective bunks, she told me that they'd stayed in touch by writing letters and phoning each other every Sunday and she thought he might be the one. There was silence for a while and I wondered if she'd fallen asleep, and then she spoke, as if she'd just decided: this was the summer she'd give him oral. I looked at the names etched with penknives into the plywood bunk above me – "Brigit '79" and "J and S forever" – and felt a weight lift that I'd not known was there. I didn't have to think about finger-banging or dick-sucking for two whole months.

The next morning, I went looking for Grum. Mom had seen us off at the dock and headed straight back home to pack for Vancouver. But since camp hadn't started yet, it was decided that Grum would sleep in the nurse's shack for the night – next door to the camp director.

I peeked into the whitewashed room.

"You up?" I whispered.

A corner of the wool blanket still covered his legs but the rest was on the plywood floor. I don't know why I did it – maybe it was because his shirt was off and he looked so scrawny and alone – but I crawled up onto the spring-coiled mattress, disrupting but not fully waking him as I curled myself around his little body. His breathing was deep and I knew that the only reason I could get so close was because he didn't know I was there.

Grum kicked in his sleep and the blanket slid entirely off. He shivered and sat up.

"Mom?"

I could tell he was confused. If he'd felt kindness from me in his sleep, the oddity jarred him now that he was awake.

"Time for breakfast," I said. "Wanna come?"

As soon as we entered the large dining room I left him to fend for himself as the LITs were expected to sit with the counsellors to go over the first-day events. But it felt nice to know that at least once, even though he was technically unconscious, I'd felt the impulse to protect him.

After breakfast, the LITs and counsellors gathered on the plateau, waiting for the campers' arrival. The camp director navigated the river in a single-engine skiff three campers at a time. Once out of the boat, the kids climbed the hill while we cheered and high-fived them, just like the counsellors had done to me every summer past. One girl with stringy blond hair, maybe ten years old, was already deep into hiccups and sobs. I walked her to our cabin and sat with her on the front steps.

"I wan-n-n-nt to gooooo ho-ho-home," she cried into her hands.

I put my arms around her and squeezed her till the shuddering lessened, then pointed to the firepit.

"That's where we have a campfire every night and sing camp songs."

"I don't know any camp songs," she said, and she threw her face back into her knees.

"You'll learn them as we sing them," I said. "Sit with me at campfire tonight." I knew this was what she needed. A wing to huddle under.

At campfire, I did as promised and saved a seat for the little girl, who curled into me as I swayed. Michelle's boyfriend, Doug, led campfire with an unveiled exuberance. It was amusing to see an almost-grown man wiggle his hips and know the hand gestures to all the songs. He must have noticed that my bravado matched his because halfway through the night he brought me up to help lead. We made a good team, getting the kids to scream and stomp their feet, working them into a mania. Michelle sat at the edge of the circle, watching us through the firelight.

A few days later there was a meteor shower. I organized a sleep-out in the field with the entire camp so we could watch the stars rip through the sky. Michelle didn't want to spend the night outside because she was scared of bats, which was reasonable – they dive-bombed us mercilessly after dusk – so I told her to take the night off and I'd stay up with the kids. The little blond girl set her sleeping bag against mine. Her name was Autumn, and so far what I'd told her had come true. She'd blossomed quickly into a slightly demonic overconfidence and I'd even had to take away her dessert at dinner for being too aggressive with the boys in cabin eight.

Doug loped over to where our cabin had gathered to sleep, a blue tarp underneath us to protect us from the morning dew. Surveying the sprawling field of teddy bears and pillows, he was so much taller than me I could smell his deodorant.

"This is gonna be a long night," he said with a grin.

The field was swarming with kids. I could almost see electricity shooting off their bodies, these little live wires who jumped and screamed in the darkness. The shooting stars weren't set to start till two in the morning so we had time to kill.

"Do you wanna do this?" Doug touched my shoulder and shrugged at the fifty or so children running wild.

"Yeah, I do," I said.

As the other camp counsellors started to slink away into the shadows to have a smoke or dangle their feet off the dock, Doug dug into his backpack and pulled out a plastic bag filled with hard candies. He threw pieces into the air and the kids rushed us. We ran, hands diving into the bag, throwing the candy forward for the kids to chase up and around the archery field, down the unfinished logging road and behind the nurse's shack. Once all the candy had been found, we corralled them back onto the tarps where I began to tell a ghost story, "The Dead Puppy Under the Bed." When I spooked a kid with a bloodcurdling scream, Doug grabbed me around the waist and pulled me to the ground. His attention made me feel outrageously confident and I realized, as we twisted our hips in unison to a song, that even though we were surrounded by kids, the performance was for each other. I'd never been this before, someone's bull's-eye. I didn't want the meteor shower to come. But just as I thought it, the first flare shot through the night.

We all lay down, sleeping bags open. It was more than I'd expected, as if the sky had become liquid silver and was pouring down on us, so many meteors streaking through space that they blurred, making the sky above us look like a time-lapse. The show went on for hours. My eyes ached from being so wide open for so long. I turned my head to rest for a minute and caught Doug staring at me, like I might be more interesting than what was above. Every part of me softened, feeling his gaze. My last thought was *I should fan out my hair to look pretty*, but before I could I was asleep.

After that night, my attention redirected to keeping Doug's focus on me. At craft time I sat close by to laugh at his jokes. On the beach, I wasn't scared of duck itch like Michelle, so I enjoyed going out in the canoe, or I was good at pretending to. Michelle and I didn't talk about how much time I spent with Doug during the day, but every night as she'd sneak out to meet him, she'd whisper, "Don't wait up," and I'd lie on my bunk, *Anne of the Island* open on my chest, as I imagined him kissing her collarbones in the chapel.

The two-week camp finished in what felt like days. The last campfire was a dramatic affair, kids scrawling phone numbers on arms and pushing final friendship bracelets up wrists. Scanning faces, I couldn't find Grum in the firelight — overwhelmed, I assumed, by all the aggressive swaying that went along with sing-alongs. He was probably in his cabin with a buddy, playing board games, so I didn't go looking for him. It felt incongruous, to be so comfortable with the emotion around the fire, but have no time for it in my own family.

The next afternoon, as we walked the campers down to the dock to be ferried across to meet their parents, Autumn clung to me and bawled harder than the day she arrived. I understood her grief. Clingy and generally quite impolite, she wasn't always enjoyable to be around, but she'd been loved anyway and she felt that. As the boat broke from the dock, I promised her I'd be back next summer. I waved till she reached the middle of the river, then turned down the planks that covered the skunk cabbage and headed back up the hill.

Summer turned the green grass brown, the songs became earworms, the food got starchier and I welcomed two more camps up the hill while Grum travelled to Vancouver to keep Mom company at the Easter Seals House, provided for out-of-town patients. The neighbours were taking care of Fred and I rarely thought about the girls. Even though I woke up at dawn every morning and fell into bed exhausted by midnight, I didn't want the summer to end.

As the month progressed, I became more militant in my flirting with Doug and left nothing to his imagination. I pranced outside, the shiny silver polka dots on my bathing suit flashing. I undid my braids and let my sunbleached hair cascade down my back like a motherfucking beer commercial. I made sure to touch him when he spoke to me, a stroke of the arm or a small hip bump. When we played flag football I tackled him and took my time getting up. I made it plain. He had a decision to make.

The weekend before the last camp of the summer, Michelle came down with the stomach flu. Having a seat free in the car, Doug invited me to the camp-counsellors-only party at the director's house, across the river and a few miles down the road. I drank a wine cooler and then another one. We went outside onto the deck and sat on a sagging couch under the stars and I knew he couldn't say anything so I decided to. I pressed my leg into his and when he got up for a refill, I danced nearby so he could feel my heat. When he was thoroughly drunk I nuzzled myself into his armpit, and once he'd passed out, I found an empty couch downstairs and lay there, wide awake, pumping with blood.

As this final week flew by, Michelle cried alone in the cabin while I maintained constant visibility. If her heart was breaking, mine was jumping out of its pants. But on the last night of Teen Camp I had to watch Michelle and Doug slow dance to "Stairway to Heaven." And the next morning, after we rolled up our sleeping bags and carried them down to the dock to be ferried back to the mainland, Doug and Michelle stepped into the boat together. She'd won. They floated away, arms around each other, and I felt a flash of humiliation. I was fourteen years old. He was eighteen. What had I been thinking? Doug looked back halfway across the river, raised his hand and smiled. They were going to another camp-counsellors-only party that night and it would be alcohol-fuelled and full of romantic finality. All that work – all summer long – for nothing. It was a bottomless feeling, like I was falling through electricity and there would be no ground.

———————

The next morning, I walked into our bright, clean house after eight weeks away, surprised to find myself happy to be home. The house smelled like the windows had been open all summer and the sheers were pulled back to let the end-of-summer glow in. Mom came out to meet me, much skinnier than when she'd waved goodbye at the camp dock, but sturdy, here. The chemo had worked.

"He said the tumours are fried and my lymph nodes obliterated. I still can't feel the left side of my chest – but who gives a shit, right Punky?" She'd just arrived home too, and spoke in a hurry as she pulled me around the garden, checking in on the potatoes and onions, the staples she asked the neighbours to water while she was away.

"The worst thing about chemotherapy," Mom said as she bent down to see if any carrots had made it, "is having to stay in that damn city. Who would live in a place made of glass?" She stood up and squeezed me with her strong arm. I leaned into her, just for a minute, and felt our bellies touch.

Taking the stairs two at a time, I found everything in my room was as I'd left it, protected under a thin layer of dust. Unpacking what I discovered to be horribly sour-smelling shorts and T-shirts, I found *Anne of the Island*, swollen at the bottom of my suitcase, and placed it on my bedside table. I'd read just enough of it this summer to find out that Gil didn't die but it took his getting close to death for Anne to admit her love. As she pressed her newly published book into his weak hands – the pages filled with the stories of home he'd told her to write about – she was finally sated, that poor loud-mouthed orphan girl.

The phone rang and I ran downstairs, knowing it was Cristal. For the next two weeks we'd take to the tracks, overgrown and ripe from a long summer without us. We'd suck on slushes and share smokes and the girls would laugh at what a drama queen I'd been. Doug already felt gauzy, far away, and my cheeks warmed at the excess I'd shown him. But it was summer camp. Broken hearts were to be expected. I just hoped I hadn't been too obvious about the whole thing.

2012

CHRISTIE AND I SPEND THE NEXT TWO WEEKS as inseparable as all new lovers — but also different, because we are the kind of olden-days new lovers who just want to get on with spending the rest of our lives together. I don't want to leave him when it's time to travel back to Mom's but there's no wiggle room in keeping my end of the bargain with God. If I do everything I can for her, Mom will live to see her (now glimmer-of-a-chance) grandchildren and I'll have no regrets. So with promises of text messages and nightly phone calls I leave Christie tucked in my bed and start the monotonous journey back through the mountains alone.

My day consists of four smokes, one bag of chips and a pee break for Midge. As I turn the Jetta into the driveway, I see Mom sitting on her stool in the carport. Out of the car, I let Midge jump from her bag and give Mom the usual tap and squeeze, not letting her get too much of a grip.

"Have you eaten today?" she says, following me inside.

"Are you hungry?" I say, trying to decode what she's asking of me.

"Oh no," she says. "When I'm alone I just snack over the sink."

I shake my head to free the image.

"What's Christie doing this weekend?"

"He's working at the mid-century furniture shop," I say, looking in the fridge for inspiration. Something light.

The kitchen is messy. Moving to the sink, there's a few open tins of tuna, not like her to leave behind. Normally she washes a dish while she swallows the last spoonful.

"What's the smell?" I say, realizing that the scent is much stronger than a few cans.

"Did he want to come up with you this weekend?" she asks.

"I don't know," I say, opening the dishwasher, "we've just started dating. I'm trying not to get weird."

Before I can slam the dishwasher shut, the smell hits. I count the days since I left.

"The cleaner sucks, Mom."

"I fired her."

"What? Why?" She's a church friend who'd been doing us a favour.

"I asked her to make me a sandwich and she said it wasn't her job."

"It's not her job, Mom. She's a cleaner."

"Not a very good one." Mom smiles.

In truth, I'm enjoying this attitude she's trying on. It shows spunk. But firing a friend is a titch over the line. I make a mental note to tell Grum and I bring the salad stuff over to the kitchen table so she can sit down while I chop veggies. But the table is a mess too, not just the normal piles of unsent Christmas cards and newspaper clippings, but also binders stuffed full of articles on cancer prevention and notes she's taken at the doctor's office. I open one of the binders and when I flip the page, dozens of chits of paper fall out.

"My schedule," she says, lunging for the scrap paper. "I had it all organized."

On top of the binders are dozens of prescription bottles, most of them empty.

"Can I throw these out, just to make some room?"

"No," she says, picking up the scraps of paper on the floor. "I need them here so I remember to take the ones in my room."

"Well, that makes sense," I say, not meaning it.

I have to find her a new cleaner. The floors are sticky and what the fuck is taped to the sliding glass door?

"It's a piece of bread, in case Zip gets hungry," she says.

I start to chop the wrinkled strawberries I've found in the fridge. My mother is an inventor. She'd rigged up her own scaffolding and pulley system so she could paint our old house without any help. She's aging but she'll always be industrious.

"What's that you're putting in the salad?" she asks.

"Strawberries."

"How do you make the dressing?"

"It's pretty simple, just vinegar—"

"What kind of vinegar?" She says.

"Apple cider usually."

"Oh, I don't have that. How about red wine vinegar?"

"That wouldn't be good," I say.

"What's that?" she asks, pointing to the pot on the stove.

"It's quinoa." I take a shallow breath. "A grain."

Mom bumbles away and I wash and toss the lettuce and cut up the cucumbers while the quinoa cools. She returns with a pencil and another scrap of paper.

"Let me just get this down," she says. "I'll never remember all the ingredients."

"Mom, it's a salad. You put whatever's in the fridge—"

"But strawberries! Who'd have thought? I'll take it to my next church-ladies night. Tell me the ingredients one more time."

"Apple cider vinegar and some oil," I say.

"What kind of oil?" she asks.

I feel like a dog, my hackles rising.

"Any kind of oil."

"Not motor oil."

The skin on my arms tightens.

"No, Mom, not motor oil. Food grade oil."

Her hand is shaking on the page.

"Then, just something to sweeten it and a bit of Dijon," I say.

"What's Dijon?" she asks.

I stop chopping. She's trying to keep her pencil steady. This is a woman who's slaughtered a chicken with one swoop of an axe. She's canned freshly caught salmon over an open fire and skinned and processed an entire bear. She's raised two kids on her own, buried all our dogs and taken sledgehammers to walls.

"You know what Dijon is, Mom."

"I've never heard of it."

She's fucking with me. My armour begins to clink into place.

"Em," she says. "Don't be such a snob. I don't know every fancy ingredient there is."

"Are you kidding me?"

"You're not so special," she says.

I've taken an oath. No regrets.

"You didn't eat an avocado until you were in your twenties," she says. "So don't get all hoity-toity with me."

I will keep her alive if I love her well.

"I just assumed you knew what Dijon was," I say.

"You didn't always know what Dee-jon was," she says. "You came from the bush. Remember?"

My mother is like a glass ball — the strongest of all forms, but if smashed the shards make you bleed.

I whip around.

"It's DIJON fucking mustard, Mother. And EVERYONE knows what that is."

She grabs at my arm. I fling it off me like she's poisonous.

"FUCK. FUCK. FUCK YOU," I scream.

I have to get out of here but she's in my way. I push past her and her body crumples into the table. Grabbing my coat and shoes, I pick up Midge and race out of the house.

It's March and the first of the pussy willows have just busted free. I pass by Nailz and Cutz and the church where we used to hide our beer. At the telephone pole, the flowers around Taylor's shrine are mush from a winter of snow. The letters are smudged and unreadable. The teddy bears, water-logged, slump over themselves, heads downcast, like they're inspecting the road. There's one fresh vase of flowers on the sidewalk, placed away from the decay. It's a bouquet of pink roses. Her mother, I assume, making sure there's always something pretty here.

Looking down the rails, the tracks are empty like no one has ever thought to use them before. I don't want to feel good right now so I don't step onto them. All my mother wanted was to know how to make a salad dressing. What is wrong with me? I screamed at her. Who would scream at their sick mother? No one. I call Christie.

"I swore at her," I whisper into the phone.

He doesn't say anything.

"I shoved her. Out of my way."

There's an intake of air.

"Am I sick? Am I mentally ill? You'd tell me?"

"You might be?" he says.

"A normal person loves their dying mother. She doesn't hurt her."

"It's a fucked-up situation, so you're acting fucked up," he says.

"It's so bad," I say.

"It really is," he agrees.

He stays on the phone as I rush back up the hill. If I walk fast enough, she won't have gone to bed yet. I'll apologize. We can watch a show together.

Hanging up before the carport, I enter through the side door with Midge in her bag. The kitchen is dark. The salad has been put away in Tupperware and the wool blankets are already tacked to the windows. Mom's door is closed. I feel a lump in my throat the size of a walnut.

I tiptoe into the kitchen and search through her prescriptions. The Ativan is easy to find. I take two and pocket the bottle for later. I'm not going to count them. I'll use as many as I need. The doctor at the walk-in clinic in Vernon will give me more if I beg him. I'll go tomorrow. I'll freak out like I'm fucking nuts if I have to. Because right now these little oblong peacemakers are the only thing that can keep me tethered to earth.

Heading downstairs, I crawl into the double bed we set up for Grum at Christmastime and put Midge beside me. I used to try so hard when Dad visited us. I entertained and asked good questions and stayed energized, hoping to keep his anger quiet. She taught me this skill, to be the polestar, and twenty-five years later, the very same tactics are being used on me. All the hovering and constant check-ins are her attempts to placate, to diffuse, as I did with him. When did his rage become mine? Heads on the same pillow, I stroke the spot between Midge's eyes until we both fall asleep.

I awake to a sound. I can't tell what it is but I know it means someone is outside. It's the middle of the night, or early morning, still pitch black out, so I only see the reflection of the window glaring back at me. The doorknob turns. Someone's trying to open the basement door. I sit up, which wakes Midge, and she runs to the edge of the bed and starts to whimper. Scanning for something I can use for protection, I crawl to the corner of the bed.

"Hello," I say. "I hear you."

Nothing.

"I have a dog," I say.

Someone raps on the window.

It's probably only neighbourhood kids trying to scare us again. I shouldn't scream. That'll wake Mom up and she'll come running and fall down the stairs.

The blow of a body crashes against the door. I open my mouth but there's no sound. Midge jumps into my lap and starts barking for me.

Someone large ducks into the room. Still in shadow, the form is tall and wide.

"It's me. It's only me," he says. "I wanted to surprise you."

A light is turned on and I can see him now. Christie. There's a blanket wrapped around him. He has a large backpack on and a raincoat underneath the blanket, making him look larger than he actually is.

"Well, you succeeded," I say.

Midge jumps off my lap and runs to the end of the bed, her tail wagging in recognition. He looks tired. He drops the load onto the floor and crawls into bed, his coat still on.

"I thought I should come and help you out before you caused irreparable mother-daughter damage," he says.

He tells me how he walked up the hill from the bus station and had taken the blanket out to wrap around himself as it was pouring rain out. He'd jumped on the bus immediately after I'd called him, hoping to make it to Armstrong before daylight.

"I'm here to help," he says.

As he rocks me, a salty balm drips out of my eyes.

"So that's how you greet a murderer?" he asks. "*Hello? Hellllloooo?*"

"I'm polite," I say. "I didn't want to offend."

That night, I fall into a deep, warm blackness that seeps through my nerves and bloodstream until my body is saturated in its loam. When I wake up, Christie is beside me. Mom will be so happy to see him. I get another day.

1992

IN THE LAST TWO WEEKS OF SUMMER, I couldn't get ahold of any of the girls to walk the tracks. Cristal had been working sixteen hours a day at the strawberry farm, moved indoors from picking the fields to packaging and transport. It was the weekend before grade nine started when I finally reached her to make plans to go to the Armstrong Fair. Mom had bought us early bird tickets and a ride pass, and when the phone rang I ran for it, knowing it was her.

"Yoodle, doodle, hoodle," I said.

"Hey. It's me," a man's voice said.

My stomach wave-pooled.

"Um, hi?"

"It's Doug," he said.

His voice sounded different. I'd only ever heard him outside, around screaming kids and splashing water. He told me he dumped Michelle at the camp party and couldn't stop thinking about me. As I listened, I tried to discern why I was disappointed to hear his voice, and what was rising instead was dread. He asked if he could come over – tonight.

"Uh, yeah, sure," I said, "I'd love to see you."

"I've been wanting to do this all summer," he said.

"Me too," I lied.

I hung up, ran my fingers through my hair and tugged at my scalp, like I'd watched Max do, trying to release the tension. I gagged a bit then shivered. He lived – forty minutes away? The house was a mess. He'd think we're poor. Oh, Cristal. I'd have to cancel on her last minute. She'd understand. I ran upstairs to scrub up.

Our first kiss was in my bedroom. I'd just given him a shoulder massage. He stood up and put a piece of gum in his mouth. Our height difference was so pronounced that he had to lean down while I reached up, my toes grabbing the carpet for balance. His lips touched mine and slowly he slid his tongue inside. It wasn't snaky, which was nice, but I couldn't find the gum. I made a few noises to make him feel good, but it was more the action of ticking another box off the list that turned me on.

He asked if we could be boyfriend and girlfriend right after, which was how it's supposed to be done. His face was thin, so thin that when he leaned in for a second kiss, I worried the bridge of his nose might poke me in the eye. He admitted that even though he was attracted to me, he was concerned with our age difference. His friends might make fun of him.

"We live in different towns," I said, sitting on his lap. "No one will have to know."

I have to call Cristal. I have a boyfriend. I have to call Cristal, was the refrain coursing through my head.

"I don't want to go home yet," Doug said and slid onto the bedroom floor.

I checked the clock radio. This meant I wouldn't be able to call her till tomorrow.

"So we'll just hang out at your place all the time?" he asked.

"We won't go out in public," I said.

On Monday morning Cristal screeched into my driveway wearing her crisp button-flies, a snap-up plaid top and her annual white sneakers. She grinned when she ran through the breezeway and I twirled a full circle in the new chapeau my dad bought me on a quick weekend visit, a green crushed velvet, with three peacock plumes pinned to its floppy brim. I threw my arms around her and as she buried her face in my hair I could feel her smile against my neck.

"I missed you at the fair, Em," she said. "We all did."

I'd told the girls briefly about Doug, but I wanted the details to be shared in person.

"How many rides did you do?"

"All of them."

"Anyone puke?"

"Max lost her cookies on the Zipper."

"How late did you stay out?

"Till closing."

"How many horse blankets did you eat?"

"Three."

I'd just missed the best weekend of the year.

We headed up the hill and I told her about camp and Doug and our first kiss. My mouth couldn't move as fast as I needed to get the words out and she laughed through the retelling, which alerted me to the possibility that embarrassing experiences translated into funny stories. But a new pool of worry started to slosh around. I wasn't as excited about Doug as I was telling Cristal about him. The one thing I liked was saying his name. Doug. I was Doug's Girlfriend now. Cristal listened as we made our way through the concourse into the student centre, the feathers in my hat tickling the few kids who came too close. When they saw us, Bugsy jumped up onto the benches and she and Aimes started to whoop like they were in the audience at *The Arsenio Hall Show*.

"Shit balls, Sym," Aimes ran at me. "You have a *boyfriend*?"

When she grinned, I saw teeth.

"Your braces are gone!"

"Finally," she said. "I French-kissed Timmy so much this summer, my tongue has calluses."

Bugsy scowled. Aimes wasn't her shadow anymore.

"What the goddamned hell Sym!" Bugsy said. "Who is it!?" Her arms were muscled from a summer of water-skiing at Shit Lake.

"I met him at camp. He doesn't want anyone to know yet."

It was weird to have imagined this scene, and now that it was here, to wish it wasn't.

The girls snuggled in closer on the benches and I smelled the heady mix of Dewberry, peach and the new oil I was wearing, which reminded me of spicy dirt.

I leaned in toward Max, who smelled only of Ivory soap.

"How was opera camp?" I asked. "Fun?"

Max's eyelids were puffy and her skin looked thin, like she hadn't spent enough time outside.

"Being away was good," she said.

"What did you learn?" I asked.

"That you can't smell vodka in orange juice."

Bugsy stood up. She'd gotten a manicure, long and mauve.

"You stopped chewing your nails," I said.

"*You* got the first boyfriend." She paced back and forth along the benches. "Oh my god. What do we do? Do we skip and go to Tuckers for fries to celebrate? This is the biggest news since Woody Allen started dating his daughter!"

I sat down, disappointed by my own lack of passion. I wanted to be back where I was, trying to get somewhere, not there yet. But to find an official boyfriend – who was eighteen and lived in a different town – within a week of grade nine starting was as miraculous as a fly finding human shit in the middle of a lake. And as word spread through the school that Emmy Symington had a boyfriend, my life became instantly easier. I was let off the hook, from fake flirtations and the allowances of side-boob grabbing, and the relief I felt from not being tracked anymore was worth the phone call I had to make every day after school, Cristal waiting patiently beside me, while I asked Doug how his day was. Soon, this freedom spread across more aspects of my life, daring me to power clash, pattern mix and add suspenders and platform shoes into my weekly rotation.

After only a month of having a boyfriend – who I only had to see on Friday and Saturday nights if his parents lent him the car – I started putting my free time to good use and signed up to be the president of our school's Amnesty International chapter. Standing outside the double doors during lunch, demanding coins, I paired flamboyance with an aggressive fundraising campaign.

"A baby dies every time you don't donate," I said to Ollie and Windex as they walked by, no attempt to swat my butt this time.

For all they knew Doug was a bodybuilder who might shank them, but more likely these boys had an unspoken code regarding their possessions. I belonged to someone now, and being claimed meant they had to tolerate some pushback.

In the kitchen after school, Mom was on her hands and knees pulling Tupperware containers out of the bottom cupboards.

"I promise, I'll never get sick again," she said into the depths. "But it's going to take work."

Cristal, Grum and I froze in the doorway.

"Anything plastic goes in the garbage," Mom said from inside the cupboard. "And if you burn toast at breakfast, don't eat it. It's a carcinogen." She chucked a plastic lid across the room. "Do you know what *carcinogen* means?" she asked, crawling back into the depths. "It will give you cancer," she said. "Burnt food gives you cancer."

"So we all must have cancer?" Grum said.

She threw a plastic tub at his head. Grum had just turned twelve and was getting funny as hell.

"With my all clear, I'm not going to be around so much anymore." Mom kept talking as if she'd been planning to give us this speech, but found it easier to make on her knees, buried inside a cave.

"You're not around now," Grum said.

"I've got to focus on my health, not just you kids," she said. "Grum, you'll have to start getting yourself to hockey."

"You're gonna make me drag my hockey bag to away games?"

There was a pause.

"I'm allergic to stress," she said. "*Stress* gives you cancer."

Cristal looked to me, her eyebrows raised. Mom was acting like a jacked-up Energizer Bunny.

"I've joined a qi gong group," Mom said, throwing a box of expired Jell-O behind her. "It's important to activate my fire."

Her chest was still burned to shit from the radiation. She'd lost thirty pounds. Why was she making herself so busy with healing?

"And I've started a meditation group for cancer patients on Saturdays."

She pushed herself to her knees and pounded a fist into her hand.

"I've been given another chance. Are you with me?"

The three of us looked at each other and shrugged.

"Great, then carry all this Tupperware outside and we'll burn it in the fire barrel next spring."

We laughed and started to gather the plastic containers. As long as she had a plan, we'd follow our little queen.

———————————

Even with the perks, within two months of dating, I started to dodge Doug's calls. He wasn't as much fun in real life as he'd been at camp. He didn't sing loudly or make up games and he wasn't as nice to Grum as he'd been around the campfire. Cristal still came over every Friday night and sometimes even waited around for him to leave. I wished she could be in my room with us, listening to the Top 40 or anything else, but instead she sat on the couch and watched movies with Mom and Grum. One night it was *Planes, Trains and Automobiles* and I could hear them laughing madly downstairs.

Upstairs was monotonous with all the grinding Doug liked to do. His favourite thing was to place his penis between my breasts and rub himself vigorously up and down, giving his "hot dog" a "bun," as we called it. I squished my breasts together while he rocked inside my boob-tube, his belt buckle hitting my chin. He'd ejaculate and I'd wipe it off with my quilt and then give him his massage. Mom liked Doug, but when we came downstairs that night, T-shirts tucked back in, she sat us down at the dinner table, looked Doug in the eye and told him that whatever we were doing up there was called statutory rape and she could send him to jail. But because he was a camp counsellor, she trusted him. Then she pulled out the ice cream and got Doug to scoop out five bowls.

———————————

Doug's house was large and white with two pillars standing on either side of the front archway, a smaller version of the facade from *The Fresh Prince of Bel-Air*. The next Saturday, Mom dropped me off on her way to her qi gong class. Doug's mom was busy making something sweet and his dad sat at the table, waiting for his dessert, watery-eyed and silent. After ten minutes of small talk, Doug grabbed my hand and pulled me down a set of carpeted stairs to the basement. He put *Ghostbusters* into the VCR and turned the volume up so his parents would think we were watching it again and I followed him up the ladder into the crawlspace where the sleeping bags were stored. I knew the drill and shimmied to the back of the narrow storage area and lay down. The space was less than three feet high so he wriggled in beside me and placed one elbow above my head for balance so he could tuck his other hand inside my tights, pull aside my underwear and stick two fingers between my folds, poking for the opening. He'd tried to find the hole on his own before and I didn't want to embarrass him so I lifted my hips, directing him to my vagina. The next part hurt. He made a closed peace sign and crammed both fingers into me, his nails catching my vaginal opening. *Why didn't he just start with one finger?* I wondered.

After a few minutes, some wetness came out, which helped him dive in fully, a relief compared to the dry burn. I made a few moan-and-groan sounds, hoping he'd think the job was done and we could trade positions, but instead, he transitioned to the next move. Inserting the peace sign again, his knuckles stayed closed, and he began to smash his fist against my pelvic bone. The moans became real. *How could he think this would feel good?* The pounding pain travelled to my ears. But he misunderstood and thought the groaning meant I wanted more, 'cause that's what I'd taught him, so he continued to punch me in the crotch, shoving me up and off the sleeping bag, till my head banged against the back wall. After many minutes of the dull *thud, thud, thud*, his forearm got tired so he pulled his hand out of my underpants — and there was blood on his palm.

"Oh sick," he said, and tried to sit up, but couldn't because we were in a crawlspace.

"Oh no!" I said.

"Do you have your period?" he asked.

"No," I said, remembering Twyla. Why couldn't my skin be thicker?

He wiped his fingers on the sleeping bag underneath us, the blood taking him out of the mood. "Let's go upstairs and see what Mom's made for dessert," and he inched backwards out of the crawlspace to turn off the VCR.

I pulled up my tights, crawled down the ladder into the rec room and looked up the flight of stairs. It was as if a puffer fish had exploded inside my vagina. I was swollen and full of spikes. I lifted myself onto the first step.

Pushing into the banister took the weight off a bit, but the grade of the stair-well seemed impossible to climb.

"That was a good one," he said, behind me. "I made you wet."

"Yeah," I said, taking another step.

He laughed and patted my bum to keep me moving.

Making it to the top, I headed into the kitchen and leaned against the counter, my hand discreetly between my legs, hoping the heat from my palm would calm the sting while I waited for the honk of Mom's car.

"Someone's flashing their lights," Doug's father yelled from the TV room.

"Thanks," I yelled back and bent down slowly to put on my shoes. Opening the front door, a gust of cold poured in.

"Shut the door," his dad yelled behind me.

The road was slushy and we had a thirty-minute drive back to Armstrong. I wondered if I should ask Mom to drive me to the hospital but decided that was too dramatic.

"I'm going to marry a boring guy," I said as she merged onto the light-streaked highway. "Was Dad boring?"

"Definitely not. I'm the boring one," she said.

I wanted to tell her that she wasn't boring. That she was creative and cool. But it wouldn't have been true. She didn't have time for those things.

"Boring guys don't leave," I said.

"How'd you get so mature for your age?" she said, her white knuckles briefly outlined by the strobe of a passing car.

As I stared into the oncoming headlights I put my hands between my legs again, and cupped my vulva like a prayer.

In early November we got our first big snowfall and Doug became busy with downhill skiing on the weekends – something I couldn't afford to do.

"How can I pay for it?" Mom yelled. "Where's the money?"

"You spent it all on reishi powder," I yelled back, and stomped upstairs.

Aimes and Bugsy were treating Jimmy and Timmy like full-time jobs, going to pit parties and dry humping on frosty gravel banks every weekend.

Even though I didn't have to accompany them – Doug only ever wanted to grind at home – I could see they were chasing the same hunger I was: to be able to let their guard down. Getting a break from surveillance and performance, when I imagined it, was an underwater calm. My body letting buoyancy hold me up, a constant rocking, tiny crackles from the coral below.

I saved all my Christmas money so I could buy a one-day pass and rent skis and poles and join Doug on the hill. His parents picked me up and as we drove the switchbacks up the mountain the snow-laden trees disappeared under cloud cover, and I prayed the car would skid out or crash before we reached the top. Barely making it off the ski lift, I snow-plowed behind his family, hating every single moment of that godforsaken hellish sport. Finally, at dusk, we trudged back to the car and I collapsed into the back seat. Doug grabbed my hand as his dad drove us down the mountain and I watched him as he looked out the window. He was going to university next summer. He wanted to have sex soon. He'd waited six months and it was a reasonable request. I'd be the first, again. But I'd break the pact – a year early.

"I'm not sure if I'm ready," I whispered behind my mitten.

"I don't want to pressure you," he said.

"I just don't want to regret it," I said.

"Me neither," he said.

I was tempted to say yes right then, cozied up in the back seat, heater on, but I had to discuss the plan with the girls first to make sure the euphoria I felt wasn't just the relief of driving away from that cunt-sniffing, waste-of-money mountain. Leaning into the switchbacks, I decided sooner was preferable to later because once it was done, he'd be locked in and I'd never have to go skiing again.

Spring came early and the ski hill closed down by March so Doug spent his weekends at my house again. We didn't listen to music or go for walks or see my friends, just straight up to my bedroom where I'd lie down and he'd lie on top of me and push his penis through the fabric of his Donald Duck boxers into my vaginal opening. It was easier to take than his knuckles, but I could feel his dick getting antsy.

"We've been together for almost a year," he said after he came on my tummy. "Camp is soon and then I move away."

"We just had our six-month anniversary, Doug," I said, counting on my fingers quickly.

"Seven months," he said and rolled back on top of me.

"I know," I said. "I'm a cock tease."

After Doug went home, Mom announced over dinner that she was taking us to Disneyland for spring break. We'd never been on a family trip before and this was the first I'd heard of the plan.

"You only get to live once," she said, spearing an underdone potato.

The plane tickets had been bought. She'd been saving up for the surprise.

"I can't go," I said, trying to take a full breath. "He could meet someone else. Or forget about me."

"Hon," she said, "he should be able to wait a week."

"But he's leaving for university in September," I said.

She rolled her eyes. She didn't understand. A wolf was ripping at my throat. If I didn't have him, I'd be alone, or I'd have to find someone else, someone less good. Doug was my protection from worse. Which meant the choice had just been made for me. I had to have sex with Doug before we left for The Happiest Place on Earth.

2012

THE SLEET HAS STOPPED its sideways slant. Down the street, the first rays of sun are spreading through the cloud cover, confirming I can leave the house. I grab my raincoat just in case it starts again and get Midge suited up for our afternoon walk. After Christie's surprise weekend visit, he drove back to the city in my Jetta, which means I'm marooned in Armstrong. In some ways being stuck here is easier than the constant question of whether or not to move home, which is relentless when I'm in Vancouver. Slipping on my rubber boots, I leave the house and Mom inside it.

Mrs. Warner is shovelling the last bits of spring detritus off her walkway, but instead of meeting me on the sidewalk to chat at length about the nasty cold spell we've just had that killed off her magnolia blooms, or how her cat Delilah has brought in her first bird, and when *her own* daughter is expected to visit, she stays engrossed in her task. Mr. Warner shuffles down the walk toward their garage, first checking the gap between the building and the fenceline in case someone's hiding back there. I'm not surprised by their caution – this is who we are now. I too peek behind my mother's garden shed before my secret joint each night, and our doors are still kept locked, even when we're home.

Now that spring has arrived, the changes around town are clear. People stopped having their Friday night dinners out – so Tuckers Restaurant didn't make it through the winter and has a For Sale sign in its front window. Happy Nickel Coffee Shop had to shut its doors due to a lack of regulars too. From its darkened windows it looks like the junk shop has been foreclosed on and I'd heard from the owner of Frugal Frocks that the used bookstore folded. People drive everywhere, even if the destination is two blocks away. Most kids still aren't allowed to walk to school by themselves, and if they do walk somewhere alone, some parents have instructed them to carry a jackknife, just to be safe.

Midge and I pass by the house where my old band teacher, Mr. Dougie, lives, and I speed up, not wanting another awkward conversation. I'd heard from Mom's friend Ruth at church that Taylor was his favourite student and he'd not returned to teaching yet. When I went to Pleasant Valley High School, Mr. Dougie was the mop-haired new music teacher from the big city. He'd moved with his young family into the biggest, most beautiful heritage house in town. I babysat his kids once and spent their nap time creeping through airy rooms filled with long tables, a piano and piles of sheet music splayed across hardwood floors. Now, he was nearing retirement and had a teenage girl of his own.

A week ago, I'd bumped into him at the gas station. Thinking that he might be a good interview for the not-yet-started CBC documentary about the tracks, I asked how his daughter was doing.

"She won't leave the house," he said. "None of her friends go outside anymore."

Even their screened-in porch, similar to the one at our old house – where mom used to hide out – was too exposed for his kids to congregate in. If the killer was brazen enough to attack Taylor on a popular thoroughfare on the busiest night of the year, the kids assumed he'd be just as likely to cut through mesh on an early spring day. Mr. Dougie was so brief with his answer, I knew better than to pull out the recorder. I wasn't cutthroat enough to risk it, and now, darting past his house, I feel embarrassed that I'd thought about it at all.

Mom doesn't seem to mind these changes to Armstrong, or it's possible she's not noticing them. Earlier this month she stopped bothering with her baggy clothes and now prefers to stay in her nightgown and slippers all day, going outside only in the morning to lie down and feel the day warm on her face. She doesn't get to enjoy a porch anymore, either, but for a different reason than the girls. Her new place wasn't built to be special, it's just a box. She's set the old wicker couch on the cement pad under her deck. Last weekend, Grum drove down from Red Deer and he and Christie built her a privacy wall out of cedar strips that crisscross into a lattice pattern. They set the wall in front of the couch, so that when she naps, the rays of sun come through the lattice but she's protected from view by all the tiny wooden Xs.

Midge looks up at me and starts to howl, her mouth making a little O shape, and I realize that all the gravel and salt on the road might be hurting her feet. I scoop her up. The sky is clearing quickly, which means Mom will want to have lunch outside. I head back up the hill, jumping over the small streams of melt coursing down Okanagan Street. Through the carport I hear the TV reporting the afternoon news. Undetected, I creep downstairs, open the back door, lie down behind the privacy screen and close my eyes. Christie's working at the mid-century furniture store during the week, and he spends his weekends picking through Value Village and alleys to find treasures to resell. It's been almost three months since the beach party but I'm not experiencing the catastrophic cycling I'm prone to: *He'll meet someone better. He'll steal my rent money.* Face tilted toward the sun I feel only calm, and because of this new settling in my belly, Mom's been easier to be around.

But the feeling doesn't seem to be mutual. Grum and I disturb her routine. Our presence sidetracks her healing. Because of the newest trial chemo she's on, her fingernails have started to split. Large, painful strips that catch on cloth and bleed. At night, she sits in her La-Z-Boy, slathering herself with thick cream and wrapping each finger in many Band-Aids, giving her hands the look of paws. She's in constant motion, shuffling more than walking, on the hunt for her address book or pills, and she forgets what she was looking for, so she shuffles back, cursing herself for her own stupidity. The woman can't sit still. Even when dying, she needs something to keep herself busy.

Upstairs, the La-Z-Boy knocks back from being reclined and I roll off the wicker couch to let her know I'm home. After a quick lunch of bread ends and tuna salad, we head out to a doctor's appointment. Mom giggles into her bandaged hand as she looks out the passenger window.

"What a cute little town," she says. "I used to live in one just like it."

It's a strange comment, but true, as she's lived in many small towns throughout her life. But when we get to her appointment I question her family doctor, a statuesque woman, about Mom's memory loss and what seems to be a growing confusion regarding her surroundings. Both the doctor and my mom agree that the trial chemo she's on gives her terrible brain fog. The doctor checks her charts and confirms that none of Mom's most recent tests show any growth or spread of tumours. She may have a few vocabulary blips and she has good reason to be frustrated with her chemo brain, but she's medically stable. Relieved to hear it, I bring Mom home and sit her at the table, and while I make us some tea, Mom strokes the kitchen walls fondly.

"I painted my kitchen in this exact colour," she says.

She had. Salmon and mint green were her go-to colour palette, and the old kitchen on Pleasant Valley Road was sponge painted in almost the same shade as this one. This childlike wonder, the way she seems to be seeing everything for the first time, makes me feel protective of her in a way I've not felt before.

"You've painted a lot of houses," I say.

"Oh, really?" she says.

"I think you helped build a few houses too."

She dips her head and smiles.

"It's strange, don't you think?" she says. "Now that it's your job to remember."

1993

I PHONED DOUG TO TELL HIM I WAS READY. He squealed into the phone like a dolphin. I felt only calm as we whispered out the plan. He'd get his brother to buy him spermicidal cream and condoms at the pharmacy and I'd skip class to go to the walk-in clinic to be fitted for a diaphragm and get the birth control pill prescribed.

The next morning, Cristal clomped along the tracks with me, chain-smoking. The bushes were teeming with green. The Nootka roses were already in bloom and I could smell something I hadn't noticed before: a liquorice scent. We'd decided I couldn't go to my family doctor for fear of him telling Mom what we were up to, so the walk-in clinic was the best option.

"How'd the fitting go?" Cristal asked as I re-entered the waiting room.

"Professionals are much gentler," I said and shoved the plastic box that reminded me of Aimes's retainer case into the bottom of my backpack.

The next morning, I whispered the plan to the girls in Mr. Wyatt's English class, while he tried to teach the *Beowulf* epic. Hopped up from being together for the first time in weeks, we crowded our desks close.

"You get to be first at everything," Aimes said.

I respected her frustration; the poor girl didn't even have her period yet.

Bugsy put her arm around me. "You'd better double up, buttercup," she said, and we all spit out a laugh at the phrase we'd heard the Brew Crew use when they'd sat above us in the stands at a lacrosse match.

"I wish that while you were doing it you could write everything down so later we'd get to read it like we'd been there with you," Max said.

Cristal looked up to make sure Mr. Wyatt hadn't noticed us. If she got one more note sent home, she wasn't allowed to work at the strawberry farm this summer. But the class was unruly as usual and Mr. Wyatt's focus had shifted to a pencil flying over his head.

"You'd better call us," Bugsy said as she leaned back in her chair and kicked her new ankle boots onto the desk. They had small crisscrossing holes punched out of the leather, like mine, except they were white, and better.

"That's what's crazy," I said. "I'm going to Disneyland this weekend. I might have to call you from the road."

"Why hasn't anyone mentioned that she's breaking the pact?" Cristal said. She pushed her chair back, making it squeak on the linoleum.

"Girls," Mr. Wyatt said. "Give me a break."

"Sorry, Mr. Wyatt," we chimed.

"No more chances."

We curled back into our circle again. I'd hoped no one would mention the pact but I'd thought through my reasoning just in case.

"Well," I said. "When grade nine ends in three months I'll *technically* be in grade ten, so I'm *kinda* breaking the pact – but you could also say I'm *testing* the pact, for when it's your turn."

"Why do you have to be so rigid, Cristal?" Aimes said. "Em just wants some vitamin D."

"Yeah," Bugsy said. "Emmy needs a big dose of Vitamin Dick, baby. Don't be harshing her mellow."

Cristal didn't smile.

Max looked out the window at the kids trying to jog around the field, dodging mud.

"I think we made that promise a long time ago and things have changed since then," she said. "Doug's a nice guy. It's your job as his girlfriend." The PE teacher's distant whistle brought her back into the room. "We didn't know that in grade eight – so I say jump his bones."

I appreciated Max being realistic about the whole thing.

Cristal shook her head, outvoted. I was glad she took our vow seriously but Max was right – I wasn't being slutty if it was my job.

"I *wish* I could have sex, but I'm holding out till I get my promise ring," Bugsy said.

The bell rang and we rushed for the door.

"Wanna get ready at my place?" Max asked, leaning against her locker.

I glanced around but Cristal had already left for volleyball practice. I'd never hung out with any of the girls without Cristal, but Max asked me casually, as if she'd forgotten the rule, and I answered ecstatically, happy to break it.

Packing up, Bugsy and Aimes sniffed around me like little possums as they pulled out the diaphragm and birth-control pills and my Obsession for Men cologne.

"Do you have an extra pair of underwear?" Aimes asked.

I nodded.

"Do you have wipes?"

I pulled them out.

"Vanilla scented, nice." Bugsy said.

"You'll call us after?" Max said.

"Pinky promise," I said, feeling faint.

They were trying to keep the mood light. They understood. I didn't want to do this. I wanted to lie on a loveseat and have him stroke my hair while I read poetry aloud, but it was too late to back out.

After hugs and pinches, Max and I climbed the school bus steps and huddled together in the middle seats, ignoring Seb and the other seniors at the back. At the last stop, we scrambled up the hill to her house, which overlooked the valley. It was mostly windows, not ostentatious, just well-built and serene. I flopped down on her double bed, firmer than mine, with a duvet rather than an old quilt. Max opened her curtains to reveal a small field of early spring wildflowers, already a few fat bees buzzing around. Amidst the wildflowers were six crosses pounded into the dirt in two neat rows.

"Whoa, pet cemetery?"

"It's my graveyard of the dead," Max said. She lay down beside me. "Trent's in there, for being a dick."

It was the first time I'd heard her say his name in ages and when I turned I saw a hard satisfaction in her eyes. She wasn't a bowl of freshly picked strawberries anymore.

"Do you ever wonder what I'll become?" Max asked, lying beside me. "And I don't mean a singer."

I rolled over to face her.

"I think you'll go to a big university," I said. "And after, you'll travel a lot."

"What else?"

I started to imagine Max as older, her hair still long, but everything else changed.

"I don't think you'll ever get married," I said. "Or have kids. You'll be too successful for that."

She smiled, like I'd given her the right answer.

"Do you wanna know your future too?" she said.

There was one thing that I wanted above all else — more than having children or a career.

"Will I fall in love?" I asked. "A good, long kind of love?"

She sat up and crossed her legs.

"You wouldn't want it so bad if it wasn't going to happen." I liked that theory. "But probably not until you're older," she said.

"How old?"

"I don't know, in your thirties?"

"That's too old."

She laughed.

"First, you'll be an actor in the city. After that gets boring, you'll get married, have two kids — and move back to Armstrong."

"I won't move back here," I said. "But I'll fall in love? You promise?"

This was the only thing that I longed to be sure of.

"Yes," she said, "I promise. You'll be chubby and happy."

"And we'll still be friends."

"Of course. When I'm not touring the world, I'll come and stay with you and your loser kids."

After a fancy dinner of stuffed green peppers it was time to get ready. I'd decided on a sailor dress, red knee-high stockings and silver platform shoes. I pulled down my underwear and sprayed cologne onto my pubic hair. Doug hadn't ever mentioned anything about my stinky crotch, which might have been politeness on his end but was more likely due to my dedicated sanitation regime.

I was to meet him at the bus stop at the bottom of the hill, so when my hair was brushed and braided, I pulled on my coat and Max walked me to the front door.

"You look like a little gummy bear," she said to me.

I didn't want to walk down the hill by myself and wait by a bus stop. I didn't want to do this thing that I could only do once for the first time. But I wanted to be done with it, too.

"Aw, Em, don't cry," she said.

"It's just the cold," I said.

Doug picked me up in his parents' car. It had electric windows and "If I Had $1,000,000" was playing. We drove into town in silence and he dropped me off as planned in the back alley where he was house-sitting for the weekend. I waited, trying to look like I belonged behind a stranger's fence, beside cans of trash. Doug unlocked the basement window from the inside and opened it as far as he could. I lay on my stomach and shimmied in backwards, my dress rising to show my underpants, and landed on a single bed in what looked to be a guest room with wall-to-wall orange carpeting, a small brown couch and a painting of a ship in the corner. We didn't turn on any lights. Slipping off my silver shoes I ran my feet through the shag. He brought a towel from the bathroom and unrolled it onto the floor.

"Let's do it down here so the blood won't mess up the sheets," he said.

I thought he might put on some music. Maybe we'd do some slow dancing? But he was anxious too.

I sat on the towel and Doug squatted beside me, a small plastic bag in his hands. I tried to keep eye contact as I lay back, my knee socks and dress still on. He reached inside my underpants and stuck a finger inside me, to make sure my diaphragm was in the right spot. I knocked my knees together while he broke the spermicidal foam from its packaging. He hadn't read the instructions yet so it took him a while to understand the steps and I crossed one knee over the other, hoping to telegraph relaxed.

"Okay, I'm ready," he said, the syringe loaded with spermicide.

I wiggled out of my underpants and lifted my hips. He poked the cartridge around my vulva until he found the hole.

"Ready?" he asked.

I nodded.

A cool liquid shot into me. He pulled the cylinder out and dropped it back into the plastic bag and stepped out of his Cheerios boxers.

"Shove over a bit," he said.

He began trying to roll a condom onto his penis. I didn't know if I should try to help him or look away, so I stroked his arm.

He lay on top of me and I felt his penis harden between my thighs. I lifted my hips, hoping he'd find the proper opening farther up, but he wouldn't stop poking around my butt hole, making me worry I might fart on his dick. I brought my hand down between my legs and guided his penis toward my vagina. He lifted himself onto his forearms. I bent my knees so he could get a better angle as he shoved the tip inside. Everything was dry. I raised my legs higher, hoping to create more space, and he pushed his penis into me in one hot slice. He began to pump, eyes closed. He didn't look handsome, eyebrows scrunched, lips pinched like a cat's asshole. I rolled my head to the side and noticed the slightly different colours of threads that made up orange shag.

I was getting tired, holding my legs in the air, so I bent them again, which caused him to open his eyes, scramble up my hips, and shove himself into what felt like my tailbone. I reached up to touch his chest, but when we caught each other's gaze we both shut our eyes again. He caught his breath, made a private noise and I felt him tighten inside me before he dropped down. It felt good to be pinned by his calm. My body softened as he kissed me on both cheeks and I tickled his back slowly, giddy with reprieve. We'd done it. It was over. He'd wait for me.

There was no blood on the towel but he rolled it up anyway to put in a garbage can down the street. We sat on the couch for a bit, in the dark, my stocking feet curled up under my bum, my crotch drippy from the spermicide. After a few minutes his nerves came back, so I climbed onto the bed and hoisted myself out the window and ran back to the gate to wait, crouched low until he pulled his car around. Driving home, he played "Blister in the Sun" on repeat and we sang along, which reminded me of camp.

The next morning, I woke to the phone ringing.

"Aren't you glad you got that over with?" Aimes said.

Watching Mom scurry back and forth, giving orders on what to pack, I laughed, noticing that in place of the usual brick on my chest there was glorious abandon.

The rest of the morning was spent packing while managing phone calls from the girls. Once everyone had been briefed, Bugsy called me back.

"Do you think you might be pregnant?" she asked.

"Why would I be pregnant?" I asked. "We used four different types of birth control."

"Well, if I'd just had sex for the first time and was going to Disneyland the next day, I'd be worried, that's all," she said. "When's your period due?"

"It's due soon," I said. "Now-ish."

"That's the worst time to do it," she said. "The sperm could have gotten through."

I hung up the phone and called Doug.

"Bugsy says we did it at the worst possible time and I might be pregnant," I said.

"What are you going to do?"

"I'll call her back and ask," I said.

Bugsy said the best solution would be if we all met on the tracks and went to the pharmacy together. First though, I'd have to get the morning-after pill prescribed, which would kill anything growing inside of me if I took it within twenty-four hours of the act. I counted quickly. Eight last night—if I swallowed the first pill by noon today I'd make it. I called Penny from Speech and Drama class, and she drove me to a new walk-in clinic in Vernon. Bugsy called Aimes who called Cristal who called Max.

After Penny dropped me off, prescription in hand, I clambered up the side of the embankment. The girls were already there, waiting for me, smoking. They each hugged me solemnly and we started carefully along the rails, navigating the puddles. We jumped off in the middle of town and took side streets to get to the pharmacy. I peered in through the window, a Valentine's Day scene still painted on, the cherubs spattered with mud from truck tires spinning out in the parking lot.

"My mom's friend Ruth is working at the front cash," I hissed.

"Shit balls," Aimes said.

Ruth volunteered with all the other church ladies at the town fair every September. She knew everyone. As we huddled up to discuss our options Bugsy headed over to a grey pickup truck, rusted out around the wheel wells, back taillights on. Through the open window she talked to the driver. After a minute the engine cut. Bugsy stepped away from the truck and both the driver and passenger doors opened and out stepped two members of the Brew Crew. Tonya, who'd pinned me to my locker last year, and beside her a skinny girl with platinum hair, black roots showing and about a hundred bobby pins holding the wisps to her head. Tonya's eyes locked onto mine as they strode towards us.

"I hear you got a problem," she said, stuffing her hands into her pockets.

"I told her everything," Bugsy said.

"So, the morning-after pill?" Tonya asked.

I looked to Bugsy and she nodded.

"It costs twenty bucks," Tonya said.

I hadn't thought to bring money. I turned to the girls who were searching their jacket pockets. Max found a two-dollar bill in her bag and offered it limply.

"I gotcha this time," Tonya said. "Ladies gotta stick together on stuff like this."

I handed Tonya the folded prescription and she walked into the pharmacy with the thin girl following behind. I looked to Bugsy, who shrugged. Cristal kicked at a porous pile of old snow. About ten minutes later Tonya came out holding a small white paper bag that was stapled shut and she handed it to me.

"You might feel sick. Try not to puke or else you'll lose the baby-killer."

"Right," I nodded.

"Take one pill now, and the other," she looked at her watch, "tomorrow morning."

"Thanks Tonya," Bugsy said. "For helping out."

"Like I said, we do what we gotta do."

Tonya and her friend walked back to her truck. When they climbed in, the thin girl leaned out the window and yelled, "Next time, double up buttercup."

They spun out, spraying sand as they peeled out onto the main road and we heard a honk as they rounded the bend. Opening the small paper bag, I cracked through the blister pack and put one small pill in my mouth and the other in my pocket, to take with me on the plane. As we walked back along the tracks, the clouds lowered, making the light dull.

"I gotta get back," Cristal said, shivering.

Hugging each other goodbye, we hopped off the tracks.

"Say hi to Minnie for us," Aimes said, as the girls disappeared down their side routes and shortcuts.

The next morning, Mom drove Grum and I bleary-eyed to the airport where we got on the plane. At 6 a.m. I reached into my pocket and took the second tiny pill out, swallowed it and lay my head against the cabin window to finally sleep.

When we landed in California, Mom's stress level began to rise incrementally. It took us two hours to get out of LAX, going from kiosk to kiosk till we found the right car rental place. As we escaped the depths of the airport and merged onto the six-lane highway, she screamed.

We found the hotel. The pool on the roof was closed for maintenance but I sat beside it anyway and wrote a postcard to Cristal about how hot it was outside. The next morning, when we walked through the great gates, my first stop was at the gift shop to buy Doug his favourite Disney character, a stuffed Donald Duck, for his birthday.

"Does a nineteen-year-old man want a stuffed animal?" my mom asked me.

About fifteen minutes later, waiting in line at Splash Mountain, I felt the familiar ache in my pelvis and an hour after we finished the Big Thunder roller coaster a wet warmth had spread between my legs. I found a bathroom, pulled down my underwear and there was a small stain of dark brown blood. I told Mom I had to call Doug.

"This is ridiculous, we're in Disneyland," she said. "Why now?"

"We're in love," I said. "I have to."

I found a payphone and called him collect and he answered on the first ring.

"Doug," I whispered, "I got my period, I'm not pregnant."

There was silence on the other end of the line.

"Oh, good," he said. "Sorry, I'd forgotten about that."

I phoned Cristal next. She said that she'd call the rest of the girls immediately. She said they'd all been on standby and they hadn't stopped thinking about me and that they were worried sick and she was so grateful I'd let them know. She told me to have a great time and send her lots of postcards and she missed me so much she was going to lose weight over it. She said she loved me more than she loved money and I giggled into the phone, giddy. I wasn't pregnant. I had a boyfriend. He wouldn't leave me. And now I had an entire week to be a kid.

Through the blur of a Greyhound bus window, I repeat everything Mom's doctor told me at the last appointment. *Her tumour markers haven't changed. No new nodes have been found in her last* PET *scan. The cancer hasn't spread.* Reaching for another Ativan I remind myself of my pact with God. Mom will live to see her grandchildren and I'll live without regret. Leaving for a few weeks of work won't change this.

I call Christie on the ride back to the city and invite him to meet me at the apartment when I arrive.

"I think I'll stay home tonight," he says.

"Why?"

"It's been a long day," he says. "I'm tired."

My tummy starts to roil but he can't know that.

"Okay. Have fun," I say, forcing cheer.

I don't know what he gets up to when I'm away. His ex-girlfriend could be at the loft waiting for him.

"You okay?" he asks.

"Fine," I say, metal gate sliding across my chest. "All good." But an old thought pops in: *If I sucked his dick he'd come over just fine.* I shake my head, embarrassed by the impulse. Also, I don't suck dick anymore. I filled my quota as a teenager. I've got no sucks left to give.

Hours later, when the bus pulls into downtown Vancouver, I'm still deciding how to handle his rejection. I'm thirty-four years old. I've trained in multiple feminist perspectives. I'm part of a radical, intersectional women's group. I go to all the marches and write cutting social satire. I should be fine with a night apart. But not wanting to, I feel a little frantic. Walking up the steps to my apartment, I wonder if I should call and try phone sex. No, I'm terrible at phone sex.

When I unlock the front door, the apartment doesn't smell stale, which means Christie's been here. Every time I've come back from Mom's he's left a treasure here for me, discovered at the Salvation Army or behind a dumpster and made beautiful again. This time my gift is a wall-mounted light in the living room. He's made it out of a broken table leg and an old lampshade and it casts a soft glow across the teak table he also found and repaired, along with the refinished bench I sink onto.

Christie's offerings are complicated to receive. I can't help but look for the strings attached, wary for when I'll be blindsided by his meth addiction or secret family. But in the months we've been together, he's been stealthily sanding down my rough spots. Still, he's not welcome to officially move in with me until he's proven that his consistency isn't a flash in the pan—because there's no way some mediocre chump is going to push his way into my rent-controlled home and feed off the tit of my industriousness. The only issue is that I don't know how much proof will be enough.

The next morning, before I open my eyes, I reach for my phone and call Christie but he's already on shift at the furniture shop and can't talk. He doesn't sound angry or guilty. If anything, the night away has made him sexier—which spikes terror in me. He's not behaving like I'm used to. Demanding. Retreating. Changing his mind. He's being straight-up and it's uncomfortable; worse than if he yelled. I shower and head down to my newest contract, which happens to be directing a play at the same theatre school I graduated from.

Entering, I find twelve students, bright-eyed, stretching their bodies in front of a mirror while a stage manager prepares the room. Their eyes follow me as I cross the floor, and I'm bemused that I'm the teacher now. Placing my laptop beside me I straighten my spine into this new role, relieved to be somewhere no one knows what's going on.

As I start introductions, the stage manager notices my phone.

"Someone really wants to reach you," the guy says. "You've missed eight calls."

"Sorry, gang, I'll just be a minute."

Grabbing my phone, I leave the room.

Grum's voice is hushed but rapid fire. He's been contacted by Mom's neighbour, Ruby. Yesterday she found Mom crying in the carport beside her smashed-up car. Mom told her that the police had revoked her licence. She doesn't want us to know.

"They'll throw me in a retirement home," she'd cried, then passed out in the carport.

Ruby called Grum. He'd jumped in his truck and drove the fourteen hours from his work site in Saskatchewan, without a stop.

"I know you just left but you've got to come back," he says. "She's not making sense."

"Is she okay?" I ask. "Is she hurt?"

"She wanted to take her dumb dog for a walk so she belted him into the passenger's seat and *drove him through the park*. There's a fence down. She hit her head. Her car's in the shop."

I tell him I'm on my way, a day behind him.

Sticking my head back into the rehearsal room I beckon to the stage manager.

"My mom's been in an accident," I say. "I have to leave."

The young stage manager grabs my coat and computer and leads me by the forearm out of the room without a goodbye to the students I've not yet met. I smile and wave as I speed out of the parking lot, hoping he hasn't picked up on my panic. I've been back in Vancouver for less than twenty-four hours. News travels fast in this town.

I'll leave tomorrow after I find a replacement for work. If I keep bailing on jobs, it won't be long before my career is over.

1993

ON THE FIRST MORNING OF SUMMER VACATION, the girls and I were on my roof, our heels dug into the steep pitch for traction. There was hardly enough room for all of us to lie down, but we wanted to look like we were the kind of girls who did this kind of thing. And because my house sat on Pleasant Valley Road, a main thoroughfare, we'd be sure to be seen. My scalp was getting stiff from the egg whites we'd coated our hair in and starting to smell from the sun beating down. Drips fell onto my forehead and cheeks, but I brushed them away, confident that this lightening trick would be the one that worked.

"What the hell is that?" Max said, pointing at Bugsy.

Her neck was covered in bruises.

"It's a Jimmy thing."

"Does he choke you out?"

"With his love," Bugsy said.

Aimes pulled down her shirt to show us her bruises too.

"They put their stamp on us," she said, "which means we're official."

"Hickeys suck," I said.

"How do you hide them?" Max asked.

"You think my parents look at my neck?" Bugsy laughed. "They don't even know I'm not home right now."

"Lucky," Aimes said.

After Cristal's parents, Kitty was the most careful of the moms. When Aimes was staying over at someone's house, Kitty would call the number Aimes left beside the phone to wish her a good night. We'd even had to get Tonya from the Brew Crew to save our ass and pretend she was another parent, hosting. Tonya didn't mind though; she preferred to stay home most weekends anyway and answering a quick call in a fake voice, to say Aimes was busy watching a movie, kept her feeling like a badass.

I rolled over on the sandpapery roof tiles to get some sun on my back. When I thought about seeing Doug tonight, my heart sank. We'd both been hired back as camp counsellors and I was holding on to hope that as soon as we got back around the firepit, my worries about him leaving for university would melt into camp spirit.

It was strange, the divide between Doug and the girls. We'd been together for an entire school year. They knew the shape of his dick but he'd only ever met them in passing. I didn't know anything about Jimmy or Timmy either, really, and I didn't care to. Trent had been showing his face again. The fuckwad. I longed for the day I could punch him in the neck. These boys already took enough time away from where we'd rather be, which was here, in the sun, stuck together on a slanted roof.

Aimes grabbed the carton of eggs from the window ledge where they'd been balanced and passed it to Bugsy, who carefully crawled over to the edge of the gable. She took an egg from the carton and threw it at my neighbour's house. She missed. She threw another egg and it missed again.

"You're wasting them," Aimes said and pushed Bugsy aside.

Aimes lay down on her tummy like a sniper and whipped an egg at the house next door. We didn't hear a crack.

"Holy shit," she whispered. "It went through a gap in the window."

"You were supposed to throw it *at* the window," I said.

"I know, but I'm a better shot than Bugsy," Aimes said.

"Do it again," Bugsy dared.

Aimes threw another egg and again it slipped through the quarter-cracked window, an almost impossible shot.

"Aimes, you're throwing eggs into a baby's room," Max said, not looking up from Bugsy's *YM* magazine.

"Do the whole dozen," I said.

I was going away to camp the next day for the entire summer and could afford to be reckless. Aimes threw the eight eggs left through the crack in the window, missing only once, which coated the window in shell and yolk. Then we heard a baby start to cry.

"Holy shit, the baby was napping," I whispered.

I started clambering up the roof toward my dormer window. There was no way we'd all make it inside before the mom picked up her crying baby and saw her nursery covered in egg yolk. I crawled through, scratching my stomach on the metal window ledge, and fell onto the bed. Max and Cristal poured down through the window after me. We rolled onto the carpet, hyped on adrenaline, while Aimes pushed Bugsy through the small window, then scuttled in last.

"Will she know it was us?" Aimes whisper-screamed.

The baby's crying stopped. The phone downstairs started to ring.

"She knows it was us," I said.

No one was home. I'd erase the angry messages. I didn't give a shit anyway. I had one last afternoon left with my girls and no dumbass baby-mom was going to take it from me.

We washed our hair, then the other girls left with promises to meet on the tracks the Saturday before grade ten started. I hugged Cristal, who was grouchy for being abandoned for the summer again. Mom ordered pizza and made her stay for dinner, so that cheered her up.

"The neighbour said something about her baby?" Mom said, mouth full, as we sat on the porch, eating off our laps.

Cristal swallowed.

"I couldn't make it out on the answering machine, but she sounded hysterical," Mom said.

I'd forgotten to erase one.

"I think Grum and his friends threw some eggs at her house yesterday," I said, thankful that he was at his buddy's for dinner and not here to defend himself.

Like I'd summoned her, the neighbour appeared on our front porch steps, bouncing her baby roughly.

"The eggs were thrown today," the woman said. "And I know it was you and your friends."

She tried to unlatch the porch screen door, but we'd screwed it shut for Operation Privacy that past winter and had forgotten to unscrew it — she couldn't get inside.

"Well maybe someone threw them at the window from the sidewalk?" Mom posited through the screen. "Kids do stupid things."

"You were on the roof," the neighbour seethed at me. "The shells have stuck to the walls and I've had to chip them off with a screwdriver. I'll need to repaint the entire room."

"*That's* not possible," Mom said. "Emmy's windows are too small to climb out of and the roof pitch is too steep."

Clammy with fury, the woman looked like she was going to jump through the screen and attack me, but her baby got fussy so she turned and stomped back to her own yard.

"I hope she finds out who did that prank," Mom said. "That poor woman has two toddlers and a newborn and a husband who drives trucks for a living. She doesn't need more work on her plate."

———————————

The next day Mom drove Grum and me along the river to camp. When we crossed the bridge I saw the beach where we used to have our river dinners. They happened a few times every summer, back when we lived in Ashton Creek — on evenings when it was hotter inside the trailer than it was out. We'd sit in folding metal chairs, our feet in the rushing water, and eat rotisserie chicken and macaroni salad from the deli section in town. On Mom's first sigh, Grum would wipe his greasy fingers down his chest and run for the sandbar and Mom and I would crack open our books. Time slowed down and the world was just us three. She'd glance up at the sheep on the other side of the bank, and I'd sip pop from a straw, batting away wasps while we waited for the heat to get less heavy. At some point Mom would bring her sunglasses to the top of her head.

"Getting to be bedtime," she'd say, shielding her eyes from the beginning-to-set sun.

Then she'd return to her book, Grum would start on a new project of trapping tadpoles using macaroni noodles as bait, and I'd move the towel from my shoulders to my lap. The light would be orangey.

"You think we should head back soon?" she'd ask no one, again. Finally, when the glare of light on the water made it too hard to read, she'd lean back, bend the page and push herself to her feet.

"Okay kidlets, time to go home to bed," she'd say, unconvincingly.

Like Mother Nature was listening, the sun would dip and Grum would smack the first mosquito and we'd have to trudge the path back through the razor grass to our car.

"Don't touch anything metal," she'd say, rolling down the windows holding her towel.

"Fire belts," we'd scream as the seatbelts scalded our bare thighs.

"Don't frazzle my nerves," she'd yell, spinning gravel as she merged onto the highway.

The warm wind would pour through the open windows, doing no good. I'd crawl up between the front seats and push aside her braid, to bury my nose in her nape and inhale. She was both musk and moisture. I'd close my eyes and nuzzle closer, my whole body wanting a taste. As she drove the windy road home, I'd go limp, chin resting on her clavicle, lips near her earlobe, breathing all of her in.

Turning away from the river, I glanced at her profile and knew if I dared to, she'd smell the same.

At the wharf, I hugged Mom goodbye for the summer and she whispered, "If he ever says he has blue balls, you tell him to go shoot off in a paper towel."

I watched her return to the car and unroll her window. It wasn't possible but I thought I could smell her summer skin all the way from the dock. I wanted to run and jump in the back seat and yell "Go, go, go!" like we were fleeing a robbery, but instead I stepped into the boat, and Grum and I crossed the river without her.

That night, before the campers arrived, all the counsellors piled into the arts and crafts hall. Once we'd tucked into our sleeping bags and the bare lightbulbs had been turned off, as the breathing around me slowed and deepened, I heard Doug's sleeping bag being unzipped one tooth at a time. Knowing what he wanted, I rolled on top of him and lifted up my nightgown. We couldn't see each other. Our friends stirred beside us, maybe sleeping, maybe not yet. He pulled his penis out and tried to push it inside me but the shaft bent from dryness. We had to move carefully against the nylon bags but with a bit of spit he got it in and I was able to lie face down and count along with the pumps, enjoying having a focus while my body was busy. When he grunted, I'd just landed on an even number and I rolled off him, a rightness in my brain.

That night I had a dream that there was a large pile of dog shit in the middle of the arts and crafts hall floor. It sat freshly coiled on the unvarnished floorboards. My camp friends surrounded me as I spooned the shit into my mouth. I had to pretend that I was enjoying the taste. That was the rule of the dream. I scooped mouthfuls of warm shit as I grinned, my teeth stained.

Before the first camp started, a new group of LITs climbed the hill, just like I had the previous summer. They looked tentative but nervy like the jackrabbits we sometimes glimpsed in the brush. My assigned LIT had unwashed hair and was stick-thin like a child. She reminded me of someone – Aimes when I first met her? I couldn't place it until we sat on our bunks and introduced ourselves to the first group of campers.

"I'm Autumn," the LIT said. "I was here last year and I loved it, so I'm back."

This was Autumn? The kid who cried into my chest? Being an LIT meant she had to be thirteen, maybe fourteen – which would have made her twelve at the youngest last summer – far off from my guess of ten. I didn't like her. A precocious child was adorable but an overly confident young woman was obnoxious and I treated her as such immediately – only leaving her with the kids after they'd fallen asleep, so I could sneak out to meet Doug in the open-air chapel.

Again, I became consumed by camp. My mind never wandered further than the bounds of the field. Every day, the same lunch time, craft time, swim time kept me going in a steady hum. Tension only presented itself when I couldn't find change for the tuck shop, or if we ran out of wool for God's eyes. Every night, Doug and I made the kids go wild with our call-and-response songs and ridiculous tandem dances. The twenty-four-hour breaks between camps were filled with jam sessions on the director's front porch, drinking warm coolers on the dock and fucking Doug silently on fallen logs, mosquitos eating my ankles and tits. The summer drove by furiously, days passing in what felt like hours and weeks rolling into each other so quickly that soon we were closer to the end of camp than the beginning.

On the last night of Teen Camp, just like last summer, we strung fairy lights through the rafters and attached streamers to fans, trying to make the humid air more festive and breezy. Doug and I swayed to the last song always played, "Stairway to Heaven," my cheek pressed against his sternum, his chin resting on the top of my head. I remembered watching him and Michelle dance to the same song last year. I wasn't scared or sad like she'd been. I'd kept him satisfied. He was going to university and I'd visit him and we were in love and at the end of the song, he dipped me and everyone clapped.

The next morning, after hugging the campers goodbye, I caught a ride home to Armstrong to wash laundry before the final camp of the summer began on Monday. Doug got into a car packed full of our counsellor friends, off to spend the night partying at the camp director's house. I invited Cristal over to have a catch up but when she arrived she was distant. She showed no interest in hearing about camp or Doug. I tried to cuddle her on the couch during the movie, but she left early, not even turning around to wave goodbye at the end of the driveway like she usually did. I fell asleep counting my fingers, because that's what I did now, throughout the day, to soothe myself.

Doug didn't call me the next morning. I did our laundry and vacuumed. He was probably just hungover. I hadn't heard from him by dinnertime that night so I sat down at the kitchen table to focus on the pattern of touching fingertips to thumb in time with the counting. If I got through three rounds of six without a mistake, he wouldn't be dead.

Finally, as I was brushing my teeth before bed, Doug called.

"Can you come get me from Autumn's house?" his voice slurred.

"What are you doing at Autumn's house?" I asked.

"We ended up here. Her parents had a lot of weed. Can you just come and get me?" he said.

I got the address and decided to take the risk of driving with my learner's permit. It was only back roads at night and Mom was already in bed.

After about twenty minutes I pulled down a dirt driveway that led me deeper into the woods. The road stopped at a cabin that looked like it was under construction, with work lights on and tarps strung up along the front and sides of the building. Bodies began to stumble out of the front door, curious about the headlights. I watched Doug and Autumn weave toward me, him using her little frame for support. She led him toward the car, her jean shorts showing knobby knees. She helped him into the passenger's seat, head on his chin, eyes closed from too much alcohol. Leaning through the window she kissed him on the cheek.

"Bye bye, Dougie," she said, and looked at me and smiled. "Hi Emmy."

I sped out in reverse, driving along the highway until we got to Vernon. He tried to rest his head on my lap as I drove.

"She's just a kid," he said. "Don't be jealous."

But it felt wrong. As he climbed out of Mom's car and stumbled toward his house, I knew something I hadn't even dared to consider had happened.

There was just one more week of camp before the summer ended but I couldn't cross back over the river. Images came at me as I lay in Mom's bed and cried. Doug and Autumn, arms around each other, swaying in chapel. Doug and Autumn laughing as they tried to lead grace together. Doug and Autumn having a water fight. *She's too young*, I'd thought. *He's being kind.* But seeing them in the car's headlights, him pawing at her while she held him up, I realized that this was the weekend that they'd been waiting for all summer, just as I'd waited so patiently last summer for mine.

Mom called the camp and told them I was sick with the flu. This was not in her character, to allow for melodrama to get in the way of a job, but she let me stay in her bed that week while I sobbed into her pillows, rather than having to watch him turn fully toward Autumn. Another counsellor called from the cook shack to tell me that they couldn't keep their hands off each other. She was pushy. She didn't care what people thought of her. Mom said it was unprofessional of Doug to be dating an LIT but wasn't I almost her age when I'd thrown myself at him last summer?

From the safety of bed my brain eventually started to sift through options. To become impenetrable I needed to get more exposed. These were opposites, I knew, but complexity wasn't a problem for me. I'd eat glass for love. I'd tear my own insides out and pin them to my chest. I'd break my own kneecaps. But I couldn't go back to camp and see him with the girl I'd been last summer — someone willing to do even more than I was to survive.

2012

ZONKED FROM THE POT AND PILLS I'd taken to fall asleep, I stare at the clock until I can read it. It's only 9 a.m. I can be on the road in an hour. I check my phone. Christie's not called yet. If I'm kind and easy for the next twenty-four hours, any decision he's made to leave me might soften. The drive through the mountains is fast this early in the morning. I keep checking my phone but he's still not responded to any of my texts from last night so I throw it into my bag. I've got more important things to deal with than how to convince Christie to love me. Fuck him if he can't manage a full-hearted, messy-ass woman. Fuck him in the head.

When I pull into the driveway in the early evening, Mom isn't waiting for me in her usual spot. I open the side door and climb the steps into the kitchen. The house is dim, curtains pulled to block out the sun as if a baby is having an afternoon nap. I peek into the living room to find Grum sitting in a chair in the dark.

"She's sleeping," he says.

He looks like he hasn't, his eyes rimmed red and bloodshot. He brushes his hand through his hair and I notice his hairline has thinned considerably. How long has it been since I saw him last? I can't help but smile. This eight-year-old who rocked his dog on the side of the road as he died, the boy who built go carts from scrap, the kid who cuddled in bed with Mom until he was thirteen. I'm able to exhale, seeing him sitting here, waiting for me, his steel-toed boots still on.

We decide to let her sleep for another hour. Grum has taken the bed in the basement again so I carry my bags into the guest room. The bed is unmade from my last visit and the lights are off. The room smells sour. It's nothing, really, but it's also everything, this unmade bed. There hasn't been a time in my life when I haven't come home to freshly washed, tightly fitted sheets. The pleasure I get from pulling the top sheet down and slipping into the firm, cool pocket she's made for me is something so ordinary that I didn't know it could stop.

I drop down. Blinders have narrowed my vision so that all I can see is the unmade bed. The violence inside rises like big teeth biting. I want to loll my head and grunt and scratch my neck in long lines. I want to hurt as bad as it does because I'm so very, very ashamed of myself. I curl up at the end of the mattress, my eyes wide. Pulling the wrinkled quilt over my body I start the slow count to one hundred, touching the tips of my fingers gently in time. *She's alive. She's here. Right now, it's okay. You're not bad. You're doing your best.* The light pressure of thumb on fingertips calms me enough that I can roll over, crack a window and head down the hall to see if she's up and ready for a snack.

After crackers and cheese, Grum and I decide that Mom needs to get her head checked out in case she got a concussion when she hit it in the accident. Grum didn't want to leave the house until I'd arrived and he's not excited about a hospital trip. After spending so much time caring for her during her first battles with cancer when he was a kid, the green hallways and bright lighting throw him into a panic. I don't share those memories as I never accompanied Mom back then — too absorbed in my own drama — so it's my turn now.

I pop two pills and load Mom into my car and drive twenty minutes along the highway to Vernon, up the steep hill to where the cement grey hospital overlooks the town. This is the same building Mom worked at as a nurse for forty years. It's where she came to get her first rounds of chemotherapy, escorted by my then-eleven-year-old brother; the same emergency department where I got my stomach pumped on my fourteenth birthday.

As we pass through the sliding doors our bodies are reflected back at us and I'm shot back in time. We've been in this vestibule before, but it had been me who'd needed help. I pause to watch us in the glass, both now and twenty years ago.

"Do you see what you've done to yourself?" she'd said.

Helping her to shuffle along I wonder if she remembers the same long-ago moment but she doesn't seem to. She grips my forearm as we approach the nurses' station.

"Hi," I say to the nurse behind the Plexiglas. "My mom was in a little accident and I just want to make sure she didn't bonk her head too hard."

The woman takes Mom's identification and indicates we're to sit down on one of the many plastic orange chairs in the vacant waiting room.

I put my arm around Mom's shoulder and she sinks into me. She seems content in silence and we've got time to kill. It's not a relaxing place to wait, though, the bright white of the walls bouncing off the floor in an unnatural glare. The sound of medics rushing through the sliding glass doors. They push a gurney with a body strapped to it past us into the emergency room. Surgical lights flood my eyes before the doors swing shut.

This is the same entrance Taylor was brought through by paramedics six months ago. And this is where her mom would have waited, I think, looking around. What chair had she sat in? I shake my head. She didn't sit down.

It was likely someone on shift that night knew Taylor, or had a kid that went to school with her — a lot of nurses commute from Armstrong to Vernon for work, like my mom had. That might have brought Marie some comfort, knowing that if she couldn't be with her daughter, another mother was. All hands would've been on deck that night. After a doctor wiped the Halloween makeup from her face and saw the severity of the blows to Taylor's scalp, her bruised and scratched neck, a nurse scraped under Taylor's finger-nails, hoping for a DNA sample. Their focus was to keep Taylor breathing, and although she didn't respond, everyone in the room coached her loudly: *You can do it Taylor. You're a fighter. Stay with us.* The on-call doctor called a sur-geon for a consult. The medical team brought in the best cardiologist in the area to keep Taylor's heart stable.

I wonder whether it's gruesome, to imagine that night in such detail, but I don't think so. It's my brain trying to filter the unimaginable. As Mom dozes on my shoulder, I picture a nurse removing her scrubs and heading to the waiting room to update Marie on what she knew. They'd have worked and prayed at the same time — that's what I think — with the same the urgency as if she was their own child. But just before dawn, behind the heavy doors her mother paced in front of, Taylor died.

A familiar scraping of curtains on their tracks brings me back into the room. The nurse calls Mom's name and I help her to stand and we're led into the emergency area. It's a quiet afternoon. A few nurses and doctors are hud-dled around the nurses' station, laughing at something on the computer. The nurse brings us to a bed and cranks it low so Mom can climb up onto the stiff paper, and the nurse slides the curtains shut, creating a temporary but cozy room. Another nurse walks in. She checks Mom's vitals and makes small talk while not making eye contact.

"I hear we've got a NASCAR driver in today."

Mom doesn't understand the joke. She sits, slumped forward, her eyes closed. I hold her across the chest while the nurse checks her pupils.

"She seems fine. Just a bump. Obviously tired." The nurse speaks like Aimes used to, in short sentences. "When you put her to bed tonight, check on her every hour. I'll get the doctor to see her before you go."

My mom turns toward her and speaks softly, her eyes still shut.

"I'm a nurse too."

"That's nice dear," the nurse says. She unwraps the blood pressure sleeve around Mom's arm and drags the curtains shut behind her.

My bag buzzes. I dig for my phone and find multiple unread text messages that span a few hours.

Sorry I missed you last night.

Have you left already?

Why didn't you wake me?

R U OK?

The strap loosens around my chest and I text him back.

Hi, we're fine, I'll call you later.

He texts back: *Miss you. Love you. Can't wait to talk. Peach emoji.*

It was all in my head. He'd never been angry. Or going to leave. Relief floods, but I'm shocked too. I'd assumed the worst. Needy mixed with dramatic is not a sexy combination and if I'm not careful, he's going to find out what a mess I am. I put my head in my hands. What will it take for me to let this guard down?

Over an hour later, a doctor brushes in, flips the chart and gives us the same information the nurse had but faster and with less eye contact.

"I was a nurse," my mom says again. Her eyes are now open but her head is still on my shoulder.

"Hmm," the doctor says.

"I worked here for forty years," she says, unaware of his disinterest.

"Is that right?" he says, eyes on the chart. "Well, thanks for your patience, hon, and it looks like you're good to go."

I help Mom step down from the stool and we travel back to the waiting room, now busier with a mom trying to entertain two sticky looking kids, a man holding his bandaged hand in a tea towel and an older woman, alone along the side wall, a strawberry-red bruise on her cheek. We travel back through the sliding doors past our reflections, and again I'm reminded that this time it's me steadying her. I have a bitter thought: I should take a picture so that she remembers.

When Grum and I put her to bed, we tuck her in how she likes it, many quilts pulled snug across her body, tucked under her feet and bum. She smiles in her drowsiness and lets her kids fuss over her a bit. Despite her independence, it's all she's ever wanted, really – a bit of a to-do made on her behalf.

1993

IN THE FIRST WEEKS OF GRADE TEN, I walked the halls like a zombie, uninterested in anything except the bell signalling that I could go home and get back into bed. I sat on the toilet between classes, hands crossed against my chest, to make sure my heart was beating at a normal rate. I thought about calling Doug from the school's pay phone, to beg him to come back to me, but managed to stop myself. Between classes, the girls floated around me like ghosts. I was still within their sphere, I could hear them speaking, but I had no ability to join in.

Halfway through the month Bugsy and Aimes became tired of my moroseness and cut directly through the student centre to the parking lot to eat lunch with Jimmy and Timmy in their side-by-side trucks. Max floated off to the band room and I couldn't get up the energy to care whether or not the shadow of Cristal was beside me.

Mom had no patience for it. After another day of shutting my door, undressing and curling up in bed, I heard her stomp up the stairs.

"Get downstairs," she yelled, throwing open my bedroom door. "You're fifteen years old and this is the least amount of pain you'll ever feel."

I didn't move.

"You wanna know what a broken heart feels like?" She turned on my lights and opened the curtains. "Get pregnant and then get left – twice!" She pulled the pillow out from under my head. "If you wanna act like an adult, grow the hell up." She turned and stomped back downstairs. "I'm back at work tomorrow." The yelling continued from the kitchen. "I'm not making lunches anymore. You're on your own." She was going back to work at the hospital, only part-time, but it surprised me – she wasn't even back to 40 percent of her usual self yet.

I stayed in bed that weekend. Mom trudged upstairs to bring me a glass of water on occasion and once she sat down and patted my arm – but soon, annoyed again, she stood up and ripped the covers off, trying to strip the bed with me in it. I rose like the undead and clawed the quilts back from her, their weight the only thing that brought comfort.

Cristal continued to pick me up for school every day but I didn't say a word, not able to risk my attention being diverted. I got dressed and grabbed an apple or piece of cold toast and walked beside her every morning, busy replaying where I'd gone too far, not held back enough, been too obvious, too crass – and who had gotten behind the wall while I'd had my guard down.

"Do you want to try for a sleepover this weekend?" Cristal asked one morning. With the coming chill, her hoodie had been switched for a winter coat and mitts.

I shook my head. I needed to go straight to bed. Only blanketed could I strategize how to defend myself against future hurts.

"Mr. Anderson was on a roll today," she tried a week later. "I counted four shirts he looked down in math class."

I kept my eyes on the few feet in front of me as we slipped along the frosty sidewalk up the hill.

"Doug was ugly and has a dumb name," Cristal said, after another week went by. "You dodged a bullet. He'll trade up again in a year."

I stopped walking. Lifting my gaze to take in my surroundings, the sky was light grey, the same colour as the sidewalk. She was right. I'd replayed every encounter. I'd considered all my mistakes. I'd regretted and begged. And as I took in the dull, frozen hillocks of dead grasses on the slope above me I realized that there was nothing left to be done.

"I bet there's a storm today," Cristal said, and like she'd just become the goddamned weatherman, a few flakes floated down.

"Can we sit for a minute?" I asked, the first words I'd uttered on our daily walk in over a month.

"Yeah, sure, where?" Cristal looked around, trying to accommodate.

I plunked down in the middle of the sidewalk. Kids could walk around me if they had to. I tilted back and a few tiny crystals landed on my cheeks. I thought there was a rule that if he got what he wanted – my body and my single-pointed focus – I maintained control, which kept me invulnerable to abandonment and attack. But he'd still left. I'd given him too much, and nothing would have ever been enough.

After a minute or two of silence, Cristal held out her arm and I used it to pull me upright. Facing the wind, a new possibility bloomed inside me like blood.

That afternoon I joined the girls in the student centre and instead of lying down, eyes closed, waiting for the next bell to tell me where to go, I borrowed five bucks from Bugsy and headed to the small canteen that was only open on Fridays and bought a twelve-inch ham and cheese sub. The kid inside the canteen microwaved it for me and I tore off the plastic wrapper and took a bite of the warm, gooey pig log.

"I'm never eating a tomato and mayo sandwich again," I said to no one, as I sat down at a table.

Aimes scuttled over to me. "Holy shit, Em, I thought we were gonna find you hanging from the bathroom stall."

I laughed and took another bite. It was nice to be able to hear her again.

"Doug was a perv. Give us a week and we'll find you a new one," she said.

Bugsy plopped down in the chair across from me. "You gonna start wearing deodorant again?" She jabbed me. "That sub must be delicious, 'cause yer eating the plastic wrapper." Bugsy pulled the plastic out of my mouth, which made me laugh, and the laughter made me gulp and I inhaled, unconsciously, but easily, for the first time in two months.

"I just took a deep breath," I said, and just to be sure, I took another one.

I didn't have to turn to see who'd sat on the other side of me because I smelled Ivory soap, and I lay my head on Max's shoulder.

"Good job Sym," she said and clapped me on the back. "Glad to have you back in the land of the not-quite-dead."

I shoved the last bite of submarine sandwich into my mouth, licked out the melted cheese at the bottom of the wrapper and looked back to our usual spot on the benches for Cristal. She stood up, I assumed to walk over and join us, and I felt the dome I'd been living under fold away and light start to pour in, and as soon as her chest was against mine I'd be okay again for sure – but Cristal turned away down the hall, face unreadable, shoulders back.

Later that afternoon, Cristal wasn't by the lockers. I'd forgotten her new volleyball schedule – or maybe I hadn't bothered to remember it? – so after school I left through the double doors by myself, this time with a plan. The sun was bright as I marched down to the only hair salon in town and I got the hairdresser to punch two holes in the right side of my nose with a piercing gun. The boldness of the act would be undeniable. I'd be seen as a rule-breaker and boys would think twice. The pain was a marker of what had changed. I left the hair salon, nose throbbing, and made my way home carefully along the tracks, which were covered in their first dusting of snow. After slipping down the embankment on my butt, I started to jog, looking forward to putting an ice cube on my new power statement.

"What have you done?" Mom said as I entered the kitchen.

"I got it pierced," I said.

"You didn't ask permission," she said.

"It's my body," I said.

Didn't she notice I was smiling for the first time in months?

"But you'll have scars." Mom clasped her hands. "Your face is ruined."

She flew at me like a crow after shiny baubles, trying to pull the rings out of my nose. I couldn't help but laugh, and the whiff of confidence only seemed to make her angrier. I backed up and she stumbled onto her knees. Grum ran between us, but with her on the ground, it looked like I was laughing at her, which I guess I was. I'd just come out of a grief coma. I felt happy for the first time in months and she'd attacked me?

"I hate you," Mom screamed.

A fire lit. Maybe it was the adrenaline of just getting pierced or the way the weather had frosted the town in ice, but I was enjoying myself.

"I'm your daughter," I said. "And you hate me?"

Mom put her hands on her knees. "I don't hate you," she backtracked. "I hate how you're behaving. I hate the things you do." She reached out to me. "I didn't mean it. I'm sorry Punky."

She pushed herself up off the floor. I had her. She'd never live this down. Grum held her around the waist to steady her shaking body. I ran upstairs, relieved that she'd done more damage than me, for once.

———————

Tonight was Halloween, and from the silence downstairs I knew I was free to do what I wanted. Without a boyfriend there were now options as to how I could celebrate. I could follow Max to a bonfire or I could go to the Sollys' party with Bugsy and Aimes and Cristal and get shit-tanked.

Heading down the tracks, like every Halloween night, the usually quiet shortcut through town had turned into a superhighway of action – kids drinking beer and lighting bottle rockets, running down the rails. The air was thick with pink smoke from firecrackers, making my depth perception confused. There was a shadow in the distance – and then, right beside me.

"Hey Em, looking good," Windex said. "You headed to the Sollys'?"

I wasn't up for his usual bullshit, so I lied.

"Nah, just looking for my brother, you see a Ninja Turtle around?"

"Yeah, he just got chased down the embankment by the cops. He was with a lion and a robot I think."

"See you later," I said, hoping he didn't follow.

I could hear the Solly brothers' party pounding halfway down the block. The yard was filled with kids, and the dormer windows on the second level of the falling-down house already had legs sticking out, beer cans being thrown onto the gravel drive below. I pushed my way into the dark, slanted house, searching for any of the girls.

"Sym," a voice screamed as a dark figure attacked me.

Bugsy pushed her hood back to show me her vampire teeth and pressed a vodka cooler into my hands.

"It's hard to chug with these things in your mouth," she said and spat the teeth onto the floor.

"You just get here?" Aimes yelled. She was doing the dead nurse costume – too easy in my opinion, but I didn't comment.

"Are you a fortune teller?" Cristal asked. She was wearing her usual plaid shirt, only she'd clipped a bow tie to her neck in acknowledgement of the night.

"I'm a space gypsy," I yelled in her ear.

"You look like your mom," Cristal said.

I had less experience at these big parties than the rest of the girls so I followed Aimes, her white jeans my beacon as she snaked through the masses.

Boys grabbed at Aimes's stethoscope and Bugsy's long wig but no one looked at me. I realized I hadn't fully considered that getting your nose double-pierced in Armstrong might be the equivalent of having a face tattoo.

"See whatchoo been missin' out on," Bugsy drawled one-eyed as she tripped forward.

Jimmy caught her from behind. "Whoa, keep 'er steady girl," he shouted and pushed her upright.

"Are you talking to your girlfriend or a horse?" I said.

"Both," he said. "Either," and shrugged.

"Sit on my face Jimmy," Bugsy slurred. "I think it's a black out night." Then she yelled, "You gonna black out with me Cris?"

Cristal put her arm around Bugsy, who looked less beautiful than normal, in poorly applied white face paint and fake blood dripping from the corners of her mouth. It was a fair question. Some nights were just about having a few in Bugsy's hot tub. Other nights were about going tits to the wind. Taking breaks to vomit between songs and finding a corner to piss in was, I was told, fun. And the mess of sickness and loss of memory only seemed to add to the girls' popularity as they became the party itself.

We glided through the house like grand marshals of the parade. We hadn't needed to ask for an invite; we'd just shown up, knowing our presence would be an addition. Cristal had a fresh pack of smokes and Aimes carried a backpack of vodka coolers. Beer pong was in the dining room, the kitchen was fairly lifeless – just older dudes slouched around the table – and there was already a lineup to use the one bathroom in the house.

"There's Max," I yelled, seeing her long hair sway in the crowd of dancers, and I left the girls, happy she'd decided to come.

It was a small living room so I had to push through some couples to get to Max. Her eyes were closed. I didn't interrupt, just leaned my chest into her back and felt her body respond. She tilted her bum to meet my tummy and I reached my arms around her waist and we began to move together. Max wasn't wearing a costume. She was stoned or drunk or both. When she saw me she laughed and turned around so we were chest to chest, our cleavage the centre-point of our motion.

"This feels cozy," she said, her eyes still shut.

The song "What's Up?" came on and someone turned up the volume. Our eyes flew open and we started to jump to the opening guitar riff. The dance floor cleared as Max and I took over. I moved my hips to the rhythm of the guitar and when the lyrics came in she started to sing in harmony with Linda Perry. Max was a rock star and I'd become her back-up dancer and we didn't give a shit because she was on fire.

Halfway through the song I opened my eyes to see everyone in the living room watching us. Cristal was in the corner and by her look she thought we were making fools of ourselves. The rest of the eyes chewed us up, like the dancing had been for them, and I felt like I'd fucked up but didn't know how. I moved toward Max and put my arms over her shoulders and she put her arms around my waist and we held on to each other and swayed, foreheads touching, waiting for the eyes to disperse.

Cristal started drinking heavily after that and Bugsy and Aimes got called outside to their boyfriends' trucks so I broke away from Max to grab another cooler and in the short time it took to scan the room, Max was gone.

Warmed by booze, I headed outside. It was fun to trip across the frosty, uneven ground. My body felt loose and I realized how badly I needed to pee. I stepped behind the shed, a bottle and smokes in one hand, lifting my skirt with the other, and a movement made me jump.

"Shit Sym, you scared me," Aimes said. She was crouched and bouncing herself dry. "I thought you were a creep."

I squatted beside her and pushed to get the stream started, painful until my bladder released and then the urine trickled and surged.

Aimes got antsy waiting for me to finish. "You seen Timmy?" She looked back to the party. "He's mad at me 'cause I look like a slut." Before I could say anything she jumped up. "There he is. Duty calls."

Without Aimes behind the shed, everything became obscured. The pounding music hurt my head. I needed to get home. I wrapped my scarves around my neck and pushed my way into the front yard till I got to the road and started to walk, my hands under my armpits. I reached the shortcut that led me to the tracks, still swarming with kids screaming and running down the rails, and I pushed through the throng. The car was in the driveway and Grum's bike was leaned up against the breezeway. They were both home safe.

I ran inside the house and cranked the heat and wiped off my bright lips and kohl-lined eyes and crawled into bed. My clock read midnight.

On Monday morning just before the bell, Aimes crawled along the bench in the student centre and motioned for us to gather close. Her hair was unwashed and her eyes flitted around above our heads, making sure no one was close enough to hear. She had something to tell us but we couldn't tell anyone – ever. She wasn't smiling. We leaned in.

"You have to promise," she said.

"I promise," we all said.

Just before sunrise, long after the party at the Sollys' had ended, Max had snuck alongside Aimes's bedroom window and rapped on the glass. Aimes let her inside and Max stood in the middle of her floor. She took off her pants and tree bark fell out of her underwear.

"What happened?" Cristal said.

He'd cornered her at the party. She'd gone for a walk with him because she couldn't find any of us. He took her to woods behind the tracks and he laid her down on the forest floor and then he lay on top of her.

"Who was it?" I asked.

"I don't know," Aimes said. "She wouldn't say."

"Was she crying?" Bugsy asked.

"Yeah," Aimes said. "She was crying."

Scared of Max's sobs, Aimes woke up Kitty, and after a long time of whispering in the hallway, Kitty called Max's parents. It was early in the morning when they picked Max up. They'd screamed at her. Then they took her to the hospital and the police were called.

"So he raped her," Bugsy said.

"She said she didn't say no," Aimes said. "So what happened wasn't his fault."

Max became hysterical that he'd find out about the drama she caused, and they'd had to sedate her.

The next day Max called Aimes from the hospital and made her promise to never tell, to never, ever talk about it to anyone again. Aimes promised.

"Is she hurt?" I asked.

"I don't know," Aimes said. "What kind of hurt do you mean?"

Aimes assumed it was Trent but Max wouldn't say. There was no reason to involve him. That's what Max kept repeating to Kitty and Aimes, and the police, and her parents, and the doctors at the hospital. He'd done nothing wrong. She hadn't tried to stop it. How was he to know?

2012

Iᴛ'ꜱ ᴀᴘʀɪʟ ᴡʜᴇɴ ᴛʜᴇ ꜰɪʀꜱᴛ ᴘᴏʟɪᴄᴇ ꜱᴋᴇᴛᴄʜ appears at the intersection of Okanagan and Rosedale. I glance up the street and see the same piece of paper fluttering off all the telephone poles: a line drawing of a man with the word ᴡᴀɴᴛᴇᴅ printed across the top of the page.

Since the weekend, all of the major media stations have been cycling through the same breaking news: there's a match to the ᴅɴᴀ found underneath Taylor's fingernails. Which means, after six months of a stalled case, the ʀᴄᴍᴘ have a suspect. To see wanted signs appear without warning feels odd, like we've been forgotten in the climax of the movie about the man who's been haunting our town.

I scan the line drawing for anything familiar. His face looks puffy, bloated. He has small, deep-set eyes. His goatee is pencil thin and runs across his jawline, connecting to his sideburns. The man looks young, mid-twenties maybe. Nothing about his features stands out as scary to me. He looks ordinary, like any guy I'd gone to high school with. Stepping back, I take in his image as a whole and after a few minutes of squinting and considering, I'm sure, without a doubt, that I don't know the man who killed Taylor.

Aborting my mission to try on summer shorts at Frugal Frocks, I rush back up the hill to tell Mom the news and when I come through the kitchen, the ᴛᴠ is on.

"He's done it before," she says, standing in front of the screen.

"What? He's a serial murderer?"

"A serial rapist," she says. "His ᴅɴᴀ connects to two unsolved assault cases in the area."

"What about Taylor?" I ask.

"The ᴅɴᴀ under her fingernails is a confirmed match," Mom says.

Whenever we speak about Taylor and the murder investigation, Mom becomes clear-headed again, no frustration or fumbling over words. A pragmatism breaks through, like how she was as a nurse.

"They've found him," Mom says, hands on her hips. "Now, they just have to find him."

———————

The next morning, the posters have spread across town — in the windows of every storefront and plastered on the community bulletin boards, tacked to every surface that'll hold a staple. Everyone in Armstrong seems to be repeating the same motions I'd done the day before. First, their heads lift to take in the sketch. Their eyes narrow, searching for recognition. Next, a step back to take in the whole picture, and finally, their shoulders drop with the same sigh of relief.

As I move through town to drop off a small bag of recycling and pick up last Sunday's bulletin from church, this is what everyone's talking about: *He's not from here.* The distinction proves what we've all been hoping but haven't been able to articulate: violence was done *to us*, not *by us*. And the shared panic we've been carrying all winter suddenly makes sense. We were frightened about the potential of another attack, but even more scary was the possibility that we were friends with a murderer. If a resident *had* committed the crime, it meant he knew that adults didn't walk the rails; it suggested he was familiar with the hiding spots and side routes and times of day kids populated the tracks. It meant he'd studied all the intimate ways kids moved around Armstrong. If it turned out the person who was capable of such prepared violence was someone we loved and trusted, that would've caused a permanent tear and turned us into fools.

"Emmy?"

I hear a man's voice behind me and turn to see Ollie, good ole Ollie Solly from the olden days. It's been a while since we've last spoken on the phone, and I haven't seen him in years.

"You back in town again?" he asks, pushing the curls off his face. His hairline has thinned and he's put on a few extra pounds, but the wide smile is the same.

"Yep," I say. "With Mom."

"How long are you visiting for this time?"

I hear the subtext. He's telling me that I'm a guest now. This is another nuance of small-town culture — it's not fair to have the best of both worlds. You've got to make a choice. And because tabs can't be kept on comers-and-goers, if you leave, the door shuts behind you.

"Not for too long," I say.

Ollie holds out a newspaper for me to see.

"Taylor Caught Her Killer" is the headline.

"Can you let it go now?" he says.

I look at him, my first guy friend, who still helps my mom with yard work when I'm not around. *Are you serious?* I want to yell. *She didn't "catch her killer," Ollie. She's dead. And being called a hero is a twisted consolation prize.* Instead, I pretend interest in the sketch on the telephone pole. I'd been prepared to see anyone up there. Mr. Dougie, the Armstrong vet — even Ollie. It would've been a shock, but also not.

When Armstrong was in lockdown those first few days after Taylor's murder, some men in town were angry that they'd been brought in for questioning. It was disrespectful, they thought, to implicate them in such a horrific event. They didn't imagine that this is how women live, wondering which good guys have a bad side and if they'll use it.

"Can I buy you a slush?" Ollie asks.

Like he has since grade eight, Ollie holds the door for me as we enter Short Stop.

After we grab slushes, we walk in silence, passing the flowerbed he found me in twenty years ago, shirt off, face down in the dirt.

"At least now you can stop wandering around Armstrong with a microphone, like a weirdo," he says.

I look at him and want to roll my eyes. I've yet to approach a single person about the documentary.

"It's a terrible tragedy," he says. "No one wants to talk about it."

How nice it must be, to think violence is a mess that can be tidied up. To not notice — everywhere you go — all the stains and frayed ends and scarring. I'd like to unleash on him but I don't have the energy to deal with his hurt feelings. He's a good guy too, like all the boys from high school probably turned out to be.

"I've got to check on Mom, Ollie," I say, hoping for a quick escape.

"I'll walk you."

"I'm fine."

I say goodbye and head back through town. But, on my way home, it feels like a wound I've been ignoring has split open. And as I turn into the cul-de-sac, old blood starts to seep out through my shirt.

What had happened to us, back then? What had they done? Was there a single sexual encounter that felt mutual, shared? With the language I have now, like *coercion* and *fawning*, the answer is no.

But the words *rape* and *assault* were saved for struggle and screaming. And we'd allowed it, a lot of the time, their ineptitude. Sometimes we even forced it upon ourselves. So, what's that called? Their demands on my body. The physical pain. My assumptions they had the right to it. No pleasure — ever. What is the name for this?

1993

THREE WEEKS AFTER THE HALLOWEEN PARTY, Max still hadn't returned to school. At the end of the day on Friday I didn't know where Aimes and Bugsy were and Cristal had left for her first away-game tournament, so I walked home by myself, made a plate of crackers and cheese, and plunked onto the couch, waiting for *Oprah* to start. I thought about calling Max again but she didn't pick up the phone the other two times I'd tried and her parents were curt when taking my messages.

The kitchen door slammed shut. Grum followed Mom into the living room and she turned off the TV, motioning for Grum to sit down beside me. I made room and Mom got onto her knees in front of us and put her hands on our thighs, as if taking communion. That's when I knew the cancer had returned.

"I'm sorry you guys," she said. "I tried to do everything I could but there are a few more tumours in my armpit."

She looked at me, something she didn't do much anymore because of my nose rings.

"How long have you known?" I said.

"Just before Halloween. I wanted you guys to have a fun night."

"Well, you should have bought me a Sega Genesis then," Grum said. His voice was changing. He had pimples on his nose and chin.

Mom smiled and clambered up onto the couch between us. She put her arms around our shoulders and squeezed us in to her.

"My kidlets," she said.

We leaned our heads on her shoulders. I started to free fall but then, like a cloak, calmness descended. *I'll do better this time*, I thought. *I'll help her get well.*

"That's not all the news," she said, her eyes back on me. "Your dad is moving to town."

I ducked out of her one-armed hug. I'd known that our fight about the nose piercing in the kitchen a month prior had pushed her over the edge but I had no idea she'd been scheming.

"I have to focus everything I have on myself right now," she said. "So I can get better for good."

"Where's Grum going?" I asked.

She looked to the carpet. "Grum's staying here, with me."

I knew I was supposed to be angry, that she was expecting me to yell, but I didn't have it in me.

"Dad agreed?" I asked.

After calling any place we'd ever lived "a shithole full of rednecks" I was surprised he'd be willing to move to Armpit, BC.

"He's rented a cabin in Vernon, just outside of town. He's going to start building up his new therapy practice. He's excited for the change."

"What are you going to do?" I asked.

"I'll do chemo again and it'll work this time," she said. "I mean it Em. I'm not going to die. Give me six months and I'll be rid of it. I promise."

Grum side-eyed me. "I get her room."

"I'm not moving out," I said.

I wouldn't leave the girls. Even if our time together was rare, they still held my guts in place.

"I'm not asking you to move out," Mom said. "You can live here on school days. I just want you to stay with him on the weekends. Your dad misses you and you've only got two years left before graduation. He's finally realized that this is his last chance to be a real dad."

I hated it when she disguised shit.

"So it's a coincidence that Dad's moving to town?" I said.

"It's good timing," she said.

"Did you ask him to move here?"

"We decided, together," she said.

I knew full well they'd never *decided* anything together – not even to have me.

"When does chemo start?" Grum asked.

"Next month," she said. "I'll do radiation in Vernon and then I'll have to travel back to Vancouver. They're gonna really nuke me this time."

Cristal walked me to school on Monday and I told her the news.

"Why are you even here today?" she asked me. "I want to go home just thinking about your mom being sick again."

"'Cause you wouldn't be there," I said.

She smiled, the first she'd offered me in a while.

All four of us huddled up in the student centre long after the last bell. It was instinctual, to gather like this. I hadn't bothered to tell Aimes and Bugsy about Mom's recurrence, figuring we could only handle so many heavy things at once. One of the group was injured and we were all feeling it. We really missed Max.

"Remember when she was singing during softball and a second base runner smashed into her, and her shoulder dislocated, and she just kept *tra-la-la-*ing?" Aimes said.

"Do you think she's as naive as she acts?" Bugsy said. "Or is she smarter than all of us combined?"

"Both," Cristal said. "She's a childlike genius."

"When is she coming back to school?" I asked.

As the stares and whispers started to filter into our circle I again noticed the usefulness of being able to feel two things at once. I was worried for my friend, and also, her absence made us visible again.

"She got out of the hospital a week ago." Aimes said. "My mom talked to her mom. That's all I know."

"Why was she in there so long in the first place?" Cristal asked.

"I think she just wanted a rest."

———

The following weekend Armstrong was blanketed in two feet of snow. Grum grabbed his GT snow racer, too small for his long legs, and ran across to the school hill to start building a jump. Mom sat at the kitchen table, tired after her first radiation treatment in Vernon the day before.

"This might be a good day for you to go to Dad's," she said.

The weekend before, he'd moved into his small cabin down a dirt road about thirty minutes away. We'd had him over for dinner once but I'd yet to see his new place.

"I've got to memorize for drama finals this weekend."

"You can do that at Dad's," she said.

"They're in only three months and I've got to win."

"He's already on his way to pick you up."

I didn't argue. In the bush, when Mom would tell us to clean the chicken coop or pick rocks, sometimes we'd forget who we were dealing with and jump on our bikes or start climbing the brush pile and she'd blindside us with a scream and a wooden spoon. This was one of those times she'd take no shit.

I slept at Dad's on both Friday and Saturday night, in a sleeping bag on the unfinished loft floor. Sunday morning I peered over the loft to see Dad still snoring on the pullout so I crawled down the ladder and found a box of Rice Krispies in a cupboard. Opening the fridge, I sniffed the milk and tipped the cereal into a bowl. As I dipped my spoon to take a bite, the winter sun streamed into my eyes, and just as I brought it to my mouth, the spoon came into focus, alive with tiny worms pouring off the sides and dropping into the milk below.

I phoned Mom.

"There's no food here," I said. "Or toilet paper."

She picked me up, citing "woman problems," and we giggled on the way home as I told her about the maggots.

"Well, nothing's changed since I lived with him," she said. "He'll always be a mountain man."

"Do I have to go back?" I asked.

"Next weekend," she said. "Before radiation. I can only rest when I know where you are."

When Max came back to school on a Monday after a month's absence, she was different and she didn't try to hide it. Her face was swollen. Her chest looked taut — like if I poked a pin in her boob, water would burst out. We threw our arms around her and we kissed her on her cheeks but Max was lacklustre. She didn't smile when Bugsy did the chipmunk face. She didn't play along when Aimes hid her pencil case.

"Give me my fucking pencils," she said.

But the biggest and worst difference was that she avoided spending time with us. As the week progressed, she hid from us as well as she used to hide from Trent. She carried her backpack with her all day so she didn't have to meet us at the lockers between classes, and she ate her lunch in the counsellor's office, by herself. I wanted her back.

After the last bell on Wednesday, we were sitting in the concourse, hands tucked inside our coats as the buses rolled up. Max was farther down the benches, where she could see her bus arriving.

"Oh no," I heard her say.

Trent was walking toward her. He'd graduated, but he still showed up weekly for his job refilling the vending machines. Max rose and turned. He jogged to catch up with her. He touched her back and she stopped. We couldn't hear what he said. We only saw their bodies. His head dipped. She smiled. He reached for her hand. She let him take it. He pulled her closer. She flipped her hair like she did when she was uncomfortable. I saw her trying to find any reason to get away, but also not being able to say no, and in this struggle I also saw myself.

Cristal's lighter was on the bench beside me. I grabbed it and stood up.

"Watch me," I said.

Trent had corralled Max over to some benches farther away, where they sat down. I walked toward them. His arm was around her, his thumb looped through her baggy jeans. Her hair was long and flat and he lifted it up and watched it fall. I was directly behind them now. He leaned in and whispered in her ear and she giggled and pulled away. The closer he tried to get to her, the stiffer she became.

I flicked the lighter and held the flame under her hair. There was a poof of black smoke. Then stink. Max screamed. She grabbed her head, not knowing what had happened. I smacked her back and neck with my hands, trying to put out her smoking hair. People started to laugh and point. Max turned around and saw me, her eyes shocked like an animal's. She grabbed at her hair and pulled it off the nape of her neck into a bunch, clenching it, then she dropped her face to her knees.

"Do you like her now?" I said to him, but not at him.

"Do you like her now?" I repeated, because what else could I do?

Trent pulled his hat low on his head, ducked and bolted for his truck.

The girls ran toward us. Max patted the hair around her face, to make sure the fire was out. A long shock had burned off. I didn't know it would happen that quickly. The flame had flown up her hair as fast as lightning strikes down. She'd needed my help; I was trying to save her but I also wanted to destroy.

The girls surrounded Max.

"Are you okay?" Bugsy leaned in and touched Max's scalp.

Max clutched her head, rocking.

"Why'd you do that?" Aimes said.

"I was trying to help," I said. "She wanted rid of him. Now he's gone."

I felt equally horrible and righteous in the act.

Max began to cry. She was angry. But more than that, I could tell she was humiliated. She didn't like being the centre of attention. It was what she avoided most and now her burnt hair was stinking up the entire concourse and she was the star of the shit show. She grabbed her bag and ran for the bus as it pulled up to the curb. I watched her climb on and the girls surrounded me, confused, not sure where to place their alliance.

All eyes in the concourse had turned to me. Seb stepped forward. He hadn't seen the act but he'd been part of the aftermath of the laughter and kids holding their noses from the stench.

"You lit Max's hair on fire," he said.

"Yeah," I said.

"Is that the girl Trent is fucking?" he asked.

"Not anymore," I said.

———

I was surprised when Max showed up for school the next day. Her parents must've made her come. The girls and I spent the day trailing her, scanning the back of her head in the hallways, looking for a bald spot, but her hair seemed to fall fine and look normal.

Previous fissures in our friendship had hurt, but this act spider-veined in all directions. That week, Max stopped bathing. She started wearing her flannel pajamas to school. She looked at the floor when she walked through the halls and didn't speak up in class, only short answers when necessary. I was conflicted because I'd solved her problem. Trent was gone. He preferred docile, not a fire starter, and the wildness of my action had been too much for him.

But I also knew that lighting her hair on fire hadn't just been charity on my part. I'd profited and was now enjoying the attention from being so bold that even the remaining members of the Brew Crew watched me at a distance. This new sense of impunity was stronger than the hurt I'd caused my friend, so I didn't push her to make up. She'd come around. Her hair was still the longest. When we gathered around the lockers at the end of each day, a shift in power was evident. No one spoke of it, but intended or not, I'd become pack leader.

AFTER A SHORT WEEKEND VISIT, Grum backs his truck out of Mom's driveway and hits the lilac bush, cracking off a branch. I put the blossoms to my nose and turn to the house, bringing her favourite smell inside with me. Mom's been bustling around these past few days, almost as if Christie and me shacking up has given her a surge of new energy. Like when you rub two dead batteries together, sometimes you generate a few more hours of charge. Qi, as she calls it, and Nell, the fake Chinese medicine doctor from down the street, says she's got more of it now that she's upped her appointments to twice a day.

Just as I turn on the kettle, the carport door opens and Mom climbs the stairs to the landing. I move the lilacs to make a scented boundary between us.

"Nell has some new intel," Mom says, blowing her nose into the corner of a tea towel. "Her eldest works for the Armstrong RCMP."

"Nell is a gossip and quite possibly a fraud," I say.

Having hitched a ride in with the flowers, a few displaced ants are trying to run across the kitchen table to freedom and I flick them into oblivion.

"You've heard how hundreds of tips have come in?" she says, grinning like Bugsy used to on a Monday after a pit party.

Two weeks after the wanted posters went up in Armstrong, they spread across the entire Okanagan Valley. It was unpleasant to see this crude drawing everywhere, at a fruit stand or in the change room at the public pool, but the assumption was that if he attacked three women in the area, he must be from around here and eventually someone would recognize him.

"Nell just told me the news," Mom says, throwing her coat on the couch, clicking on the TV. "Have you heard?"

"No, what news?"

"He's been caught."

The line drawing takes over the screen and the video cuts to a flat, shabby motel with a reporter detailing how this was where the accused had holed up.

A photograph of the man appears in the top right portion of the TV and his image looks remarkably like the police sketch.

"I don't understand," I say. "They found him?"

"Yes," Mom says. "He's been arrested."

Mom cranks the volume and I rush back to the kitchen to turn off the whistling kettle. After spending so many months looking over my shoulder – this is how it happens? Today is the day, just like that? The events unfolding in front of us feel both sinister and anticlimactic.

"The killer's father. He lives in Cherryville," Mom says, repeating what she's hearing off the news.

I rush back, balancing two steeping cups of tea. A reporter stands in front of a small, shuttered house. An older man tries to cover his face with his hands as he's pushed into the back of a police car. The segment cuts to the newsroom and a picture of Taylor in her bronze prom dress, then to her mother, Marie, giving an interview at the Vernon courthouse, microphones in her face, questions being yelled off camera. The TV cuts back to the news-room again and I lower onto the edge of the couch. After hearing of his son's capture, the father cooperated with the police. He admitted to lying about an alibi. He'd bought his son fake identification so that he could escape the province. He'd suggested a jumbled social insurance number when his son applied for a job.

Mom asks for milk in her tea and I jump up, happy for the distraction.

"I love my children but I wouldn't do that for you," she yells.

I don't know why I'm not glued to the TV. After six months in suspension, now I can't stop moving. Opening a cupboard, I search for cookies.

"He was well known," Mom yells.

"Who, the father or the murderer?"

"The murderer." Mom listens for a moment. "The girl he tried to rape six years ago recognized him. She'd ID'd him correctly before, but his dad gave a fake alibi then too."

A sourness rises in my throat, that a father is given more credit than a girl.

I bring in the milk and a roll of Hobnobs on a tray, as a quote from the father to his son when he was in hiding ticker-tapes across the bottom of the screen: *Stay away. It's hotter than a firecracker here.* The camera pans back to the reporter standing in front of the father's house, a police cruiser driving away as reporters run after it. The anchor wraps up by explaining that now there will be two trials — one for the serial rapist and murderer and another for his dad.

Mom and I look at each other. She pushes herself to standing and walks to the front door. Unlocking it, she unlatches the screen and hip-checks the mesh till it pops free. Cold air rushes inside as Mom yells "Good riddance to bad rubbish!" into the cul-de-sac for everyone to hear.

———————————

The change to Armstrong is striking and immediate. As if a lid has lifted off our valley, bright light floods the streets, a hyper-colour that makes us squint. We must look like a town of foals, wobbling around on too-long legs, engaging in a bit of prancing but mostly stunned. The murderer is hand-cuffed, in jail without bail, waiting for trial. We've seen the photos.

Like everyone else, Mom is further energized by the confirmation that Armstrong can return to itself. She focuses on her caloric intake and physical health. She ups her appointments with Nell, the pretend Chinese medicine practitioner, who tells her that lung cancer is related to unprocessed grief, and for Mom to have any hope of living long enough to meet her grandchil-dren, she must "work harder at being happy." I tell Mom that this statement is an oxymoron and she tells me that she won't tolerate any more negative ions in her house.

Across town the wanted posters are ripped down. They disappear one night and are never seen again, not in a recycling bin or under the tire of a parked car. Even the staples are taken out of the telephone poles. Engines rev as kids open up their garages and start to tinker under their hoods. Short Stop returns to its late-night hours and Tuckers takes down its For Sale sign and reopens for weekend dining. The church ladies have met and decided to reclaim Armstrong. Under the leadership of Taylor's mom, Marie, they will build a walking trail along the tracks in Taylor's honour. They'll start by tearing out all the dead brush and planting bright perennials. They want to hang strings of lights above the path so that the trail feels safe to walk, day or night. There will be a monument placed at the spot where Taylor was found, with pictures of her with her friends and family lacquered to it. Armstrong will pay for it all.

As the days get longer and warmer, construction on the trail begins. Money is raised and plants are donated and a fence is built. But however close Mom and her friends get to the tracks, a line of little old ladies on their knees, digging up roots and tearing out brambles – no one steps onto the rails. Not adult or child, not for rebellion or a Sunday stroll. And even though the new lights that hang along the fenceline are bright, they don't penetrate the shade that edges the path.

––––––––––

I don't use the trail. And one afternoon I decide to follow the old rails out of town – toward the heat shimmers that bend the distant rails – to catch summer's arrival in full. Daisies already dead along the gravel edges. Dandelions, my familiars, thick and strong. The Nootka roses have almost broken their buds, light pink flesh peeking through green bodices. The lupines already high like weeds.

I'm stopped. There is a group of girls on the sidewalk at the junction where the tracks meet the road. They look young, maybe twelve or thirteen, their feet too large for their legs. There are four of them, huddled together around a bench. If one glances across the street she's going to see a middle-aged woman hiding in the high grass holding a chihuahua, so I cross the road to pass by them, pretending nonchalance. I smell hairspray. One of them pulls out lip gloss. They scuttle down Rosedale Avenue toward the park and once they're around the corner, I double back to inspect the bench they were gathered around. Excel gum and an empty pack of smokes have been left behind. I head home to tell Mom that I might have a radio doc to make after all.

Balancing iced tea and an egg salad sandwich on a tray, I find her sleeping on the wicker couch downstairs, the sun shining across the lower half of her face and a dry snore coming from the back of her throat. Depending on her weekly white blood cell count and if she's stable enough for chemo, my twice-monthly trips have increased. I don't keep track anymore. Slow mornings lead into a doctor's appointment and a few errands. An afternoon nap and a light lunch are usually followed by an evening fight, and when the heat lessens we try to pull a few weeds before bedtime. I've not yet felt the clarity I was told will come when it's time to move home, so I assume it's not time yet. She stirs when the sunbeam hits her eyes and as she sits up I pass her the sandwich and tea.

"Are there flax seeds in this bread?" she says, pulling a bite out of her mouth.

"I don't know."

"Flax pokes through my enzyme barrier," she says, spitting the bread onto the plate. "It gives me leaky gut. I won't eat it."

"Fine," I say, "but there's no more bread in the house."

"It's all connected, Em," she says. "A flax seed could take away one of my days."

Her neck is crepe-like ribbons and I want to reach out and stroke it. How is it possible to feel such revulsion and ache at the same time?

I decide that now's finally the right time to start the interviews I've been putting off and after two more weeks of keeping my eyes peeled for the group of girls, I find a half-finished slush cup and another empty pack of smokes on the bench. It seems always around the same time each day that they meet at the corner of Okanagan and Rosedale and travel a few blocks more than the last time. As summer peaks and the light stays longer, the girls stretch their legs all the way down to the fairgrounds, leaning against the fence of the outdoor pool, their shin guards still on from soccer, but still, I don't approach them. Heads down in a tight pod, they take the long way through town, on the sidewalks only.

Because of the heat, Mom wants to nap longer into the afternoon, so I adventure along the rails farther than I've ever gone before, past the gulley with the rusted-out cars at the bottom of it. There's a patch of the yellow flowers that Max used to collect when we'd go walking and talking. I crouch and take a photo and text it to her, an old number, and I don't expect a reply. She probably lives in another country. That was her plan. After college, we'd worked on some art projects together, but there had been an escalation of fights until the worst one six years ago. It was late at night and Max was yelling at me from across my apartment kitchen table. She said I was a shitty friend. She told me that I was selfish, just like my dad. She'd looked at me with her polar-ice eyes and smirked, knowing how much that would hurt. The next morning, she behaved like we hadn't fought and I wondered if I'd made it all up, but we haven't talked since. Maybe it had taken her this long to get mad at me. I'm Facebook friends with Aimes and Bugsy and we wish each other happy birthday. Cristal keeps me at a distance. I heard she moved to the woods, with her partner and their dog. The only way to move on was to let go.

I slip my phone into my pocket and turn toward home. I've walked for almost two hours and heard only birdsong. Even though I'm glad that the Armstrong girls are leaving their houses bit by bit, my solitude is confirmation that the tracks are gone for good.

Late summer, we heard rumour of a trial date being set. It's scheduled for over two years from now. I catch Marie on TV speaking to the reporters about her desire for a swift first-degree murder charge. The news coverage amps up again but the story seems to be transitioning to pulp as reporters have a new frenzy to attach to: what he plans to plead. Rumour is he's claiming to have been drunk and on drugs the night he killed Taylor, therefore unaccountable, with no planned motive. I think about Marie as I drag Midge on our daily walk, but I don't dare call her. What would I say? *I'm sorry your daughter was killed. I just want you to know that her place was my place too.*

If Taylor's innocence was forcibly removed, Armstrong's is eroding at a slower pace. My initial impression of a new beginning came too soon. The few restaurants are open again, but we're not returning to normal as hoped, and an irritable resentment has set in. It feels unfair that we can't just be a country town with a main drag and high school named Pleasant Valley anymore. Now, we shop and go to church in a place where a girl can get beaten and strangled to death at 6 p.m. on a Monday night.

IT WAS JANUARY WHEN MOM LEFT for a month of chemotherapy in Vancouver. The roads were clear and the sky a bright winter blue. We were doing better these days. In her instinct to put herself first, I felt closer to her. I still didn't want to move out but I didn't want to have to beg to be allowed to stay either, so I was hoping when she came back from chemo she'd renege on the decision that I had to live at Dad's part-time. After we waved her off, Grum wiped his eyes with the back of his hand and jumped on his bike, headed to a sleepover at his buddy's house.

"Be back by tomorrow night," I yelled after him.

I ran back inside and called Bugsy.

"Mom's just left for chemo. We're having a party tonight. Tell everyone."

I drew myself a bath in the clawfoot tub just off the kitchen and waited for it to fill with bubbles. I had the weekend before Dad came to get Grum and I. He'd just moved into a house with his girlfriend and her kids in Vernon and he wanted to show me my new room. But he'd had something new to show me every few months of my life and I couldn't keep up, so I shoved the plan to the back of my head to deal with after I threw the party of the year. Since I lit Max's hair on fire, something in me had toughened. Or maybe it was her rejection of me that had forced the shift. I felt detached and floaty now, and when Mom had backed out of the driveway I'd felt none of the usual worry.

I stepped into the tub. I didn't know who'd be coming or if anyone would be interested, but my hoo-ha would be ready. Stretching out, above me was a dusty light fixture, and I was brought back to the day we moved in. Grum jumping into the large empty tub and proclaiming, "Em, we could raise ducks in here." At the trailer, our hot water tank was delicate enough that we only took a bath once a week, and shared the same water. Mom went first because she liked it hot, then me because I was a girl, and Grum got the cold-dead-skin-soup finale. Tonight, I stretched out along the porcelain, my head and toes barely touching either end, and I let the bubbles rise up past my ears to hear them crinkle.

After my float, I soaped up my crotch and scrubbed it like I was washing a potato. Ever since having sex, I'd become vigilant in vaginal hygiene. At camp, I'd carried scented personal wipes in my backpack at all times, just in case Doug wanted a quickie in the woods. When I showered, I lifted a leg onto the side of the tub so that I could get in there with a loofa. At school I washed up with wet paper towel and liquid soap every time I peed, and I'd taken to finding empty classrooms several times a day where I could do a quick check. The problem was that no matter how much I scoured, my vagina still smelled off to me. It was like the skin itself was leaching odour. Imagine if some dumbass like Windex cornered me in the gym and tried to cram his hands down my pants and they came out smelling like fish?

An hour later, Bugsy, Cristal and Aimes arrived first, banging through the breezeway.

"Are you sure you want to throw a party Sym?" Aimes asked, kicking her winter boots across the kitchen.

"Why not?" Bugsy said, unravelling from her scarf. "It's the perfect time. She's got all weekend to clean up."

Cristal sat on the wicker couch. "Can we lock your mom's door, so no one can get inside her room?"

"It's Armstrong," I said. "I'll kick out any skids who don't listen."

"I've told Timmy and he's told his crew," Aimes said.

"And Jimmy and his brothers are coming," Bugsy said.

"Do you think Max will come?" I asked.

"Do you think the sky is made of cotton candy?" Bugsy said. "She's in bed with her Walkman on."

Usually her absence would've had me anxious and counting in even numbers for an hour but tonight it didn't bother me.

At 7 p.m. we plunked ourselves down around the kitchen table and started taking shots from Mom's china teacups, and at some point we moved onto the porch to watch the sun set.

"See. No cotton candy sky," Bugsy said.

The booze warmed me. Was this what being an adult felt like? Not giving a shit? Reaching for the mickey, I knocked it over and it spilled across the floorboards of the porch.

"Shit balls Sym," Cristal said and ran to the kitchen for a dishtowel.

My head was getting heavy and harder to turn. I let my eyes fall and the noises began to encircle us. The crunch of tires on snow. The slam of a truck door. Cowboy boots on ice. The back door opening and slamming shut. Bugsy ran to greet the guests but Aimes and I stayed put, smoking and ashing into the teacups. A yell. The Offspring turned on in the living room. The porch was in complete darkness now, just the cherries of the smokes showing. We were drunk and it was hard to stand. There was a crash. I didn't care.

Eventually Aimes and I stumbled into the front foyer. All the lights in the house were on and from this vantage point, my house wasn't mine anymore. People I didn't recognize were packed into the living room, dirty boots standing on my mom's circular green rug. Looking into the dining room was even more confusing: some people were leaning against the glass doors where Mom kept her pottery and others sat on her dining room table flicking bottle caps at the chandelier above them. An older girl sat her ass down on the piano keys and her friend joined in. I didn't know them and didn't dare tell them to stop. I turned back to the foyer and Aimes was gone.

Cristal emerged from the kitchen, weaving toward me. She grabbed my hand and we charged through the house, pushing past men wearing oilskin coats and girls sitting on their laps.

"Do you know any of these people?" I asked.

"No idea," she yelled.

We ran up to my room. It was empty. I opened the curtains and looked outside to see our snowy yard filled with cars, the driveway boxed in by trucks and people on flatbeds jumping, making the hydraulics bounce.

"I'm fucked," I said.

We heard yelling downstairs and I took the steep attic steps two at a time. I ran into the kitchen to see boys holding each other off. A punch was thrown.

"Get outside," someone yelled.

"Shut up, ya townie," said a man inside the circle of rowdies.

"Who are you?" Ollie yelled back. I was surprised to see him here. I hadn't seen him in months, even at school. "Go outside if you wanna fight," he said pushing the man roughly through the door. "Not in Judy's house."

I couldn't help but smile, imagining Mom, in Vancouver by now, proud of Ollie for looking out for her.

"Bugsy, what the fuck?" Cristal screamed from Mom's bedroom. "Get out of here."

I ran to the bedroom and saw Bugsy and Jimmy pulling up their pants, his muddy boots on her cream carpet.

"I fucking told you," Cristal said, trying to make my mother's bed.

There was a mickey of gin, unfinished, on Mom's bedside table. I chugged it, not wanting to know what happened next.

The noise got louder. Not sure how I climbed the stairs, I leaned over the toilet and heaved. It was nice here, my cheek resting on the bowl. Something began to tickle me. A spider. I pushed it away. I puked again and the crawling sensation returned, climbing up and around my breasts. Hands. I puked again and the fingers began to tug at my tits like a baby goat. Shoving them away again, I missed the toilet and puked on the wall. I raised up onto my knees to try and hit the toilet at a better angle. The hands jumped off my wet boobs and I felt the fingers travel down toward my crotch. *See, you just never know*, I thought, relieved that I'd remembered to scrub up earlier that afternoon.

I woke up in bed with Cristal on the floor, the sun streaming through my windows.

"Shit balls," I moaned.

She laughed.

Flashes from last night: A fight. Bugsy and Jimmy screwing in my mom's bed. Heaving like a cat while someone snatched at me. I couldn't draw up a face and was glad not to know. I rolled out of bed, contemplating this new layer of callus I felt inside.

I got up to pee and Grum's bedroom door was shut, which was odd. I tried to open it. It wasn't locked but barricaded somehow. I pushed my shoulder against the door and it opened a crack.

My bravado crashed. Who'd hide in a thirteen-year-old's bedroom?

"Who's in there?" I said.

"Em?" Grum's voice answered.

"Grum, it's me," I said. "Open up."

I heard him moving furniture and he opened the door, looking tired.

"I thought you were having a sleepover?"

"I changed my mind," he said. "I missed Mom so I wanted to come home."

Standing there, hand on the doorknob, I realized what must have happened and what he might have seen.

"What were you thinking?"

He started to cry, my little brother, now taller than me.

I looked farther into his room to see the TV balanced on his twin bed, plugged into the wall.

"So I wouldn't get bored," he said.

"I'm sorry, Grum," I said.

"You're gonna kill her you know."

Grum, Cristal and I picked our way downstairs, surveying the damage. There were beer cans everywhere and some broken glasses. I'd have to mop the walls, but no windows had been broken, or furniture. It would take me the weekend to clean up but nothing was permanent. We walked through the breezeway to have a smoke and Grum trailed behind us. The armoire that held all of our winter gear was open. He looked inside.

"They stole everything," he said.

"What?"

He opened the chest that sat beside the armoire, more storage for winter boots. It had been emptied too.

"Our cross-country skis, my GT snow racer – all gone," he said.

Nothing was left, not a single second-hand Gore-Tex jacket or crappy pair of Sorels. Our basket that held handmade mittens and all of Mom's scarves and tams had been taken too. I pushed through to the back of the armoire. They even took my grandmother's fake fur. Mom had a deer-hide jacket from the Arctic that she was planning to donate to a museum. This was where she'd stored her dead father's long johns. Every piece of warm clothing we'd ever owned was gone.

————

Mom got a phone call early that morning. I hadn't thought that she could be reached at the Easter Seals House but they had a direct line and an hour before her first chemo treatment she took a call from our neighbour, who'd never forgiven me for The Unsolved Case of the Eggs in the Baby's Room. The woman stood on our side porch, smiling, hair unbrushed, the stupid kid on her hip, as she delivered the news.

"Your mother says you are to go to your dad's and not come back," she said, giving the toddler a bounce. "She said you're to clean the house, pack your room and be gone by tomorrow."

I tried to shut the door.

"Your mother has cancer and you threw a party," she said. "You should be ashamed of yourself."

I turned away. I didn't feel bad. My skin was thick.

I cleaned up the best I could, washing all the surfaces with vinegar and spot washing boot prints off the pillow shams. I vacuumed the furniture and floors and took a soft cloth to the chandelier, polishing every piece of cut glass. But I didn't pack up my room like she'd asked me to. Instead, I locked it, called Dad to tell him we were ready to go and waited downstairs with a garbage bag of clothes and a Ziploc bag with deodorant, a toothbrush, mascara and lipstick stuffed inside.

Dad pulled up just as Grum and I were walking out of the breezeway. In his car, I sat with the garbage bag on my lap. She'd kicked me out and she didn't want to talk about it. I looked up to my bedroom windows, dark, dead wisteria hanging on, and I began to cry.

"It's hard being a shit disturber isn't it?" Dad said.

I nodded.

"You were being a kid, having fun, and it got out of hand." He skidded out of the driveway onto Pleasant Valley Road. "I bought you a dresser at the auction and a four-poster bed," he said. "The rug is one of those Oriental ones, so it looks pretty fancy in your new room."

I wiped my eyes as he took the highway out of Armstrong.

"If you stay with me for more than three months, I'll buy you your own car," he said.

"That sounds like a bribe."

"Call it what you like, I want my daughter to live with me."

"But I have to get myself to school on Monday."

"Okay, fine," he said. "I'll buy you a car this weekend."

I smiled.

"A car with a sunroof?"

That Monday morning at school, I walked Cristal around my new 1980 Honda Accord. No sunroof, but I was the first of my friends to get her own vehicle.

"I can pick you up for school now," I said.

"Nah," Cristal said, circling the car.

"But you picked me up for years, now it's my turn."

"It's not the same thing."

As winter broke to spring, I drove the stretch of highway between Vernon and Armstrong twice a day. If I went twenty over the limit I could get to school in just under fifteen minutes. Dad's rule was that I had to be home at 6 p.m. every night, so I was free for a few hours after school and on some days the girls and I returned to the tracks, pulled by the verdant green emerging along the rails.

"Do you ever bring guys up here?" Aimes asked.

"No. Never," Bugsy said and flicked her half-smoked cigarette onto the ground.

Cristal looked at the unfinished cigarette lying between the rails, a waft of smoke rising, and shook her head as if to say *what a waste*.

"Bringing a guy up here would be like sucking dick in a church," said Aimes.

We laughed but Aimes was right. No matter how far we'd gone in stretching the pact — or in my case, completely breaking it — no one dared to screw around with the sanctity of this place.

Cristal looked at her watch and jumped up.

"Time to head," she said. "DQ."

Cristal hopped on her bike and rode down the embankment toward her new after-school job. Aimes and Bugsy, who were applying lipstick, followed, on their way to the park where J and T were smoking cigarettes, waiting for them.

"LYLAS," I said and turned toward Rosedale, where I'd parked my car, to drive in the opposite direction of home.

———————

By the end of grade ten, with all the back-and-forth to Dad's, and travelling to out-of-town drama competitions, I had less and less time to spend with the girls. They didn't seem to notice my absence. Bugsy and Aimes were in the bathroom every break, Aimes trying to console a sobbing Bugsy after Jimmy had broken it off for no good reason. Now that I drove, without the daily pick-ups and drop-offs from Cristal, our time together wasn't guaranteed either. So when Bugsy invited me to a party at her cousin's house as an afterthought, I agreed immediately. I scrubbed up with a soapy washcloth, stepped into a new crushed velvet bodysuit and high-rise jeans, and drove myself to the address.

Bugsy found me coming out of the bathroom and we each chugged two beers to loosen up. I didn't know anyone, which made me less concerned, and I started to feel the beat of the music in my ass and spine. Heading outside for a smoke, we ran into Cristal and Aimes, and we all laughed uncomfortably at the impromptu reunion. I grabbed two folding chairs from the side of the house and wiped the cobwebs off them.

"For my girls," I said, placing the chairs behind Bugsy and Cristal for them to sit in.

Bugsy giggled and sat down but Cristal looked away.

"We miss you, Sym," Aimes said, dropping into the chair.

"I miss you too, Aimes," I said. "I'm coming home soon. Mom's done chemo now, so I'm hoping to be back by the end of the month."

I could feel Cristal roll her eyes. I'd been using the same line for three months now. Mom had never yelled at me, and the few times I'd shown up to grab clothes, she'd made me dinner, but I'd not slept in my own bed since the chemo party.

"Holy shit is that Twyla?" Bugsy leapt up and pointed through the mess of kids at a girl with a high, bleached-out ponytail, standing next to the trampoline.

"Yeah, she's got a boyfriend from Vernon now," Aimes said. "He must not know about her slut baggage."

Jimmy and Timmy pushed through the screen door and Bugsy became distracted, so I headed over to the trampoline with a cider to watch the drunk kids bounce. Twyla sidled up next to me, the same type of cider in her hand, raspberry dazzle.

"Do you go to PVSS still?" she asked.

"Yeah," I said, getting out of the way of a double bounce.

"I never see you with your crew anymore."

"Well, you're gone too," I said. "I haven't seen you in science for weeks."

"I've just been with Ben. Cuddling up. Ya know?"

"So all you do is lay in bed all day and screw?" I said.

"No, we just cuddle," she said again. "He's a cuddler."

I looked to Ben, shaggy hair and a big smile, and realized I didn't know what cuddling with a boy felt like. Turning away, I found a half-drunk beer on the grass and I finished it. Someone handed me a plastic cup full of something sweet and I chugged that too. I swayed, looking back to the party, and heard the first heavy beats of "Zombie" come from the living room. It was time to dance – I needed all eyes on me, to be sure that I was still here.

I followed the music up the stairs to the back deck. I couldn't see the ground anymore—it was dark out and I was too high up—just the flickering lights of town in the distance. Dizzy, I rested my head on the cool metal railing, and out came the first few stars. I ralphed. Hands came up from behind me. I didn't bother trying to push them away this time, too sick to care. But the hands surprised me and instead of heading toward my breasts, they grabbed my braids. The hands held each braid up and away from my face as I puked. It was the most romantic gesture I'd ever felt, to have these hands hold my hair back as I hurled onto the sagebrush below.

After a while I slid down the glass wall onto the deck. The boy who held my braids smelled good, like car freshener. His hair was strawberry blond.

Squinting, I was taken aback to see that he was not a boy at all, but a man, broad shouldered, with stubble and pockmarked cheeks, like a sports hero. He looked about twenty-six.

He patted my head. "What's your name?"

"Emmy," I said.

"Well Emmy, you're too cute for your own good."

I leaned into him.

I woke up in the passengers seat of someone's car and the man was beside me, his hands running up and down my bodysuit, trying to find an opening. I slipped myself out of the top to give him boob access as a gift for being such a gentleman. He pulled the bodysuit down past my belly and over my butt. Not what I'd intended. I was tired. I had school tomorrow.

No, I might have said.

He was kissing me, hard and sloppy and his mouth tasted of smoke and burps. I turned my head to the side to get a breath as he continued to lick around my chin, like he hadn't noticed where my lips had gone. Not as gallant has he'd been on the balcony.

"Please don't," I tried again.

But he was busy trying to get his pants off while negotiating the gear shift.

What are you gonna do, push him off and crawl through the car window like a shithead, leotard around your ankles? He was on top of me now. His hands holding my torso down, for traction, as he shoved himself inside.

Don't make it a problem, I thought. *Like a day of downhill skiing, just get it done.*

Eventually, he dropped onto me, winded. Now I could go home and sleep. Looking around the interior of the car, I realized it was mine, with the keys in the ignition.

"Drive me to my friends' house," he said, as he did up his pants.

Leaving was easier than going back inside to find the girls, so I backed out of the driveway onto the highway. He lit a smoke as I gunned it along a straight stretch. Past the town limits, I shut my eyes. If I didn't crash by the time I got to ten, my mom wouldn't die. I counted evenly, with my eyes shut, and when I opened them, we were fine. Still in my lane. I did it again. Eyes closed. Counted to ten. If we didn't crash, my family would be safe. Good.

Easy. Again. The third time I waited till we rounded a bend and a truck passed by. I counted slowly. My eyes wanted to fling open but I squeezed them shut to make the deal work. This was my last chance. I'd bet my life on it. Eight, nine, ten. Headlights were in front of me. I brought the car back over the centre line. The man kept smoking, not noticing the roulette I'd just played. My whole body went limp. I was back in control.

I pulled up to his buddy's house. The man took a drag on his smoke. "Coming in?"

"Nah," I said. I was exhausted, like a toddler who just fell asleep in her Cheerios.

"I like you," he said, and flicked the cigarette onto the road. "Let's hang out again."

"Sure," I said. "Call me." and I smiled for his sake.

It was shocking how cold I felt inside and how easy that was to hide from him.

Driving up Dad's street, I parked a few houses away so the muffler didn't wake up the house. When I stepped out of the car, I realized I didn't have any shoes on. I grabbed my purse and looked under my seat. They were my favourite pair. Dad had bought them for me in Victoria.

I turned and headed up the centre of the road in my stocking feet. Staying between the streetlamps, I couldn't stop thinking about my silver shoes and where they'd gone. They were metallic silver, with platforms, which made me look taller than I was, but the heels were sturdy, so that I could still run.

———————————

At school that Monday, switching binders between classes, I recapped the party as I hadn't seen the girls since I'd gotten shit-faced and lost my shoes. I was embarrassed by it all, how he'd held my braids, then held me down.

"Twyla was hilarious," I said, hoping to draw them in. "She's got a boyfriend. And he's nice to her."

Max glanced up and I thought I noticed a small smile before she turned away, but Cristal's eyes narrowed as she spun off.

"What's her problem?" I asked.

Bugsy sighed as she watched Cristal walk away.

"Sym, you've been ignoring her for months," she said.

"Not true," I said. "I talk to her non-stop."

"If you're talking about yourself maybe," Aimes said. "Did you ever think that we might have stressful things going on?"

She popped a Starburst and scowled. Aimes had never spoken to me in this tone before, like she was above, commenting down.

"Do you have a mother with cancer who just kicked you out?" I spat back, hoping to sound shark-like, but it came across more like a plea.

Bugsy grabbed me by my shoulders and pushed me toward English class.

"She picked you up and walked you home for years. She helped your mother make dinner while you sucked dick upstairs, and now – ever since you've moved – you've got no time for her."

I stopped in the middle of the hallway and a group of grade eight girls veered to avoid running into me.

"Maybe she should get her own life," I said, not meaning it.

"Your family is part of her life and it's killing her you're not around," Bugsy said.

"You're being a bitch," Aimes said.

"What did you say?"

"You move away, don't call us, and are fucking I-don't-even-know-who?" Aimes hissed through the rush of students.

"We know who she's fucking," Bugsy said. "She went off with my older cousin."

Was that who the man was? They'd been talking about this without me around.

Aimes strode down the hall toward the back doors, hiking her large purse over her shoulder. Bugsy and I ran to keep up.

"The party was embarrassing, Em. You don't even remember what happened to you."

Aimes pushed through the doors that led onto the field and started toward the dip. Bugsy and I followed, charged up by her rage but wanting to stay behind it.

"Cristal's a mess," Aimes said. "You're her best friend and you've disappeared," she said. "She's been talking to Mr. Dobbs three times a week, for months. Haven't you noticed?" Mr. Dobbs was the school guidance counsellor. And I hadn't.

"I thought she had volleyball practice."

We headed into the grasses, already at knee level. Coming from the expanse of the field into this sloping terrain felt quieter, more contained, but Aimes kept yelling.

"She hasn't played volleyball in over a year."

Aimes sat down and Bugsy and I crouched beside her.

I was trying to figure out how to get out of the twilight zone I'd just stepped into. The last time Cristal and I'd hung out, she'd been sitting with Mom in the living room watching *Frasier*. I was stressed so I went upstairs and rehearsed for drama nationals. That's what friends did, I thought – do their own thing and take each other's shit.

"How long has she felt like this?" I asked.

"Since Doug," Aimes said.

"She says there's something wrong with you," Bugsy said. "Says you're more than boy crazy –"

"She says you're sick," Aimes said.

"Tell her to say that to my face next time."

I stood up, trying to brush all the tiny seeds off my patchwork pants.

"She would never tell you, Em. She's hanging around to make sure your mom's okay," Aimes said.

"She hangs around because her parents are dicks," I said.

"No, they're not, Sym. They're British," Bugsy said. "They might be shy but they've always been nice to me."

"What about when her mom chased me down the street that time?"

"It was dark out on a school night," Aimes said. "She thought you were breaking in." She crossed her arms. "My mom would've done the same thing."

"But they make her stay in the basement."

"She moved *herself* downstairs for the privacy," Aimes said, standing. "And guess what Em?" Aimes moved her hands to her hips. "She keeps her room clean on purpose. She's had it exactly like that since grade three. Her shirts are colour coded. Her walls are bare. She's a fucking minimalist."

"Why didn't she ever tell me?"

"Because you never asked."

Bugsy started back toward the school, pushing through the long grasses. "Mr. Dobbs said you sound – what was the word, Aimes?"

Aimes caught up. "Entitled. Mr. Dobbs says you are entitled."

"I don't even know what that means."

"It means –" Aimes looked to Bugsy.

"It means you think you should get what you want." Bugsy stopped so I could catch up.

"Of course I think that," I said. "Who doesn't?"

"Not Cristal."

They were showing me a world I didn't recognize. They'd been talking about this for how long? Like how we talked about Max? This was absurd. They weren't going to pin this on me. We'd made our choices together.

"You guys were obsessed with getting noticed," I said, thinking back to Aimes and Bugsy hanging around the machine shop every lunch hour during grade eight, pushing each other into the vending machine to attract attention.

"Not really," Aimes said. I could see her relaxing. She hooked her arm through mine as we turned back to the school. "Timmy and I just had our one-year anniversary."

"But you went to all those parties and got shit-faced and grinded with dudes?"

"I kept the pact," Aimes said.

"Aren't you doing it with Jimmy?" I turned to Bugsy, begging for some camaraderie.

"It was the only way he'd get back together with me. It's the end of grade ten and I'm going to marry him," she said. "I followed the rules."

"What are you saying? We're not friends anymore?"

I stopped in the middle of the field, waiting for an answer.

"What choice do we have?" Bugsy said, eyes softening.

"You promised," Aimes said. "You made us all promise that we'd take care of each other and leave no one behind."

My guts loosened. I tried to take off but Aimes blocked my path.

"We don't want to have to say it Sym." Aimes looked to Bugsy and back to me. They were taking their job seriously.

"I'm out?" I said, staring past them to the back wall of the high school, where runt-o-the-litter had made my lip bleed.

Aimes kicked at the cleat-marked grass. "I just wish you weren't so desperate."

"It puts us in an uncomfortable position," Bugsy said. "You're acting like a skid."

"More than that," Aimes said. "She's a *skid dog*."

"A what? You just made that up," I said. "It doesn't mean anything."

"So what if it's made up," Aimes said. "It means whatever we want it to."

"Slutty and trashy combined," Bugsy said.

I bolted.

"Bye Sym," Aimes called out after me. "See you in history."

2012

ONCE SUMMER VACATION IS OVER and Armstrong kids return to school, I try to take action, like a real journalist would. I start the trek up to my old high school, recorder and microphone in my bag as kids race past me. *I'm not here to stir up pain*, I coach myself. *I just want to know if these Armstrong girls loved the tracks like we did.* I can't explain why this question has been haunting me since Taylor's death, so I pray the principal, Mr. Mitzel, doesn't ask. Pushing through the slate-blue double doors the smell hits me immediately. Pine-Sol. It's the same foyer, only smaller, and the student centre off to the right only has one kid in it, wearing all black, head down on the table like she's sleeping. I enter the office, pretending I'm the hard-hitting reporter I'm not, and I see a familiar poofy head peeking over her cubicle.

"Oh, my gosh," I say, over the counter. "Are you Jimmy Robson's mom?"

The woman leans back in her chair and scowls. She has the same spongy red hair she had twenty years ago. She makes a motion that I decide is a nod.

"You were my high school secretary. Yeah?"

She shrugs. Obviously.

"I'm Emmy. Bugsy and I were good friends. Remember?"

She looks through me – computing my age, my weight and all the internal changes that must have altered me so drastically, Emmy is proving hard to find.

"Oh yes," she says, unconvinced. "Emmy. Of course."

I sidetrack the plan for a moment, excited to be only one degree away from Bugsy.

"Can you tell Bugsy that I say hi? Can you pass that message along for me? Do you have her phone number?"

"I don't," the woman says.

She turns and starts typing again.

"Do they still live out east? Jimmy got his Red Seal right? How old are their girls now?"

"Bugsy and Jimmy got divorced last year," the woman says in a voice that tells me whose fault she thinks that is. "I don't have her new number."

"Well, if you hear from her, can you tell her that you saw me? Can you send her my love?"

A kid enters the office to sign in late and Jimmy's mom is relieved to have something else to attend to.

A few minutes later, the principal waves me into his office. I'd called yesterday and explained the gist of the situation: *I don't want to talk about Taylor. I want to talk about the tracks.*

"I'll hold you to it," he says now, leaning back in his swivel chair. "We had to lock the kids inside the high school the first month after Taylor's murder, reporters skulking around, pretending to be students."

I nod.

"I found some girls who said they'd talk to you – drama nerds mostly." He paused. "A CBC Radio documentary about railroad tracks?" That was as simply as I could express it to him on the phone.

"Yes, about how the girls use the tracks, or if they do at all? They won't be identified and I really appreciate their time."

He looks up and waves behind me. "They're here," he says. "Happy to get out of science class." He shakes my hand. "Artists are weird. Wanting to know about the feelings of the railroad?" He chuckles like I'm a goddamned clown and leads me to the room the girls are waiting in, the old counsellor's office.

The girls are sitting around a large table. Five of them, shifting in their seats.

"Thanks Mr. Mitzel," I say. "We'll be done in less than an hour."

"You've got fifteen minutes," he says. "I'll be in my office." He nods to the girls. "If you need anything."

I put my bag on a chair, pull out the recorder and slide it to the centre of the table.

"First off, if you change your mind, I can erase it," I say. "Second, if you don't like how you sound, we can re-record. And last, thank you for meeting me."

The girls nod deadpan. They're the kind of small-town kids who are comfortable enough around adults to have no affectation. One is grabbing gummy worms from a small plastic bag. Another takes a sip of a slush. And with their chicken legs, greasy noses and long hair, I see us.

"I'm Emmy and this is a bit weird—"

They stiffen.

"Are you a reporter?" The tallest girl leans forward. "'Cause we don't talk to the media." Her blond ponytail is tucked through a baseball cap.

"I'm not a reporter but I do have a recording device—" I point to the recorder again.

"Don't bother," the girl beside her says and crosses her arms, tanned like Bugsy's used to be. "We've got nothing to say."

"I don't want to talk about Taylor," I say. "I want to talk about the tracks."

A girl with a half-shave throws an arm around her friend's shoulder. "What do you wanna know? Trains go on them. Once a day."

These girls are giving off heat and I realize what's going on. Adults don't get to know what happens on the tracks and the fact that this protocol is still in place means something.

"We met there almost every day after school," I say. "At the same spot."

The girls look at me, heads tilted like birds. They're being cautious, or maybe a better word is vigilant. The short one sucks on her slush. Ponytail crosses her arms.

"I went to high school here," I say. "Grad '96," and I pull an invisible train horn like a loser.

"Why do you want to know about the tracks?" the short one with the slush asks.

"I grew up on them. I want to know if it was just me."

"You could ask my mom." The tall blond lifts an eyebrow. "She grew up here in the olden days too."

I laugh and press record.

"We used to call it walking and talking," I say.

"That's what it's still called," Half-Shave says.

My heart jumps but they're getting shifty again. I don't have much time.

"You know what I didn't realize until I was an adult," I say. "The tracks were a reminder that there's always a way out."

A girl who hasn't spoken yet, the one I've pinned as an actual drama nerd, leans forward.

"I don't know the street names in Armstrong but I can get to anyone's house from the tracks."

I sit back in my chair and she moves in closer, like a horse nosing for an apple.

"In summer, when the leaves are the biggest," she says, "you're right in the centre of things but you still feel hidden, ya know?

"I used to live out there till the stars came out," says another girl. She has bleached-out hair and purple lips and reminds me the most of myself. "Autumn days were the best," she says. "When it's just you and your girls and balance practice." She nudges the girl with the half-shave. "You won't fall off and the sun never goes down."

"Exactly," Half-Shave says. "I don't feel lonely, but I get to be alone."

There's a knock. The door opens and a familiar face pokes his head in.

"I hear Emmy Symington is back at school."

It's Mr. Dobbs, the old high school counsellor, sent in to check on me.

"How's your little brother doing?"

"He's good," I say. "He has a cement business. He's happy."

"I always liked that kid. And Max. She must be a singer now right?"

"She's got a double doctorate in the creation of sound," I say, and we laugh.

"Tell her hi for me, will you? Tell her that she often pops into my mind."

I smile and nod, knowing I won't.

He closes the door and my attention returns to the group.

"Why don't you want to talk about Taylor?" Ponytail asks me.

"I'm not allowed to," I say. "You're minors and I haven't asked your parents' permission."

"It's not like we aren't thinking of her all the time," Drama Nerd says.

"You can talk about Taylor if you want to, I just can't ask," I say, making the rules up as I go.

"We know she fought back," Half-Shave says.

"And you don't walk the tracks anymore?" I say.

"No," the short one with the slush says. "We don't."

It hits me, how tired these girls must be.

Shorty throws her empty slush cup in the garbage. "I'm just confused," she says. "What hurts more? Walking the tracks after what happened, or staying away? How can I have opposite feelings about the same place?"

There's a knock at the door. My time is up. I look to the recorder that's been collecting their voices. I've just asked these girls to drop their defences, and now they've got nowhere to go to deal with it.

"I'd love to talk with you again, anytime."

"No thanks," they say in unison.

"But thanks for asking us better questions," the tall blond says.

The girls pick up their bags and start to file out of the room. I can feel their alchemy as they walk away. It's undeniable, even though they have no idea it exists, the charge pulsing off them, just by being together.

1994

On THE FIRST DAY OF GRADE ELEVEN, after an entire summer apart, I thought we'd be overcome by nostalgic hysteria, but Aimes, Bugsy and Cristal only looked up from the back of homeroom briefly before going back to their whispers. Between classes, Cristal avoided me in the hallway and when we had to stand next to each other at our lockers to get our books, her face flushed red, as if my presence gave her internal hives.

Max surprised me though. After months of not seeing each other and no mention ever of the hair-on-fire incident, in the first weeks of school we'd found ourselves sitting together in honours history. Maybe it was because we shared a competitive streak and we'd already tied for highest marks last year, or she felt an affinity with my lowered status, but when we passed each other in the halls she'd sometimes reach out for my hand, and if we found ourselves in the smoke pit together she'd sit beside me. She'd made some sort of agreement with Mr. Dobbs, that if she doubled up on grade eleven and grade twelve schoolwork, she'd be able to graduate early.

In Mr. Wyatt's English lit class, I'd moved my desk from the back of the classroom, where I'd sat with the girls for three years, to the front. Hearing giggling behind me I felt a flicker on my back. I turned around. Aimes and Bugsy and Cristal laughed into each other's shoulders as they shot spitballs at me. *Is this a shitty teen movie?* I thought. *Am I the girl who's gonna get pig blood poured all over her right now?*

After school I took the long route through Armstrong to pass by the house but Mom's car wasn't in the driveway. I pulled up to the breezeway, all her dahlias in bloom, and felt a familiar pride for the beauty she'd made us. I snuck up the stairs and unlocked my bedroom door to take a nap in my old bed. It was heavenly, the cold sheets and stale air. Without Cristal acting as referee it was hard to negotiate being around Mom. Once this summer I'd come by unannounced and she looked up from her crouch in the garden with the same flash of veiled disappointment I saw whenever a church friend dropped in and she had to dust off her knees and be good company. She'd been given the all clear – again – and had joined a dragon boat team for cancer survivors, so she wasn't home much anymore anyway.

I drove back to Dad's, alone. He was working sixteen hours a day with therapy clients and it was odd to be with his girlfriend and her two little kids when he wasn't around, so I headed upstairs to read.

There was a knock on my bedroom door. It was Max. She'd come over to study, and in my ennui, I'd lost track of time. We'd begun to meet up twice a week in the evenings to do practice tests. There was something new about Max. Since the rape last Halloween she'd stopped all pretense. No more faking it, or playing dumb for our sakes. This sense of self made her comforting to be around.

It was muggy in my new room. The plum tree outside scented the air and neither of us were in a big hurry to work. I wondered if we could be honest now. The girls had taken care of each other precisely by *not* talking directly. But look where that had gotten us.

"Why are you the only one still around?" I asked her. "I lit your hair on fire."

"That was the worst day of my life," she said.

"I never said sorry," I said.

"I knew you were."

Max lit a smoke, took a drag and blew it at the ceiling.

"Smoke it out the window, so we don't get caught."

She waved the smoke toward the cracked window.

"Why didn't you get mad?" I asked. "Why didn't you freak out?"

"If you were crazy enough to light my hair on fire, what else would you do?"

"You didn't want to wake the dragon?" I said.

Waking the dragon was what we called our fathers' rage. Over the years, we'd shared tactics we'd found useful when we saw them start to lose it. Strategies that might bring them back from the edge.

"Exactly," Max said.

Once again, it was hard to hear that who I thought I was, I wasn't.

"I knew that you were fucked up," she said.

"You were fucked up more," I said and steamrolled onto her.

"That's true," she said.

"Well, I'll never let anyone light your hair on fire again," I said.

She laughed at the ridiculousness of the assertion that I'd protect her from myself.

"Did you ever think that maybe Twyla wasn't a slut?" she asked.

This was new to us, speaking honestly, not through other people or in code.

"She was a slut." I remembered my chat with her at the party in June beside the trampoline. "But she's not anymore."

"So how do you know she ever was one?" Max asked. Before I could say anything, she answered. "I just wonder who gets to make these decisions, ya know?"

Mid way through grade eleven and on my own, the need for affection became relentless. I hardly ever saw Bugsy, Aimes or Cristal, except in the halls between classes, and Max was busy trying to graduate early. So when I wasn't studying for a test or memorizing lines for a play, I began to spend more and more time with Penny, from speech and drama class, following her to grad parties in Vernon, where the kids were older than me and had cottages and ski chalets. In this new environment I could re-create myself. Get my fix.

As the weekends progressed, softened by alcohol, I continued to grind against older boys I'd just met at parties in Vernon, wiping up with frozen leaves or on the upholstery in the back seats of their parents' cars. I tried not to have intercourse with one-night stands. But Sunday mornings became an exercise in trying to remember who'd been down my pants. I usually couldn't draw up a face as it had been dark out and my eyes were slurry. It didn't matter as the exchange felt like a fair trade. They got to squeeze my c-cup boobs and for the evening I felt attended to, seen.

The key to satiating and staying sated, I'd discovered, was in the acting. To not placidly allow sex to happen, as I had with Bugsy's cousin, but to pretend I was ravenous for it. If I initiated, I retained a semblance of dignity. A girl who loved dick might be considered impressive, or at least rare, and you're not a victim if you've asked for it.

Some nights before bed, I'd get on my hands and knees in my favourite flannel nightie to practise in front of the mirror, simulating the different positions I might find myself in – what angle to keep my neck at so there was no double chin, and how much I needed to suck in my stomach to show off my ribs – so I'd know what I'd look like before it happened.

There were nice moments. During the Christmas holidays Bugsy invited me over to hang out with Jimmy and Windex (his younger cousin, who knew?) while her parents were out drunk-carolling. The pot lights were off in Bugsy's formal living room, so it was only the fifteen-foot Christmas tree that cast a glow. Bugsy and Jimmy went downstairs for a hot tub. I didn't want to do anything with the skeez – he didn't offer back the same sense of value for product – but I was exhausted by the hassle of not, so I stretched out on the white pleather couch, he pulled his penis out of his corduroy pants and before I could find a pillow, he'd shot his load all over my shirt. I was surprised when he asked if I wanted to cuddle after. He'd started *Silence of the Lambs*, which was too scary to watch with no Cristal to burrow into, but his arms gave me the deep breaths I needed so I stayed put, and I passed the time by counting the presents under Bugsy's tree. Sixty-two.

THE FAIR COMES TO TOWN on the first weekend in September, as it has for the past 113 years. Everyone in Armstrong involves themselves in this three-day event, whether it's raising hogs for the agricultural exhibits or growing pumpkins for the pie competitions. The churches in town rely on the Famous Fall Fair Roast Beef Dinner Fundraiser to pay their ministers for the year, so the job of the parishioners is to get fairgoers to buy plates of roast beef smothered in gravy and the different congregations compete for business. We never have to worry. Our church always sells out. Mom and I usually stand side by side, slopping the meat, potatoes, buttered carrots, peas and gravy onto paper plates, warning customers to hold them in the middle, for fear of collapse. I prefer the gravy-pouring job but so do most of the old ladies who complain of weak wrists, so my secondary tasks are usually plate clearing and coffee refilling, jobs that take dexterity to manoeuvre through the tight rows of bodies trying to eat quickly, on their way to the next grandstand show. Christie's come up to spend the weekend with me. He's never been to a rodeo before and even though some city people think a small-town fair is an ironic event, he takes Armstrong's business seriously.

We head down the hill and he follows me to the back entrance of the fairgrounds where we get stamped as volunteers and zigzag through the growing crowds to get to our shift. On the first day of the fair, it's mostly kids and parents, no roughnecks or Hells Angels yet. Christie stops at a kiosk that promises a blender so strong it will cut through a spoon.

Our fundraiser is held at the far end of the fairgrounds, under the grandstand that hosts the heavy horse pull and chuckwagon races. This means that every few minutes, when there's a win, a thousand feet stomp above us, dropping bits of hay and dust onto the patrons gobbling their meals below.

No one dares mention it. The dinner is run primarily by women between the ages of sixty and eighty, and those ladies drive the hungry crowds through with a firm hand.

"Just one more booth," Christie says. He's noticed another demonstration: a vacuum cleaner guaranteed to suck up lug nuts.

I lean against him as he listens to her countdown.

"Have you ever seen blood sucked up a tube?" the rep yells into her headset.

The midway's getting busier and the smell of fried donuts makes my stomach grumble. I check my phone.

"We're late," I say, pulling him toward the grandstand.

The dinner lineup already snakes around the large building. Christie and I sneak through the cowboys to find the ladies running the length of the hall, percolators in hand, eyes flitting down rows of papered tables. I wave, to catch Mom's eye. She exits the rush, grabs me by the arm and pulls me into a corner.

"Are you trying to make a fool of me?" she says, in front of a table full of Jell-O squares topped with whipped cream.

"What job do you want us to do?" I ask, hoping Christie's presence will calm her down.

"All I asked was for you to volunteer for one shift and you waltz in whenever you feel like it."

The tray she's holding to her chest is shaking and her pupils are bead-like.

"We're here now," I say. "We'll help."

"You take nothing seriously," she says.

A few of her friends are floating in our periphery, listening to the argument.

"It was only half an hour. I wanted Christie to see the fair."

I'm trying to act like nothing's wrong for our audience but I don't know if I've seen her angrier. Small but ferocious, Mom's secret power has always been her ability to hide the fact that she has any power at all. It sneaks up on us. And it's the frenzy attached that always surprises me, like she might reach out and yank my hair.

"Go tell Enid you're here so she can rewrap her wrists," she says.

She rushes away, one hand holding up her too-big jeans, the tray of Jell-O in the other.

Christie's put in charge of taking out the garbage before the wasps find the corn. The church ladies send darts of panic my way when I chat too long with a rancher. A few huddle around the coffee urn, glancing at me. I appreciate their loyalty to my mom and as I head toward the refill station Lydia steps out and touches my arm.

"How are you faring dear?"

"Fine," I say. "Great."

Lydia checks back with the gaggle of women around the urn. They've decided they need to say something.

"You mother isn't as able as she acts, dear," she says.

"I know," I say.

"You don't know or you wouldn't have been late," she says.

Before the reproach breaks me, Lydia squeezes my hand and smiles, then she points to a man seated nearby.

"The one with the big mustache who smells like manure," she says. "He's had two desserts. Don't let him sneak a third."

Near the end of our shift I scan for Mom but I can't find her anywhere.

She must have slipped off and gone home without saying goodbye. We'd planned to walk through the fairgrounds together and show Christie the first-place poultry winners. Shame mixed with self-preservation means I can't indulge her any further, so I grab Christie's hand, still damp from washing dishes, and pull him out the back exit.

"Should we check on her?" he asks.

"That's what she wants us to do," I say, the wall up.

As we enter the midway we're hit with spinning discs of light and the squeal of helium balloons. It's the same path the girls and I used to loop, hot pink feather clips in our hair, bright from sugar, holding hands, eyes peeled for the Brew Crew.

"Do you want me to win you something?" Christie asks and points to the stalls with basketball hoops and batting cages.

Kids are spinning in cages above me. The girls' screams pierce through every other fairground noise, so much delight in their terror. When Cristal's sister Ford was in grade twelve, on the last night of the fair she ran off with a carny. They'd fallen in love at the ring toss and after spending the weekend at his booth, she hitched a ride out of town when the fair closed up on Sunday night and no one ever saw her again.

The music gets louder and I grab Christie's hand as we weave between the kids being dragged toward the exit signs and head to what I hope will be his favourite part. The agricultural buildings are long aluminum barns full of animals and whenever I breathe in the musk of wool and feathers mixed with the tang of sawdust and urine my eyes droop and my breathing slows down. But before we get there Christie stops me.

"Here's a ride for you," he says and points to the Ferris wheel.

The baskets revolve, framed in strings of multicoloured lights.

"I don't do rides," I say.

He steers me into the line and the operator ushers us into a small box that sways as soon as I sit down. The safety mechanism is only a thin metal rod that he lowers over our laps and so for an extra safety measure Christie wraps one arm around my back and the other around my belly. In the first few months of being together, every time he touched me, I'd jump – my body nervous, ready to be taken by surprise. It's been only this, his slow steadiness, that allows me to lean into him now.

As soon as the ride starts I know I've made a mistake. The seat tips forward, toward the ground, so I lean back to counter the movement which makes us dump backward. I start to whimper as the basket reaches its full height.

"Fuck, god, god, please, fuck, god, no," I chant as we begin the descent in what feels like a free fall.

Christie starts to laugh as the second round begins and the movement makes the small box shake. I shut my eyes. I cannot help the sounds coming from my mouth.

"Don't fucking laugh!" I yell at him.

He laughs even harder.

"Stop," I say. "Stop laughing, stop moving. Stop."

This makes him laugh more.

"I hate this," I moan, my fists clenched around the thin metal rod in front of me.

At the bottom of the circle again, I have time to take a sip of breath before the heart-catching lift that continues until we make it to the top, where we dangle like a Christmas tree ornament. No matter how still I sit, it feels like large hands are going to pick me up and eject me into the night.

"Open your eyes, Em," Christie says. "You can see the whole town."

I peek. Below me, people stroll the midway, small pink and purple puffs in their hands. Ahead, the fairground gates and ticket booths are covered in fairy lights. Above is Pleasant Valley Road, with cars parked wherever they can fit. Past the road, above the dense brush, are the tracks, stretching out past the bend into the woods. The rails flash red and green from the lights spilling onto them. Taylor had two months of life left, last fall fair. I bet she was a ride girl.

After a few minutes of stillness, the Ferris wheel jolts back to life and I yelp.

"We're almost done," Christie says. "I'm right here."

I sink into Christie, not for protection, but because I'm trying to believe him.

The operator laughs as he brings us to the ground and unlatches the safety.

"Don't take her on the teacups," the operator says. "She'll piss herself."

Rowdier than an hour ago, the midway is keyed up with an edge that makes me want to go home.

Exiting through the fairy lights, we cross the road and climb up the scree to the tracks. We're at the spot where kids used to sit and chug beer before they jumped the fence. Where they'd hang out after the gates closed, to smoke and compare rides.

We walk the rails side by side. Fog hangs low and in the far distance I think I see an animal. I grab Christie's arm and squint to listen, but it's too misty to see so we keep walking. In all his time in Armstrong I've never taken Christie to Taylor's spot, or my own. We've kept him too busy with dump runs and cooking dinner. I take his hand and lead him to where Taylor was attacked, almost a year ago.

"This is the spot," I say.

"Taylor's spot," he says.

I see her there, the outline of her body curled in the ditch. The grasses are high again and the earth has crumbled and curved around her and I don't want to disturb her rest.

I scan the distance and again I think I see movement ahead. Off the tracks, Christie follows me into the trees and it's only when I crouch, to get lower than the fog, that I see them, sitting in the centre of the rails, just past our old spot. A wisp of smoke rises, signalling a shared cigarette. Their voices are too low to make out, but constant, like the faraway tone of a train. I stare at the circle, trying to make out any details. A flash of silver – maybe an earring?

They've returned.

I don't realize I'm holding my breath until Christie pulls me to standing. "It's weird," he says. "Hiding like this."

We step back on the rails and the girls, three I count quickly, hear our footsteps and turn toward us.

"Adults," one girl yells, and they take off, braids and scarves behind them.

"It's okay," I yell, "it's only me," and I laugh at how stupid I sound.

The girls slow down their run and then they stop. From about half a school field length away, we face each other. Their legs are spread wide across the rails. I can see their breath rising and the outlines of their bodies, thin and tall. I nod to them and without turning, I step backward, motioning Christie to follow. The tracks aren't mine anymore. They're telling me to go.

IT WAS EARLY SPRING, right around the time sweaters were packed up and windbreakers brought out, when I looked out the window in Chemistry 11, the sky a piercing blue, and decided to cut school and walk the tracks by myself. I grabbed my bag and drove down the hill to the intersection where the tracks met the road and parked in the preschool's lot, turning away from our old spot, heading instead toward the woods. When I stepped onto the rails, like always, the world softened. The cold sun beat down on the dead grasses and dry wild wheat and made the tracks shine.

We used to take balance practise very seriously. It was a sign of status, how fast you could travel along the rails. The first step, I remembered, was to balance without moving. That was beginner shit, but I did it anyway. I hovered. I said hello, reintroducing myself to the rails. The next step was to close my eyes. I wavered but held my balance, feeling the warmth of the rails radiate up my legs as I counted to thirteen, the number we'd chosen to mean we could continue to step three, which was walking.

Stepping forward, I tried to remember how long it had been since we'd all stood in a circle together. One year at least. Nearing graduation, we weren't overtly mean to each other anymore. Everyone just seemed worn out. There was a fatigue behind our eyes, visible only to those who shared its origins. A week ago, we'd lapsed for a moment. In the locker room after gym, Aimes let a tiny fart squeak out and Bugsy said, "Holy shit, Kitty's home, hide," and Aimes and Bugsy and I dashed to the showers laughing, then caught ourselves, embarrassed we'd forgotten we weren't friends anymore. Cristal's birthday was coming up soon. Mom usually made her a cake. Had she done it last year? I couldn't remember.

I was moving slowly now, my toes and chin up. The real skill was pretending confidence, that's what'll help you run. I'm not bragging but it's hard to do and looks fucking cool. It's also exhilarating because if you do fall, you'll get a shitty road rash, so the brilliance to the game is to run fast enough to outpace your thoughts but not so fast you lose control. I wasn't going to try to run today. There was no way I was that good anymore.

I heard a yell behind me.

"Hey, Sym!"

Turning, I saw Aimes, far down the tracks, waving to catch my attention. She trotted forward, big purse hiked over her shoulder, smoke in hand.

"You skipping too?" she said. "I saw your car. I'm headed to Tuckers for fries with Tim. Walk me there."

I smiled, and because we'd not spoken in so long, we both dropped our heads to focus on the rails.

"You seen Max around lately?" she asked.

"Only in History."

"You hear about Cristal?"

"She's got a boyfriend now?"

"He drives her nuts," she said. "It's just for show."

"Hey, Windex struck again," I said, remembering the brief encounter on Bugsy's couch at Christmas.

We laughed, but this time a more tired sound came out.

"Windex is a slut," Aimes said.

"Nah," I said. "He's a perv."

"Why don't guys get called sluts?" Aimes said.

"Good question," I said. "You called me a slut last year."

"'Cause you are one," Aimes said.

She fell off the rail, then hopped back on.

"I don't do it because I like it," I said.

"But you go looking for it," she said.

"Yeah, I do." I said, aware that there were complications to my actions I couldn't explain.

"What don't you like?" Aimes asked.

"Faking it," I said. "I wish they could tell the difference."

"They can tell," Aimes said. "They just don't care."

I shook my head. This whole time, my bravado—the sexual performance

I'd gotten so good at—hadn't been for the boys' benefit at all. I'd only been trying to convince myself.

We wobbled for a while, still.

"Sucking dick is as enjoyable as washing a dog," Aimes said. "As soon as I marry Timmy—*zzzzzip*." She zipped her mouth shut. "Closed for business."

We laughed. She lit a smoke and took a drag.

"Has anything ever felt good to you?" she asked.

"The best it's ever felt is fine. Doable."

"What about when you masturbate?"

"I don't," I said. "Why bother if a guy's not around?"

Having Aimes beside me again felt like light in my veins. Her questions calmed me, as did being in our natural habitat, performing our old motions.

"What the hell, Sym?" she said. "Now you're going to tell me you don't know where your clit is."

I shrugged.

"Are you kidding me right now?"

Aimes walked to the brush, cracked off a stick and drew an oblong shape in the fine gravel. Then she dug four dots down the centre of the egg shape.

"Butt hole, dick hole, pee hole," she pointed like a teacher. She circled the top of the drawing. "This little bump is your clit!"

"Wait a sec," I said. "The dick hole and the pee hole are two separate holes?"

"Yes," Aimes said. "Absolutely."

The dudes had been flicking on my urinator this whole time.

"It's weird that you're such a skank, but you're also a total prude," Aimes said, and stepped up to re-balance.

"Stop calling me that."

"Maybe that's the difference between being a slut and a skid?" Aimes said, reaching into her purse for a piece of gum. "Sluts like having sex and skids have to have sex."

"That makes sense," I said, trying the definition on for size. "So, I'm a skid then."

"A skid dog," she said.

"That makes you a skid dog too," I said.

"Aren't we all."

I stopped balancing. I'd never heard her so brazen. I turned.

"Have you ever smelled a stinky crotch?" I asked.

"Have you ever gone camping?" she said.

"What does a normal vagina smell like?" I asked, finally positing the question after so many years of worry.

"Sweaty," she said.

"Can I smell yours?"

"What?"

"Can I smell your vagina?"

"Gag me with a spoon," Aimes said.

"I think I might have a problem," I said. "If I smelled yours, I could compare."

"Emmy, get a grip. Sometimes you just don't feel fresh, even after a shower," she said, reciting that stupid fucking Massengill commercial.

"There's a scent—"

Aimes checked both ways down the tracks, then she crouched so that her nose touched my paisley skirt.

"I'm real close up and I don't smell fish so I'd say you're fine."

"Are you sure I don't stink?"

"It smells like you," Aimes said. "Musky."

We were close enough to town that we could see the grain silo up ahead. I was getting hungry. It had to be around 3 p.m. by now.

"Why are you even talking to me?" I said.

Aimes stood to face me. "Because we used to be best friends."

"We haven't hung out in over a year."

She put her foot up on the rail. "You're the one who demanded we make a pact and then broke it."

"Aimes, you broke the pact too," I said. "We all did."

Aimes threw her jacket on the ground. "I held him off for three months till we'd been together a year. Three fucking months. You know how much shit that got me into?"

She was bringing pain onto the tracks. This hadn't happened before. And it was medicine, the walking and talking.

We'd just passed the protection of the trees and were about to enter town. The wind had picked up. I grabbed Aimes's jacket and passed it back to her.

That's when we heard it. Without speaking, Aimes and I bolted for the grain silo. Max's voice rang out over the rails, so large and vibratory I couldn't believe she was the only one making the sound. When we made it to the silo door I reached to open it but Aimes grabbed my hand.

"She doesn't want us in there."

Max was singing in French. I knew what she'd look like inside. Eyes closed, standing in the centre of the cylindrical room, palms together under her sternum, like I'd seen her practise. We backed away from the aluminum door. Aimes was right. We weren't welcome anymore.

"Shit, I'm late," she said, and started to cross the tracks. "Duty calls."

I wanted to grab her and not let her go. I wished she'd stay here, with me, and fill up on Max's song.

"Love you, Sym," she said. "See ya later, skid dog."

"Takes one to know one," I yelled back.

Flippancy, the only layer of protection we had left.

2012

I AWAKEN TO THE SMELL OF PORRIDGE. Mom's already up, coat on, tying her shoes, hair crunchy from bed head.

"Oh good, you're coming," she says.

I have no idea what she's referencing.

"The meditation group," she says. "I asked you to come yesterday and you said sure."

Oh. That.

I pull on a pair of tights and a T-shirt and let Christie sleep. If I wasn't in trouble from the fair, I wouldn't be going, but to make amends I won't put up a fight. Mom founded a meditation group after her first bouts with cancer when I was a teenager and she's led it every Saturday afternoon since. I've never been, as it's for terminal patients and their loved ones, but I've heard it explained over the phone to new clients countless times. *In a darkened room, the volunteers will lay their hands on you. They might stroke your body or hold still, depending on what you need.* My mother has spent years touching people gently on her lunch hour, but she's always been too busy to receive the healing herself.

We drive to the church and head down the carpeted stairwell. It's chilly as we descend into the basement and the volunteers give us homemade slippers to wear. There are five other sets of people gathered for healing touch today and we start the session by sitting in a circle. The requirement of being here is that you're dying of cancer or you're caring for someone dying of cancer and a volunteer invites us to share our names and the reason why we've come. When it's my time to share I don't know how to answer. I don't think I can classify myself as her caregiver.

"Oh," I say. "It's amazing when faced with this kind of difficulty, how all the bullshit drops away and you can finally appreciate someone for who they truly are."

My mom smiles and the older bald woman to my right nods in recognition and I feel like a fraud.

The volunteers lay foam mats covered in fabric on the cement floor and we lie down in the darkened room. Mom puts her mat beside mine and reaches across the floor for my hand. Reflexively, I pull it away from her.

One of the volunteers comes by and drapes an old quilt across my body and I'm reminded of the ancient circle of women who sat together as I spied on them that drunken night so many years ago. This quilt could be one of theirs. The volunteer places a heavy cloth over my eyes to take away any light and she sits at my feet and begins to press into my heels. After a few moments of her hands kneading and the weight of the quilt on my body, I start to feel prickly. It's uncomfortable, like a crack and a peeling that I haven't let happen in a long time. No sound – only tears pour out of my eyes, pool in my ears and drip onto the mattress.

She just wants to hold my hand. Why can't I let her hold my hand?

Because I'm punishing her, I think. For not holding my hand when I was a kid. For making me so self-sufficient that I don't know how to reach back. For never letting herself rest, so now I don't know how to either. If she'd taken better care of herself maybe she wouldn't have gotten cancer. And now, because of all her damn dignity, I won't have a mom to teach me how to become one.

It's here, age thirty-four, under the blanket, when I admit I need her. I need her to tell me how to raise my unborn kids so I can scoff at all the suggestions. I need her fashion opinions that I will never in a million years adopt. I need her to ask me what baba ghanoush is – one more time. And I'm terrified that she's going to die. I'm so fucking terrified that my eyes roll to the back of my head. How did I miss the call that I was told would be so clear? I reach across the floor, ravenous, clutching, find her hand and grab at it. She reaches back and we fumble our fingers together until they mesh.

"I'm sorry, Mama, I'm so sorry," I say over and over again.

We lie there, and I let my mom stroke my hand, silent tears pouring from my eyes. She pats it for a time, and cups it within her own palm and rolls my fist into a ball and squeezes it closed. She knows what I need and she gives it to me and I take it. Just like what daughters and moms do. Her oncologist recently told us that the cancer has spread to her brain lining. Hard to detect, it's been growing for a while, which explains the increasingly odd behaviour – like finding her on the kitchen floor in the middle of the night, a tub of Moose Tracks ice cream between her legs, and her crooning from the taste of sugar.

The volunteer signals the end of class by ringing a small bell. Everyone rises but Mom and I stay put, squeezing each other's hands. The volunteers begin to pack up the mats and chairs and the other participants tiptoe out and we're alone now. I take her hand and place it on my belly, still a secret and nothing to show yet, but I want her to know – even if I'm not getting out of this without regret, she might still get her last wish.

"I need you to stay alive, Mom." Now that I've softened I'm turning to mush. "Miracles happen. You can have six more years. You'll get to watch your grandkid learn to ride a bike. We'll do camping trips. They'll remember you."

She pushes herself upright, thin hand on her chest, eyes wide, her mouth dropped into a grin.

"In seven more months," I say. "You'll get to meet them. You just have to start taking better care –"

She stops me.

"Enough with the sap," she says, throwing off the quilt. She can't stop smiling. "We've got a lot of work to do before I go."

1996

WE DID WALK THE TRACKS TOGETHER one last time. It was June. That morning, a Friday, I'd hung up my mom's old red wool coat in the closet under the stairs and taken out a lighter one, the only other jacket that hadn't been stolen from the chemo party, checkered red and black, something she'd made for herself when she was my age. Mom just had her two-year scan and the oncologist said she was still all clear. I wanted to spend as much time as I could at home with her before I left for theatre school.

We all found each other in the student centre. There was a week left of high school. We were waiting in a lineup to get our grad photos taken. I was happy with how my homemade prom dress had turned out, a maroon velvet with criss-crossing golden ropes that shaped my bodice, like the Lady of Shalott. Max had dressed as Mozart's wife. She'd borrowed a period costume from Asparagus Theatre and put talcum powder in her hair to turn it white. Cristal was stiff in her sister Ford's unworn black off-the-shoulder grad dress. Thankfully both Bugsy and Aimes looked the part of prom queens, with satin gowns and sprays of rhinestones and high French rolls with ringlets. Aimes was making us take a group shot. I'd rolled my eyes when she'd first suggested it but she was adamant.

"We grew up together," she said. "You're going to look back when you're fat and forty and want a picture."

"I won't," Cristal said.

But she'd cornered Max and convinced her that we needed a record of us, and with her buy-in, here we were.

Cristal had started dating a boy with long blond hair, but you wouldn't know it as she walked the halls in front of him. Max only attended one class a week, for extra credit, as she'd managed to graduate early. Aimes and Bugsy had spent the spring side by side in J and T's identical low-riders, waving to each other from the passenger seats while the boys gunned it at the one traffic light in town. They'd both been given promise rings on Christmas morning, but Aimes's had been much smaller than Bugsy's, the size of the head of a pin, something she didn't mention but I knew ground her down. So at prom two weeks ago, when Jimmy proposed to Bugsy on bended knee, with "Kiss from a Rose" by Seal playing in the background, Aimes got so angry at Timmy for not keeping up that she broke up with him, tiara on, drunk in front of the Sev.

And now here we were, in our old corner of the student centre, the carpet stained with oil and gum. The Brew Crew was long gone. Trent had disappeared. Ollie, officially subsumed by his older brothers. We'd made it to the top of the food chain, but hadn't had the time to notice or care. Maybe the red stones that had lit up between our legs so many years ago had a homing effect too, pulling us back together in hopes of a final charge.

The young photographer was already sweating when we entered the dark room. He'd set out fake flowers and cardboard hats and three stools to sit on.

"What a lucky guy to be surrounded by so many pretty ladies," he said, and Cristal's face flushed, although she'd heard it every picture day of her life.

Aimes perched on Bugsy and threw her feet up onto Max's lap. I sat on Cristal's lap and put my feet on Aimes's outstretched legs. Bugsy grabbed the fake flowers and Max put on one of the hats. We weren't pretending comfort, we just were.

We tried to smile into the camera but we couldn't keep our faces straight.

"Look into your futures," he said.

This made us snort more.

We turned the stools inwards to face each other. Across from me, Aimes smiled at Cristal, which made me smile at Max who smiled across to Bugsy. It was perfect and fast and he got the shot. And that's when it was decided: to return to the tracks, all five of us.

"Wanna head?" Bugsy asked, nodding to the door.

We grabbed our bags, stripped off our dresses in the bathroom and ran outside.

It was quiet as we trekked down the hill. We didn't hang out anymore but the reasons why had become gauzy. Something to do with fear and shame. When we hit the intersection, we jumped on the rails and headed past our old spot. The farther we walked, the stiller the world became. It didn't matter anymore, who turned on who or why. We all seemed grateful to return to the familiar ping of stones on rails and softening light.

At the ravine underneath Aimes's place, we jumped off the tracks while she clambered up the hill to get flashlights. When she passed them out and we began again we still didn't talk much, just kept walking farther down the rails than we'd bothered to venture before. I hooked my arm through Max's. Cristal started up balance practice, a strong level three, even after all her time away. She'd made her goal of $3,000 and bought herself a motorcycle. The plan was to share a dorm room with Aimes in college and drive her around town on the back of her new ride.

Aimes and Bugsy started to shove each other into the bushes like idiots, an old routine that still made us laugh. If high school was a death by a thousand cuts, the walk couldn't help but feel like a slow fade out.

Maybe an hour later the call of a train sounded, so we hopped off the tracks and ran down a steep hill into a gulley of rusted-out cars. As it turned to dusk, one by one we flicked the flashlights on and began to skulk around, reaching inside the metal skeletons as the train blew by on the embankment above. It was eerie at first, scouting this empty valley by ourselves, but soon we were climbing through the cars like cats.

"We don't know what we're looking for," Aimes yelled.

"But we'll know what it is when we find it," Max yelled back.

Bugsy crouched to take a pee and Aimes pushed her over midstream. Bugsy stood up, giggling, and shook her butt dry.

"Would you rather do it with Chad Chud or eat cat shit?" she said, starting the game.

Aimes, Max and I agreed that we'd rather eat cat shit.

"I'm not playing," Cristal said.

"Cat shit is the worst kind of shit to eat," Bugsy said as she climbed through the open windshield of a car. "I might have to pick Chad Chud."

"Cristal. Play?" Aimes said.

"No. It's a bullshit question," she said.

"It's *cat* shit," Bugsy said, "and you have to pick the least worst option."

"I'm not going to eat shit *or* fuck a chode," Cristal said.

Aimes and Bugsy started to push on a large boulder, hoping to overturn it. I poked around by myself in the high grass. Cristal stuck to bouncing on a sagging bumper – and that's when Max found them. She yelled for us and we all dropped what we were doing and ran. There were five old silver radio control dials sticking out of the front dash in what was now the shell of a car. They were rectangular and short like erasers. We each took a turn tearing one of the silver dials out of the dead radio. They came out clean, with a snap. We stood in a circle, the sky almost dark, and we raised the silver sticks above our heads, like priestesses enacting a spell.

"Friends forever," Aimes said. "Promise?"

"I promise," Bugsy said.

Cristal curled her hand around the metal dial. "I promise," she said.

"I promise," said Max, knocking her dial against each of ours, making a *ting* sound.

The girls looked at me, waiting.

"Forever means – no matter what, wherever you move, whoever you become – you all better keep yours," Max said.

"Of course I promise," I said.

Aimes checked her watch, "Oh shit, it's late."

"Don't tell me we missed *Friends*," Bugsy said.

"We should head back," Cristal said, looking up the gully to the tracks.

We shoved the silver radio dials into our pockets and raced back up the hill to the rails. The moon hadn't fully risen. The tracks ahead were dim. We started into the darkness in a line, one after another, separate, but with each other's shape in view. We kept our flashlights off as we entered the corridor of trees, and let our eyes adjust in their own time.

I DON'T WANT MY MOM to be in the delivery room while I'm in labour.

"But I was a nurse for forty years," she said, over the phone. "I know how to read a cervix."

She means well but Mom is far from stable and I don't think she can hack seeing the blood and hearing me scream through my butthole. So, we wait, and as soon as my son is born, Christie calls Mom from the hospital with the news.

"You're a grandma, Jude," he says. "You did it!"

I also say that she can't come to Vancouver to meet her grandchild until the weekend. Airport pick-ups, stress around where she'll sleep, and her mind—not all there—aren't going to be useful while I'm trying to learn how to breastfeed. I've become pragmatic within the high-stakes situation. My mother is dying. I have a newborn. We can all wait three days.

But she doesn't wait. When she gets the call that Arthur's been born, she packs herself a bag and drives the mountain pass by herself, to Vancouver, without a driver's licence. I'm upstairs in bed. Arthur is sleeping beside me. I can tell it's her by the sound of her knuckles rapping on the front door.

She bustles inside, her coat still on, and climbs the stairwell to meet him. I sit her in the chair we've bought off Craigslist, that lateral rocking kind that's supposed to be great for sleeping and feeding in. Mom is so tiny now, she looks like a little kid, her feet dangling free. I wrap Arthur up tight and place him in her arms, and she holds her grandson. She leans back, one hand on his bum, the other cradling his body, and her sense memory takes over. I don't need to worry. She knows how to hold a baby. I go back to bed and watch as my mom rocks my son. She moves him gently to her knees and bends over so they are nose to nose.

I close my eyes, grateful for a moment to myself. Even though I tried to forbid it I'm glad she came as soon as she did. They sit together rocking for a long time, her whispering things and cooing and I pretend to fall asleep. After I don't know how long Mom brings Artie back into the bed with me. She leans over. "Thanks, Em," she says. "For making me a grandma." And then, she leaves, only an hour or so after she's arrived. She tiptoes downstairs, whispering something to Christie about not wanting to disrupt the new little family and she drives herself the seven hours home.

She sees Arthur again a month later. This time I come to her. She's in and out of lucidity and sometimes his presence comforts her and other times, his cries are distressing. I take him for a walk so she can nap, and again, I try to work up the courage to call Taylor's mom. The documentary about the tracks has been made. It won an honourable mention at a big New York festival. I want her to know it exists. Still, when the answering machine comes on I'm relieved. I sputter something about growing up in Armstrong and how, since the two-year anniversary of Taylor's murder is approaching, she's on my mind. Within five minutes Marie calls back.

"I heard that documentary," she says. "I didn't catch who made it. I was driving, and I had to pull over. I was so happy someone thinks of her as much as I do."

"It was me," I say. "I told that story."

"I didn't know other girls used to walk the rails," she says. "I thought it was just a thing Tae and her friends did."

"I guess it's been going on for a long time," I say.

"They'd be out 'til all hours," she says. "All the girls."

"Us too," I say.

After we say goodbye, I look across the street to the tracks. The air above appears gossamer, like on the first day we met, only wider, more than I'd previously imagined. Not a shield at all, but a web. No need to pull it down from the sky. We are everywhere.

Acknowledgements

THANK YOU to Aislinn Hunter, who taught me how to write a book while I was writing it. My teacher, editor and now dear friend – may everyone have a mentor in their life as brilliant and generous as Aislinn. Thank you to Anita Rochon, my lifetime collaborator at The Chop. How lucky am I to get at least twenty more years making art with you, my family. Thank you to Caroline Skelton, the most whip-smart, sensitive and ruthless editor around, and Pam Robertson, my copy editor, for your precision and finesse. Hilary McMahon, my agent at Westwood Creative Artists, who saw what I was trying to do and got excited about it – I'm forever loyal. Also, Anna Comfort O'Keeffe at Douglas & McIntyre: you too took a risk on a new voice and I'm indebted.

I've had many women's circles in my life. The Six Pack, thanks for letting me tell our story slant. Thanks for some of the most riotous, joyful moments of my life. I love you girls. My women's group that spanned twenty years – you taught me about the kind of feminist I wanted to be. Christina, my chosen sister, and Kamaljit, my non-sexual wife for life. Thank you for the soft home. Thanks to my Hawaii dolphin sister Rachel and our many years of retreating together. My Necessary Creatives crew, the radio ladies and my MarcoPolo girls (Jody, Jen and Medina), who always bring me back when I want to go for milk.

I want to acknowledge SFU's Writer's Studio and their graduate program. JJ Lee, you lit the spark and were so generous with your mind and time, as was Madeleine Lamphier, my first reader and dear friend.

Thank you to all my past mentors, who taught me the rules and how to break them: John Turner (Mump and Smoot and Pochinko Clown), Karen Hines (Pochsy and Neo-Bouffon), Nadia Ross (STO Union) Karen Levine and Kathleen Flaherty (CBC Radio) and Suzan, my fairy godmother.

To the kids and teenagers I love and admire: Arthur, Obie, Maya, Norah, Eleah, Jasper, Cosmo, Marike, Jannic, Saoirse, Isla, Aoife and Aleen. This gang's changing the world and I'm so lucky I get to watch it happen.

To my dad – thank you for letting me share one version of events. Graham – you're the best brother and I love you. Auntie Jo, thank you for my love of books.

To Christie, my spouse: Thanks for loving all of me, nurturing our boys, respecting my art practice and making me laugh the hardest. I'm stuck to you for life. To my mama, we love you and in the boys you live on. Marie Van Diest, thanks for trusting me with Taylor's story.

Great thanks to the Canada Council for the Arts, the BC Arts Council, the Penny Lou Writers Residency and Caravan Farm Theatre, who helped with financial assistance and resources.

Finally, I want to thank the stewards of the traditional territories of the Secwépemc Nation, the land I grew up on and wrote some of this book from. Since time immemorial you've been the caretakers of the place I get to call home and for that I give great thanks.

Photo by zev tiefenbach

EMELIA SYMINGTON-FEDY is an international theatre creator and the founding co-artistic director of The Chop, with over twenty-five playwriting credits spanning her career. A graduate of Studio 58 (Langara College) and The Writer's Studio (Simon Fraser University), Emelia is a frequent contributor to CBC Radio and has told personal stories about motherhood, addiction, grief, her body, and other forbidden topics for over twenty years. She is also a guest lecturer at UBC and SFU and hosts retreats on creativity. Emelia lives in the Shuswap with her family. *Skid Dogs* is her first book.